YUKON RIVER

ALASKA

Holy Cross

Kodiak

n Islands

Dutch Harbor

Unalaska

Queen
Charlotte
Islands

Vancouver Island

Estevan Point

JUAN DE FUCA STRAIT

Fort Stevens

Brookings

SAN FRANCISCO

CANADA

SEATTLE

COLUMBIA
RIVER

PORTLAND

Bly

UNITED STATES

PACIFIC OCEAN

Goleta

LOS ANGELES

MEXICO

HAWAIIAN ISLANDS

Pearl Harbor

RETALIATION:

OREGON STATE MONOGRAPHS
STUDIES IN HISTORY
Clifford Trow, Consulting Editor

RETALIATION:

Japanese Attacks and
Allied Countermeasures on the
Pacific Coast in World War II

Bert Webber

ドウリトル空軍　日本奇襲への反撃
大日本帝国軍の北米太平洋岸攻撃史

Corvallis:
OREGON STATE UNIVERSITY PRESS

オレゴン州立大学プレス
コーヴァレス市郵箱６８９
米国オレゴン州（９７３３０）

Library of Congress Cataloging in Publication Data

Webber, Bert (Ebbert T)
   Retaliation: Japanese Attacks and Allied Countermeasures on the
Pacific Coast in World War II.

   (Oregon State monographs: Studies in history; no. 6)
   Bibliography: pp.
   Includes index.

   1. World War, 1939-1945—Pacific Coast. 2. World War, 1939-
1945—Japan.   I. Title.   II. Series.
D769.1.W4   940.54'28   75-11692
ISBN 0-87071-076-1

Contents

CHRONOLOGY
World War II Events along Pacific Coast

Preface

People tend to divide into three groups when it comes to knowledge of the events of World War II. There are the old-timers who lived through the period as adults and who either took part in the global struggle or received daily news of it by radio and newspapers. Many of them stuck pins in wall maps at strange-sounding places like Benghazi, Stalingrad, Oahu, Bataan, Marrakech, Salerno, Guadalcanal, St. Lô, Okinawa, Bastogne, and Hiroshima. They knew the faces of Montgomery, Eisenhower, Bradley, Patton, Doolittle, and Nimitz. They recognized the voices of Edward R. Murrow, William L. Shirer, and Winston Churchill. They watched for the byline of Ernie Pyle, for Bill Mauldin's cartoons of Willie and Joe, Pathé newsreels, and "The March of Time!"

There is a second group, those a little younger, including that huge segment of the population known as the "war-baby crop" who know something of the war from hearing Dad talk about his adventures in far-off places. They have an impression second-hand from those who stayed stateside and suffered from shortages, blackouts, restrictions, and rationing. They have an impression and perhaps memories of patterns of life disrupted, mobility, industrial expansion, marching troops, rumbling tanks, and long lines of olive-drab trucks.

Today's school and college group, the teens and the yet younger, know about the war mostly through what they read in required history courses or pick up in exaggerated versions on the late-night television movies. To them the 1940's seem like ancient history, and they find World War II a little hard to distinguish from conflicts that came before and afterwards.

The majority of all three groups know little or nothing about the series of attacks—some pathetic, some ingenious, all daring—which the Japanese made on the continental United States. For example, a recent perusal of the holdings of a secondary school library on a military post—the only post in the U.S. mainland to be shelled by the guns of a foreign enemy since the War of 1812—revealed no books, charts, or other materials telling of the role which that fort played in World War II. The librarian, who was also the social science teacher, said that he had "heard something once about an enemy attack here, but I really don't know anything about it. Maybe someday somebody will write a book."

Here is that book.

1

There are several reasons why so little is generally known about the Japanese attacks on North America in World War II. At the time of the attacks military secrecy prevented wide publicity. Authorities did not want the populace to become panicked. They did not want the Japanese to know how successful the attacks had been. Also, more earth-shaking events were taking place elsewhere around the globe, and they received most public attention. Even after news restrictions were removed in the closing days of the war, there was bigger news elsewhere to absorb the public's attention. What has been published about the attacks since the war is scattered, scarce, and contradictory.

This book is designed to unscramble and assemble pertinent details and anecdotes about the attacks and the circumstances surrounding them. It deals generally with Japanese operations off the west coast of the United States and Canada, with defense measures taken to lessen their effects, and with Japanese attempts to strike blows into the American homeland as retaliation for the Doolittle raid on the Japanese homeland.

In launching these attacks, the Japanese high command may well have had in mind a broader purpose than retaliation for one enemy action. In addition to whatever actual damage bombs dropped in North America would cause, there was the possibility of creating panic, disrupting the American war effort, and providing worldwide propaganda favorable to the Japanese, but to the men in the field, the attacks were a means of "getting even." As the first pilot to bomb the United States says, "It gave me great satisfaction to get some revenge for the bombing of my homeland by Doolittle's raiders." The balloon bombing of North America also appears tied in with the April 1942 U.S. attack on Japan. The home islands had been violated and the Samurai code required satisfaction for the insult.

The shore attack on southern California came before the Doolittle raid and could not have been part of the retaliation for it, but it has its own particular retaliatory implications.

The Japanese landings on the Aleutian Islands of Alaska were part of a grand strategy that included an attempt to occupy Midway Island. Because the operations in Alaska are well documented and information about them is readily available from other sources, they are not treated in detail here.

The main area of concern in this book is the Pacific Northwest from northern California into British Columbia, and especially the state of Oregon. In what were then the 48 states, Oregon was the only state where a fort was attacked, the only state where an aircraft bombing occurred, and the only state where lives were lost as a direct result of enemy military action. More of the bomb-carrying Japanese balloons were discovered in Oregon than in any other state.

Sifting truth from rumor, fact from fiction, and actual from imagined events always presents a problem—and especially so after a lapse of thirty years.

I checked on a story that a submarine, presumably Japanese, had shot at the Southern Pacific's *Coast Daylight* train number 99 as it skirted the beach south of San Luis Obispo. The shell failed to hit the train but exploded on the beach close enough for fragments to pepper the side of the kitchen section of the dining car. Three dining car workers were hit, two of them only slightly, but Vertie Bea Loggins—on her first day on the job— was struck by a jagged shell fragment that nearly severed her arm. Physicians on the train and in San Luis Obispo attended her.

Could this have been a hushed-up incident of enemy action that the government did not want to become public knowledge? I tried to find out. Fred Ehlers of Klamath Falls was the Army inspector in San Francisco that night who counted 33 holes in the side of car 10257 and ordered them repaired. Robert A. Sederholm, a public relations representative for the Southern Pacific, searched for old-timers who could remember the incident and Congressman John Dellenback of Oregon found material in Washington. The following is probably the true story of the incident.

A field artillery unit firing on the range at Camp Cooke, California, had fired a 105-mm howitzer, mounted on an M-7 tank chassis. The shell ricocheted, skidded along the ground, went over a small knoll, and became airborne just as the streamliner purred northward along the edge of the beach. The shell went over the train and exploded on the beach—so much for this "enemy attack."

Throughout the war "submarines" sighted along the coast turned out to be whales or floating logs.

One of the thousands of bomb-carrying balloons launched in Japan landed in the Sacramento Valley of California. It was found draped over power lines, the deflated envelope on one side and the ballast gear, three sandbags, and two incendiary bombs dangling on the other side.

A letter and other materials from Kou Maki (in Japanese) gives credence to declarations of men of the 248th Coast Artillery who have insisted for decades that they saw "submarines" in the Strait of Juan de Fuca and in Puget Sound. Although no enemy "submarines" entered the Strait, the Japanese did engage in a little trickery. Maki wrote that in order to deceive coast watchers, Japanese crewmen launched many "dummies." These devices were lengths of bamboo painted black, with a rock tied to one end and a piece of glass affixed to the other. The rock weight caused the bamboo pole to float vertically and the current kept it moving—just like a periscope!

As recently as 1972 a skin diver reported finding the hulk of a Japanese submarine off Cape Kiwanda, Oregon. United Press International distributed the story. The Associated Press in Portland asked me to comment. I responded that according to Japanese records, which account for all of their undersea craft, none of their submarines was lost off the U.S. west coast. Readers with facts to the contrary were urged to get in touch with me. Several did, but none of their "facts" checked out.

Rumors have persisted that in addition to direct attacks on military and merchant shipping, losses occurred because of sabotage. For example, at Yakutat, Alaska, on January 11, 1942, a fire broke out in the hold of the *M.S. Clevedon*, threatening its cargo of ammunition. This was one of the ships, incidentally, that had carried Regular Army troops staged at Camp Clatsop, Oregon, in 1941 to Kodiak and Dutch Harbor. When the fire broke out, the crew abandoned ship. The *S.S. Taku* passed a line and towed the *Clevedon* away from the port and let her run aground at a safe distance. Soon a tremendous explosion rocked Yakutat and the surrounding villages and forests. What was left sank.

Could this have been sabotage? Rumormongers pointed out that there were Japanese living in the vicinity. But no evidence of sabotage ever came to light. A careless crew member or faulty electrical wiring is a more likely possibility.

"The Strange (and Beautiful) Story of a Jap Sub and a Garbage Scow" was related by the San Francisco *Chronicle* on January 27, 1942. On December 20, 1941, it was claimed, the scow *Tahoe* on a routine garbage-dumping run off the Farallon Islands, had sighted, rammed, and apparently sunk a submarine in broad daylight. Drydock inspection

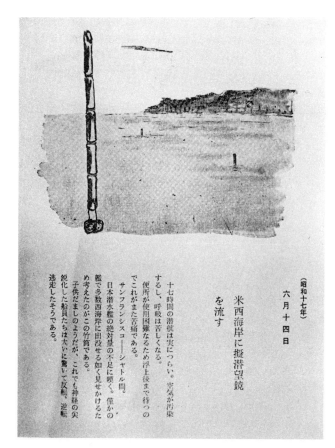

Kou Maki, a Japanese submariner, describes how dummy periscopes were dropped along the west coast of the United States to make up for the lack of submarines. "The bamboo poles," he says, "were made to deceive the enemy as if there were large numbers of submarines around, but the actual number of submarines was small. It was like tricking children, but it was reported that nervous [U.S.] sailors were frightened and turned their ships to flee."

later revealed that the 37-year-old former lumber ship had indeed "struck a steel object" that had cut a gash a foot wide and 80 feet long in the hull. The U.S. Navy disavowed any knowledge of the incident. The Japanese have never mentioned it. Their submarine *I-23* was in the vicinity at the time, having put a shell through the side of the Richfield Oil Company tanker *Agwiworld* the same day off Santa Cruz. But if the *I-23* was hit by the *Tahoe*, the submarine was not sunk, as alleged. It survived another two months before it was lost with all hands in the mid-Pacific. The *Chronicle* praised the *Tahoe* skipper, William Vartnaw, for having "lived up to the highest traditions of the sea."

Incidents like this have enlivened the search for the facts which have been collected for this book, and may someday be collected into a volume of slips, fluffs, near-misses, and other boners that form the human record of any war.

Actually, stronger than rumor, stranger than fiction, are the true stories of what was planned and what happened—and what was planned and did not happen. It is not generally known, for example, that a few days after the Pearl Harbor attack the Imperial Japanese Navy issued orders for their nine submarines fanned out along the west coast of the United States to fire simultaneously on shore targets on Christmas Eve 1941. If one shivers at the thought of this threat today—thirty years later—what might have been the reaction just after the disaster in Hawaii? Americans had not yet recovered from the "anything can happen now" feeling. Civilians and the military alike worried about the possibility of a Japanese raid or an invasion of the west coast.

What would have been the effect on morale at Yuletide parties if news had come that Japanese submarines had shelled the lighthouse beacons at Capes Flattery, Disappointment, Blanco, and Mendocino? If shells had struck San Francisco or the Golden Gate Bridge? If the submarines that lay off Monterey Bay, Estero Bay, San Pedro, and San Diego had surfaced and lobbed shells shoreward? What would that kind of Christmas greeting have done to jittery America? Fortunately, orders for these mass attacks were rescinded and the plan was never revived.

The true story of the balloon bombings skirts on the fringes of science fiction. Many readers, I believe, will be as fascinated as I have been in learning of the ingenious simplicity of the bomb-carrying balloons that very nearly proved to be effective offensive weapons. Only a strenuous defense by members of the civilian sector, a few flaws in technology, and wet, frozen forests rendered the balloons relatively harmless.

In the search for accurate information for this book I have gone to sea and into the air to reconstruct events. I have climbed trackless mountainsides, combed volumes of documents, read the limited selection of magazines and newspaper clippings that pertain to the attacks, and persuaded reluctant clerks to delve into yellowing files. An especially pertinent source, at least to my mind, is the people who were on the scene when the attacks occurred and who vividly remembered what happened. I have talked with and corresponded with hundreds of them and taken reams of notes and boxes of pictures. I early found that I needed to use a cross-checking system, which tended to reinforce some testimony and suggest that other time-warped recollections be discarded.

I have tried to be accurate, to use reliable sources, and to choose what appears to be the most plausible of conflicting stories. If this effort has missed points that readers feel are pertinent, I hope they will tell me about them.

In selecting material to be included, in organizing it, and in preparing the manuscript, I have had the good fortune to have the beyond-the-call-of-duty assistance of two members of the Oregon State University Press. Jesse Bone, chairman of the Board of Governors of the Press, and Ken Munford, Director of the Press, have used their talents to see this book through to completion. The inquisitive minds and alert blue pencils of copy editors have done much to polish the manuscript.

Others deserving of a special note of appreciation are translators Mari Suga Schwartz, Keiko Nakamura Thurston, and Matt Amano and typists Dale Webber, June Rettig, and Ginny Knowles. The contributions of hundreds of others are identified in the "Sources, Acknowledgments, and Notes" at the end of the text.

To my wife Marjorie Jean—"Suzy" to me—who actively assisted me, at my side and in the background, I am forever indebted.

BERT WEBBER
Medford, Oregon

December 31, 1974

The *Tahoe*, a garbage scow owned by the Oakland Scavenger Company, reported ramming a partially submerged submarine west of San Francisco on December 20, 1941.

TOKYO BOMBED

The Oregon Statesman
POUNDED 1851

The Inside
Your complete morning newspaper. The Statesman offers you pertinent comments on war news of the day by Kirke Simpson, Washington analyst.

De Gaulle
NEW YORK, April 17—(AP) Gen. Charles De Gaulle, leader of the free-French forces, is scheduled for a Saturday broadcast to this country via NBC and Blue networks at 12:25 PWT.

NINETY-FIRST YEAR   Salem, Oregon, Saturday Morning, April 18, 1942   Price 5c.   No. 328

Japs Announce First Raid On City

In Tokyo, volunteers fought a fire caused by a bomb dropped by one of Doolittle's Raiders on April 18, 1942.

Radio Declares Three Aircraft Shot Down; No US Confirmation

Stimson Says Army to Start Offense Soon

Stresses MacArthur Is in Command; 'Things Moving'

WASHINGTON, April 17—(AP) Secretary Stimson said Friday the army would be ready for the offensive soon, no matter what difficulties might be encountered. At the same time he emphasized that Gen. Douglas MacArthur had "over-all strategic command" in the southwest Pacific

(Later in the day news dispatches from Australia said MacArthur had received a directive from Washington clarifying his powers. Newsmen at US army headquarters in Australia were informed the directive was com-

'Inhuman Attack' Is Averred Made On Schools, Hospitals

TOKYO—(From Japanese broadcasts)—April 18—(AP)—The Tokyo region was raided by enemy planes this afternoon, a Japanese official announcement said today. The raiders came from several directions.

Three planes were declared to have been shot down in the raids, the first of the war on Japan's imperial homelands.

"It is confirmed that three enemy

Over Yokosuka Naval Base in Japan, Lt. Richard Knobloch snapped this picture from the co-pilot's window moments before a 500-pound bomb was dropped on a submarine tender being converted into an aircraft carrier. Four submarines were dry-docked nearby (see page 153). Two of them, *I-25* and *I-26* later participated in retaliatory raids on the west coast of North America.

6

Introduction

In the early 1940's, the nations bordering the Pacific Basin engaged in a mighty struggle to determine whether or not the Japanese Empire should expand in southeast Asia and dominate the southwest Pacific. Japanese forces invaded Indochina in 1940 and the Philippine Islands in December 1941. Japan declared war on the United States, Great Britain, Australia, Canada, New Zealand, and the Union of South Africa on December 7, 1941, and joined the Axis Powers, Germany and Italy, who were at war with Great Britain, and who had forced France to surrender in 1940.

Japan's actions plunged the partially mobilized United States into the global conflict as a full participant rather than as a neutral with anti-Axis leanings. The struggle in the Pacific lasted nearly four years, from December 1941 to September 1945. But once the basic issue was settled, when Japan clearly saw that its dream of imperial expansion was not to be realized by military force, a remarkable transformation took place. The Japanese people accepted the judgment of battle and set out to make the best of their new international situation.

In the intervening years, Japan and the United States have developed a congenial relationship. They have become industrial and commercial rivals in international trade. They depend on each other for mutual political assistance. They promote cultural exchanges. Camera-clicking tourists flow through each other's homelands. And in many areas the Japanese and Americans have achieved a relationship that is more mutually beneficial than that which normally exists between allies.

It is therefore possible now to look at what went on during the war years from different points of view. Official reports from both sides, classified documents, correspondence, and a mass of comment and analysis have become available for examination. Personal memoirs of participants have been published. Former officers and other officials on both sides of the Pacific, including the only pilot who bombed the U.S. mainland, have delved into their memories, searched archives, and spoken freely of their wartime activities.

Grand strategy

The main thrust of Japanese expansion was southward into the Philippine Islands, Micronesia, Indonesia, and Southeast Asia. In order to protect their eastern flank the Japanese strategists knew

7

U.S. Coast Guard Station at Woman's Bay, Kodiak Island, Alaska, 1974. In May 1942, a plane launched from the *I-25* Japanese submarine made reconnaissance flights over this base, then a naval air station.

they would have to neutralize the U.S. forces in the Pacific, cripple the U.S. seapower, and delay American attacks that would upset their timetable for conquest and occupation.

The boldest phase of their plan was to make a surprise attack on the U.S. Naval Base at Pearl Harbor in the Hawaiian Islands in an effort to destroy American naval power in the Pacific. All the world knows how effectively this strategy was carried out and the extent to which the United States was caught napping and left embarrassingly unprepared for speedy counterattack.

This is not to say that the United States and Canada were completely unprepared for a Pacific war. Canada was mobilized and participating in the European war. Because of that war and the uncertainty of Japan's intentions in the Pacific, the United States was partially mobilized. Manpower and equipment for the Army and Navy had been expanded. Beginning in 1940, National Guard units and Reserve personnel had been called into federal service.

Large contingents of land, sea, and air forces had been assembled in the Hawaiian Islands. That is the main reason the Japanese chose that spot for their initial surprise attack.

Coastal defenses, some of which will be described later, had been established along the U.S.

west coast for nearly a century. The Panama Canal zone had been fortified.

In Alaska three main bases had been authorized by Congress in the late 1930's. These were located at Sitka in the southeast panhandle, on Kodiak Island at the base of the Alaska Peninsula, and on Unalaska Island in the Aleutian chain. Both the Army and the Navy had establishments at these locations. They were garrisoned by regular Navy and Army personnel and later augmented by National Guard units. Across the bay from the Dutch Harbor naval station on Unalaska Island the Army manned Fort Meares. On Kodiak Island the Navy had Kodiak Naval Air Station and the Army, Fort Greely.

The Aleutian bases, which were expanded after the war with Japan started, had a dual purpose: to prevent a Japanese stepping-stone advance across the north Pacific into Canada and the United States, and to provide a springboard for a similar advance by U.S. forces in the opposite direction. To some extent they achieved both purposes. In June 1942, enemy aircraft raided Dutch Harbor, and a few days later Japanese troops occupied Attu and Kiska, 600 miles to the west of Dutch Harbor, and later a third island, Agattu. The combination of frequent bombing by American forces and the extreme weather conditions—equally bad for both

8

sides—contained the Japanese. By mid-1943 the Japanese were beaten on Attu and had withdrawn from Kiska under cover of bad weather. The United States then built airfields in the western Aleutians from which Japanese bases in the Kurils were photographed and attacked by air.

The Doolittle raid

Nations at war set up box-score boards like those on a baseball field on which to record their wins and losses. The Japanese marked up wins first: Pearl Harbor, Guam, Wake, the Philippines, Indochina, Burma, and the southwest Pacific. For weeks, for months, the news for Americans was all bad. True, there was individual as well as unit heroism in those grim early days of the war, but in general, it was Japan that was scoring.

Americans hoped for a Pearl Harbor-or-equal battle won by the United States, but all was silent until April 18, 1942. On that date Lt. Col. James H. Doolittle, with 16 twin-engined B-25 bombers of the Army Air Force, took off from the Navy's aircraft carrier *Hornet* and bombed Tokyo and other parts of the Japanese home islands. Score one for the United States!

The Doolittle attack (which the Navy refers to as the Halsey-Doolittle raid), in which Army medium bombers built to operate from landing fields were launched from an aircraft carrier, was unique in military history. It shocked the Japanese military planners and brought on a severe case of public jitters. American planes had been seen flying at

A U.S. Army Air Force Mitchell bomber (B-25B) of the type used by the Doolittle Raiders.

low altitude in the middle of the day and dropping bombs on Tokyo, Yokosuka, Kobe, and Nagoya.

As various historians point out, face-saving on the part of the Japanese was mandatory after the Doolittle raid. Physical damage done by the bombers was not great, but the attack was quite injurious to morale. Japanese newspapers played down the raid. Yet the realization that the United States was unified and able to reach out and damage the homeland this early in the war seemed cause enough for the warlords to be wary of larger attacks sure to come in the future.

The feeling on the Japanese home front is reflected in a letter the air-ace Saburo Sakai received from his school-girl cousin, whom he later married.

I know you are in the thick of combat and your successes against the enemy are of great comfort to all of us at home. The bombing of Tokyo and several other cities has brought about tremendous change in the attitude of our people toward the war. Now things are different. Bombs have been dropped here on our homes. It does not seem anymore that there is such a great difference between the battle front and the home front.

In his account of his war experiences, Sakai comments,

Officially the government disclaimed any heavy damage . . . but the attack unnerved almost every pilot at Lae [New Guinea]. The knowledge the enemy was strong enough to smash our homeland . . . was cause for serious apprehension.

Almost like a return-mail reply, the Imperial High Command ordered that something be done in retaliation. But what? The American homeland was thousands of miles across the ocean. Many of the *I*-class long-range submarines were equipped to carry and launch reconnaissance planes. Perhaps they could also be used to drop bombs. A study started years earlier on free-floating gas-filled balloons as offensive weapons was scrutinized. Some means had to be found to wreak havoc on the American homeland. ☐

American base at Dutch Harbor, Alaska, after the Japanese attack on June 3, 1942.

JAPANESE ATTACK ON DUTCH HARBOR, JUNE 3, 1942.

The 357-foot-long B-1 type Japanese submarine was equipped with a seaplane hangar and catapult on the fore deck. It could carry a small reconnaissance floatplane and mounted a 14-cm gun on the after deck. Three of these submarines shelled targets along the west coast. One of the planes dropped incendiary bombs on Oregon forests.

I

The War Below

ALTHOUGH THE ATTACK ON PEARL HARBOR was primarily by air, submarines played an important part in Japanese operations. Before and during the war, Japanese naval architects used great ingenuity and skill in developing a wide variety of versatile undersea craft, ranging from tiny submarines with two-man crews to huge submersible transports 400 feet long. The Japanese designed and built torpedoes capable of high speed and exceptional range. Some of the larger *I*-class fleet submarines were equipped to carry midget submarines as well as torpedoes. Others were designed to carry aircraft. This was not an entirely new concept. The British had tried the idea and discarded it.

At the start of the war, Japan had about a dozen *I*-class submarines capable of carrying small reconnaissance aircraft. Eventually they built others that carried two or three aircraft, but these did not get into the war in the eastern Pacific. In all, according to records available now, Japan had a total of 42 aircraft-carrying submarines, but not all were available at any one time. Some were lost early in the war, while others were not launched until weeks before the war's end.

Those designed or adapted for carrying aircraft that were in operation at the beginning of the war included the *I-6, I-7, I-8, I-9, I-10, I-15, I-17, I-19, I-21, I-23, I-25,* and *I-26*. There is evidence that all but *I-23* and *I-26* actually carried planes at that time. The *I-6* and *I-7* did not have assignments along the North American coast, but all of the others came into U.S. or Canadian waters at least once. The *I-17* made two trips, both off California; *I-25* made three trips and *I-26* two trips to the north Pacific coasts.

The GLEN aircraft

Allied intelligence apparently knew little about the Japanese plane designed and built with great secrecy for submarine transport. After it was discovered and classified, it was given the code name GLEN—and sometimes referred to as the "Erector Set" because it had to be assembled each time before it could fly. It was a small, light, slow monoplane with a 340-horsepower engine, a top speed of 153 miles per hour at sea level, and a 550-mile range. It had a crew of two, was armed with a small machine gun, and after being modified for bombing could carry a payload of two 76-kilogram (170-pound) bombs.

According to Japanese nomenclature it was classed as a ZERO-type reconnaissance seaplane, designated as YOKOSUKA E-14Y-1. This plane should not be confused with the other, more-famous ZERO's, especially the highly maneuverable fighter called ZEKE and its floatplane version called RUFE. The "ZERO" terminology merely meant that it went into production in the Japanese year 2600 (i.e., in 1940).

The GLEN had a wing span of 36 feet (10.96 meters), a length of 22 feet (8.54 meters), and a height of 9 feet (3.68 meters). William Green gives this description:

Destined to be built in larger numbers than any other submarine-borne aircraft, the E14Y1 was of mixed construction with a welded steel-tube fuselage covered forward with light metal panels, aft with fabric over light wooden formers and on the underside with metal sheet, and the wings had light metal spars, wooden ribs and fabric covering. The single-step floats were attached to the fuselage by transverse inverted W-struts, and these could be detached from the fuselage and struts for stowage aboard the submarine. The wings could be detached from the fuselage at the spar fittings, the flaps and ailerons folded under the wings, and the V-struts hingeing at the wing attachments to fold up against the lower surfaces. The top section of the fin and the ventral stabilising surface below the rear fuselage were also detachable, and the outer sections of the tailplane folded upward for stowage.

The E14Y1 was powered by a 340 h.p. nine-cylinder Tempu 12 radial engine, and this was started up while the aircraft was still inside the submarine's cylindrical hangar. After removal from the hangar the wings, fins, and floats were attached, the tailplane unfolded, and the floatplane catapulted from the deck of the submarine [by compressed air]. Production of the E14Y1 was begun in 1940, and the first deliveries to the J.N.A.F. began in the late summer of 1941.

The GLEN-type aircraft was used for reconnaissance in the central and southwest Pacific and in southwest Alaska and the Aleutians. On two occasions one of them dropped incendiary bombs on Oregon forests (see Chapters VI and VII).

Submarine operations

Preparatory to the attack on Pearl Harbor, scheduled for December 7, 1941, an advance expeditionary force of 27 submarines was sent out in late November. Most were the long-range I-type. Five of them carried midget two-man submarines 41 to 45 feet long, attached to the mother ship with heavy clamps. About eleven of the submarines carried aircraft.

The principal operating base for the Japanese Sixth (Submarine) Fleet, which consisted of forty

Imperial Japanese Navy Submarine I-25 Principal Particulars		
Standard Displacement		2191.9 LT
Principal Dimensions		
Length (overall)		108.7 m
Length (waterline)		107.0 m
Breadth (extreme)		9.3 m
Depth		7.9 m
Mean draft (normal)		5.14 m
Surface Displacement		
Normal		2,584 t
Full		3,233 t
Speed & Power		
Surface		23.6 kts/12,400 HP
Submerged		8.0 kts/ 2,000 HP
Endurance		
Surface		16 kts-14,000 SM
Submerged	3 kts-	33 Hrs
Armament		
14 cm/45 cal gun		1
25 mm machine gun (twin)		1
53 cm torpedo tube		6
Aircraft		1
Submergible Depth		100 m
Complement		97
Mitsubishi Heavy Industries, Ltd.		

submarines in mid-1941, was at Kwajalein atoll in the Marshall Islands. On November 18-20 the advance expeditionary force of submarines left Kure and Yokosuka for Kwajalein, where they refueled and took on supplies. They then departed for the Hawaiian Islands and took up picket positions at varying distances around the islands.

One of them, the *I-26*, which was using space in the deck hangar to carry extra fuel tanks in place of a GLEN aircraft, broke off from the other ships and moved toward the North American coast. Three more of the big submarines, *I-19*, *I-21*, and *I-23* came into Hawaiian waters before December 7 to provide the Ship Lane Patrol for the Pearl Harbor Striking Force.

The five submarines that carried midgets launched them shortly after midnight, Sunday morning, December 7. Sighting one of these was the first indication of enemy action the Americans discovered, but news of its presence did not reach Pearl Harbor soon enough to alert the U.S. Navy. The midgets did no damage. Three were located and destroyed; the other two disappeared. The hull of one of the latter was found twenty years later.

The *Cynthia Olson*

At about the time bombs began to drop on Pearl Harbor, the *I-26* patrolling 1,000 miles northeast of the Hawaiian Islands sighted the *Cynthia Olson*, a 2,140-ton lumber freighter under charter to the U.S. Army. Arguments still pop up from time to time over which came first—the attack on *Cynthia Olson* or on Pearl Harbor.

The commander of *I-26*, Minoru Yokoda (who changed his name to Minoru Hasegawa after the war), explained the situation to me by letter in 1973:

The claim I wish to make clear here is that my attack on *Cynthia Olson* was *after* Pearl Harbor.

Minoru Yokoda,
commander of *I-26*

I had had a strict order from Japanese Navy Superior *not to do anything* before 3:30 a.m. December 8, 1941 TOKYO TIME, the planned time to attack Pearl Harbor, so that Pearl Harbor might be the real *sudden* attack against U.S. forces.

The most important element in the entire debate as to the event seems to be that throughout the world the Japanese Navy was using *Tokyo time*. Thus the day of Pearl Harbor was to us the 8th of December, while it was the 7th to you.

I did not come up to the sea-surface until 3:30 a.m. Japan Tokyo time to attack *Cynthia Olson* to keep the silent secrecy for the entire Navy Force of Japan about to attack and start the war.

I did not use any torpedo against *Cynthia Olson* but gun-shells as the attack was from the surface. Having come up on the surface exactly at 3:30 a.m., I took some minutes to prepare the gun. The attacks were made as follows:

(i) I shot a shell so that it would not hit the ship directly but go over it as the *warning to stop*, and gave them some chance to escape from the ship.

(ii) Men left the ship in smaller rescue boats.

(iii) Our radio man caught the SOS from *Cynthia Olson* which *S.S. Lurline* was said to have heard. And we noticed a mistake in their message, that they were saying of being attacked by "torpedoes," when actually they were *gun-shells*.

(iv) Having given some time for the men to escape from the ship, we shelled the ship effectively, but at that time we could not sink it.

(v) In order to avoid the counterattack from the air force in reply to the call, our *I-26* went into the water without seeing the last moment of the ship.

The *Cynthia Olson*, first merchant
ship sunk in the Pacific war.

Cynthia Olson slowly sinking as photographed by Saburo Hayashi from
the bridge of *I-26*.

(vi) After a while I came on the surface again and saw the ship now on fire but yet not sunk. I shelled some again and went into the water again to avoid the possible counterattack.

(vii) For the third time, when I came up to the surface, I could see it almost sunk. I could not see in person the very moment when the ship sank into the water.

(viii) Then *I-26* went on southward on the surface of the sea.

At that time, in 1941, there was a 4½-hour time difference between Tokyo and Honolulu (now it is 5 hours). In 1941, 3:30 a.m., December 8 in Japan was 8 a.m., December 7 in the Hawaiian Islands. The Pearl Harbor attack began at 7:55 a.m., Hawaii time, only five minutes before *I-26*—according to Mr. Hasegawa—rose out of the sea to attack *Cynthia Olson*. Although crew members entered lifeboats, they were never heard from or seen again.

Submarines in the eastern Pacific

None of the reconnaissance planes carried on submarines took part in the Pearl Harbor attack. The first operational sortie of one of these float-planes took place at dawn on December 16, when *I-7* assembled and launched its plane so that observers could see what damage had been done at Pearl Harbor. The *I-19* successfully completed a similar mission by moonlight during the night of January 4, 1942, and again on February 23.

None of the three U.S. aircraft carriers assigned to the Pacific Fleet was in Pearl Harbor at the time of the attack. The *Lexington* was en route to Midway Island, *Enterprise* was returning from Wake Island, and *Saratoga* was entering San Diego harbor.

The Japanese submarines were eager to find the American carriers. The *I-6* reported sighting a *Lexington*-class carrier on December 10 in Hawaiian waters and pursuit was ordered. The same day planes from the *Enterprise* spotted and sank *I-70* (*I-170*), the first Japanese vessel lost. For the next few days U.S. destroyers and the *I*-subs played hide and seek without doing any further damage to each other. The subs were after bigger game—aircraft carriers—specifically the *Lexington*, which was believed to be heading for the U.S. mainland.

The *I*-subs were more successful against freighters and tankers. In addition to the *Cynthia Olson* on December 7, they shelled and sank the S.S. *Lahina* 700 miles northwest of Hawaii on December 11; torpedoed and sank the S.S. *Manini* not

far from Honolulu on December 17; and torpedoed and sank the S.S. *Prusa* 150 miles south of Hawaii on December 18. Other merchant ships including the tankers *Agwiworld*, and the *Emidio, Samoa, Larry Doheney, Montebello,* and *Absaroka* were attacked off the California coast before Christmas.

Unable to locate the *Lexington*, the Japanese submarines dispersed toward the U.S. coast—to attack shipping and to be in position to shell coastal targets. Their disposition (see map) was as follows:

I-26 off Cape Flattery, Strait of Juan de Fuca, Washington

I-25 off Cape Disappointment, mouth of the Columbia River

I-9 off Cape Blanco, Oregon
I-17 off Cape Mendocino, California
I-15 off San Francisco, California
I-23 off Monterey Bay, California
I-21 off Estero Bay, California
I-19 off Los Angeles, California
I-10 off San Diego, California

According to records translated after the war and published in Japanese Monograph No. 102 by the General Headquarters, Far East Command, the Submarine Force Detachment had been scheduled to shell the coastal cities of the United States on Christmas Eve, but "in the latter part of December the antisubmarine measures taken by the United States became very severe and the Submarine Force Detachment . . . was ordered by the Combined Fleet Headquarters to abandon the plan."

What the "very severe" antisubmarine measures taken by U.S. forces along the U.S. west coast may have lacked in the way of trained personnel and adequate equipment was overcome to some extent by vigor and innovation. Small boats of various types put to sea and any type of military plane that could fly as far as the coast was put into the air in weather which was especially bad in the Pacific Northwest. Trainers, observation planes, photomapping and pursuit planes, and a limited number of medium bombers went on patrol schedules up and down the coast. Many months later the U.S. Navy opened the Tillamook Naval Air Station, which maintained a number of blimps for offshore patrol, but in the first month of the war the makeshift arrangements carried the load and became an effective deterrent to coastal attacks.

One of the earliest recorded incidents involving a Japanese submarine off the Oregon coast was told by Clarence E. Gillingham, an engineer-gunner on a B-25 Mitchell bomber stationed at the Army Air Corps field in Pendleton. Gillingham recalls a mission on December 24, 1942:

We were flying out of McChord because the weather was so bad we'd not been able to get back to Pendleton the night before. We left the airport so as to hit the Oregon Coast off the mouth of the Columbia River about daybreak. At pre-flight briefing, we had been told to fly at 1,000 feet altitude, so the Bombardier (Pfc. [later Colonel] George R. Hammond) set his Norden bombsight for that level. We were loaded with 300-pound bombs.

About 12 miles off the coast, we sighted what looked like a submarine. Because of the heavy fog we were flying only about 500 feet above the water. Radioman Pvt. John O. Van Marter was told to radio that we had sighted a sub

and we were attacking. Our first bomb overshot the sub because of the wrong altitude setting on the sight. I was ordered by the aircraft commander, Lt. Brick Holstrom [Brig. Gen. Everett W. Holstrom, USAF (Ret.)] to keep the sub in sight while he turned and made another pass. I was in the top turret where I could get a good view while he racked the plane around. When we came out of it, our props were picking up water from the ocean. As we came back up, the bombardier salvoed the load and I saw one bomb hit right in front of the conning tower. Another went just to the side of the sub. The submarine had been under the water but the hit brought it back up near the surface, then the vessel went back down again. I could see air bubbles and oil. The shock nearly took our plane with it. We radioed we had hit the sub and were returning to base.

When we arrived at McChord Field, we found the field socked in so we went north toward Seattle, heading for Boeing Field. The ground crew had left the airspeed indicator cover on, when we took off, so we couldn't tell how fast we were going. So we called for fire trucks to be on the field because we might stall out, but we landed okay. Brick Holstrom called the Second Bomber Command from a flight operations office telephone, and we were told that the Navy had confirmed the sinking. The Navy checked all reports because whales had been killed by bombing under the mistaken impression that they were submarines.

Lt. Ted Lawson, piloting another B-25, flew over the area shortly afterwards. "The oil was coming up in greasy bubbles," he says, "as if some awful thing was throwing up under water."

Brig. Gen. John B. Brooks, Acting Commander of the Second Air Force, ordered a special review for Lt. Holstrom and his crew, at which Holstrom, his copilot Lt. Rosstrom Wilder, and Bombardier Hammond were each awarded Air Medals.

For years investigators have searched for details, verifications, and proof-positive that a submarine was sunk. We know now that the Japanese *I-25* had been off the mouth of the Columbia River anticipating the Christmas Eve shelling, and we also know that she was not sunk, for she returned twice more to the Pacific coast before being lost in the South Pacific in 1943. The Japanese War History Office confirms the report that *I-25* was in Pacific Northwest waters on December 20 and that it was ordered to head for Panama. No other Japanese submarines are reported to have been in the area at the time. The U.S. Navy states that there was no American submarine in the area at the time.

General Brooks wrote a Salem, Oregon, *Capital Journal* reporter in 1961 that his letters of commendation were issued on the basis of existing reports and that strict criteria for determining sinkings had not yet been laid down. "I was proud of my command," he said, "and decided to make the awards." The Navy's Action Assessment Sheet, Incident No. 72, 2 Sept. 1942, rated the attack on the submarine as "D—probably damaged, no evidence of destruction."

General Holstrom, who piloted the B-25, wrote me: "I saw the submarine. There was no claim made by me or the crew beyond the fact that we saw the sub and we thought one of the bombs had made a hit. I simply reported to the Navy what happened."

Incidentally, the B-25B, which pilots Holstrom and Wilder were flying that day, is one of the planes that flew over Tokyo with the Doolittle raiders a few months later. "As far as I know," General Holstrom says, "except for the test crew at the North American plant, no one ever flew that airplane but myself until it was destroyed in China."

The *Mauna Ala*

Although not a victim of direct enemy assault, the Matson Navigation Company's S.S. *Mauna Ala* was wrecked because of conditions attributable to the war. At the time of the Pearl Harbor attack, the ship was 750 miles at sea, bound for the Hawaiian Islands. It was ordered to turn back and speed for refuge in the Columbia River. It never made it because aids to navigation along the west coast of North America had been turned off to thwart enemy vessels from entering harbors at night. Nearing the Columbia on December 10 and running at full speed, the *Mauna Ala* plowed into the sands of Clatsop Beach and stopped 700 feet from

Christmas cargo from the wrecked *S.S. Mauna Ala* littered the sand of Clatsop Beach.

shore. The Coast Guard took their 52-foot motor lifeboat *Triumph* alongside and rescued the 35 men aboard. The pounding surf broke up the ship and spewed its holiday cargo of 60,000 Christmas trees, hundreds of turkeys, and other goods for miles along the beach.

The *Emidio*

The first submarine attack on commercial shipping immediately off the northwest coast came a few days after the beaching of *Mauna Ala*. On December 20, the General Petroleum tanker S.S. *Emidio* was riding empty out of Seattle for San Pedro. Captain Clark A. Farrow, the tanker's skipper, said later that he was on a course set by the U.S. Navy, who had told him there were no submarines in the vicinity. The Japanese submarine *I-17*, with Commander Kuzo Nishino at the helm, sighted the 6,912-ton tanker near Blunts Reef off Cape Mendocino, California. Within sight of land at about 1:30 p.m. *I-17* surfaced, turned its 14-cm deck gun on *Emidio*, and fired six rounds. Five shells struck the tanker. The *Emidio* crew took to lifeboats and about twelve hours later reached Blunts Reef lightship, where they were taken aboard. The tanker did not sink. She drifted onto a rock off Crescent City, where years later (1959) the Coast Guard declared the hulk a menace to navigation and a wrecking crew broke her up.

Toward the end of December the submarines spread out along the west coast were ordered back to Kwajalein for resupply and refitting and by the middle of January had reached their base.

Submarines in the North Pacific

In February 1942 and again in May, some of the submarines returned to the North Pacific. Before the Battle of Midway, June 4-6, 1942, a diversionary attack on the Aleutians was part of the Japanese master plan. The patrol and reconnaissance group that accompanied the northern task force consisted of the submarines *I-9, I-15, I-17, I-19, I-25,* and *I-26*. All but *I-26* carried GLEN floatplanes.

In the Aleutians, one of the submarines, *I-17* or *I-19* (probably the former), was caught on the surface by a U.S. patrol plane. It escaped but had to abandon its plane, which, unfortunately, was destroyed, although it might possibly have been captured intact. None of this type of aircraft is known to have survived the war.

The tanker *Emidio* before and after being attacked by the *I-17* on December 20, 1941.

The *I-25* cruised within flight range of Kodiak and launched its plane. Circling high above Pyramid Peak at 9,000-feet altitude, the pilot and observer had a bird's-eye view of the U.S. Naval Base on Woman's Bay and of early morning Army life at Fort Greely, where barracks and other buildings were planted in neat rows between Mt. Barometer and Lake Louise, a few miles west of the Navy installations. What a target for machine-gun strafing! Could this thought have occurred to the pilot, Warrant Officer Nobuo Fujita, and his observer Petty Officer Shoji Okuda? Their aircraft was designed for observation, not attack. It was armed with only a single 7.7-mm machine gun. Strafing Fort Greely would have been more dangerous to Fujita and Okuda than to the Americans. They would have been an easy target for the 215th Coast Artillery (Minnesota National Guard) antiaircraft batteries if they had

deviated from their look-and-see orders and attempted anything bold.

None of the American skywatchers on Kodiak apparently saw the Japanese plane. Col. Eugene E. Kent (USA Ret) of Medford, Oregon, who was Post Signal Officer at Fort Greely, told me in 1972 that the Army was not aware of it. "If General [Charles H.] Corlett knew about it," he said, "I'm sure his staff would have been told."

Such a flight in that vicinity was not without hazard. There were something like 105 U.S. Army planes and 27 Navy planes in Alaska at the time, most of them within range of Kodiak. Except for the transports and trainers, any one of them could have blown Fujita's GLEN out of the sky without the least bit of trouble or if they had followed him back to the *I-25* they could have given the submarine something to worry about.

Camouflaged barracks on the main post at Fort Greely, Alaska, in late spring 1942. Black window shades and light-tight doors helped conceal the fort from aerial reconnaissance at night.

Enemy plane over Seattle?

After the *I-25's* reconnaissance over Kodiak on May 21, 1942, she and *I-26* were directed to the coast of the Pacific Northwest, where they arrived the first week in June. One mission of the *I-26* was to see if there were any Canadian or U.S. naval units in the Vancouver-Seattle waters which could be dispatched to the Aleutians. The Japanese wanted to know if there would be any major naval interference with their landings on Attu and Kiska. According to Morison, Holmes, and other sources, the *I-26* sent up a plane to reconnoiter Seattle, but it was never observed or reported. In light of new information, it appears that this flight could not have taken place. Mr. Hasegawa, who was Commander Yokoda of *I-26* at the time, replied to a question I submitted to him in 1973:

During the reconnaissance mission in June 1942, I did not fly any aircraft over Seattle, since there was no aircraft on *I-26*.

The aircraft spotters who have been chided for letting a Japanese reconnaissance plane fly over Seattle undetected and unreported need not feel any embarrassment. Whatever reconnaissance the *I-26* conducted was from the surface of the sea. It did not even try to enter the Strait of Juan de Fuca.

The *Coast Trader*

On Sunday afternoon, June 7, 1942, the *I-26* sighted the *S.S. Coast Trader* of the Coastwise Line at 48°15′N-125°45′W. With Captain Lyle G. Havens in command the 3,286-ton freighter was carrying a cargo of newsprint from Port Angeles to San Francisco. Mr. Hasegawa recalls:

It was our *I-26* that torpedoed [the *Coast Trader*] near the Strait of Juan de Fuca. I did not go into the strait; it seemed too dangerous for us to enter. We attacked *Coast Trader* as she came out from the Strait.

We could not see the last moment of her [but we saw] many things from the boat floating on the surface. I did not meet any U.S. forces in that area, except one patrol frigate-type boat cruising eastward. But we could not ascertain its nationality whether American, Canadian, or other. However, we were much aware of the aircraft frequently flying above us.

When the torpedo struck the ship, the explosion damaged its radio antenna. No distress message was sent. The freighter floated for 40 minutes before sinking, giving the crew of 36 and the Army gun crew of 26 time to abandon ship in two small rafts and one boat. A fishing vessel, *Virginia I*, sighted the lifeboat about 24 hours later and towed it to Neah Bay. The next day a Canadian corvette, guided by a Coast Guard airplane, rescued the men on the rafts and took them to the Port Angeles Navy Section Base. One man died, apparently from exposure. The injured were taken to a Port Angeles hospital.

Patrol craft *YP89*, a Coast Guard surf boat, and several aircraft were sent to look for the submarine. The Canadian corvette *H.M.C.S. Edmundston* and the armed yacht *Sans Peur* searched waters to the north. The U.S. destroyer *Fox* put to sea in such haste that a liberty party was left behind. Regularly patrolling PBY Catalinas of Navy Patrol Wing Four were especially alert in the search area. On June 9 the air search group reported sighting a submarine 420 miles northwest of Tatoosh Island. This was probably *I-26*.

The board of inquiry into the *Coast Trader's* loss came to conclusions not shared by the survivors. The report, dated July 1, 1942, said that the loss was due to "an internal explosion and not to a torpedo or mine." The Navy apparently did not want to publicly acknowledge Japanese submarine activity on the Pacific Northwest coast. The Navy directed the late Nard Jones of the Seattle *Post-Intelligencer*, then a Navy lieutenant, to "give the matter negative publicity."

The *I-9*, on Aleutian patrol, cruised east toward Kodiak Island. In mid-June its aircraft, following Fujita's earlier pattern, reconnoitered the Kodiak Naval Air Station. Like Fujita's flight, this one was also apparently undetected by U.S. forces. The *I-9* cruised east from Kodiak into the Gulf of Alaska, and on June 19 intercepted the *U.S.A.T. General Gorgas* at 146°46′W-56°17′N. The submarine attacked with its deck gun, but the transport managed to evade most of the shells and steamed out of range, taking only two hits and minor damage in the action.

The *S.S. Coast Trader.*

The *Fort Camosun*

On June 20, about 70 miles south-southwest of Cape Flattery, the *I-25* intercepted the *S.S. Fort Camosun*, a new, coal-burning cargo vessel under charter to the British Ministry of War Transport. Making her maiden voyage under Captain T. S. Eggleston, this Victoria-built ship was loaded to capacity with zinc, lead, plywood, and other raw materials consigned for England. At 12:06 a.m., a torpedo from *I-25* struck the port side below the bridge. The explosion opened holds number 2 and 3 to the sea. At 1:20 a.m. the attacking submarine surfaced and fired a shell across the bow of the disabled ship. Half an hour later another shell struck the starboard side amidships. The Vancouver *Sun* later described this as a "determined attack."

At 2:30 a.m. the Canadian corvette *Quesnel*, returning to British Columbia after convoy duty, and the corvette *Edmundston*, on antisubmarine patrol, sped to the scene of the attack. After nearly six hours at flank speed *Quesnel* sighted the damaged vessel, attacked what seemed to be a submerged submarine nearby, and with the *Edmundston* providing cover, rescued the 31-man crew of *Fort Camosun* from lifeboats.

The area was getting too crowded with enemy warships for Commander Meiji Tagami of *I-25*. He turned south and departed, claiming *Fort Camosun*, now lying dead in the water and slowly settling, as a sinking. When I queried the Japanese War History Institute in Tokyo in June 1972, the Institute confirmed the attack, "*I-25* . . . sinking tanker *Fort Camosun*." The records, apparently, were based only on the original report from the *I-25*, because the ship was a freighter, not a tanker, and it was not sunk.

Near midnight, 24 hours after the torpedoing, the *Edmundston* put a towline on *Fort Camosun*, which was now low in the water but still afloat, and headed for port. The stricken ship, like most modern vessels, had steering engines to move the rudder. Without power the effect was something like an automobile with power steering when the engine is cut off—except that the *Fort Camosun* did not have any manually operated steering gear!

About 2:30 a.m., June 22, two more tugs arrived—the *Henry Foss*, a large commercial seagoing tugboat from Tacoma, and the *U.S.S. Tatnuck ATO-27*, a 149-foot fleet tug of 1919 vintage mounting a 3-inch gun. At dawn, all three tugs took *Fort Camosun* in tow. At 3 p.m. a fourth tug-boat, *Salvage Queen,* joined the party. Although the torpedoed ship was deeper in the water and yawing wildly, the task of getting her out of the ocean and into the Strait of Juan de Fuca was accomplished. Her condition was still critical. As an emergency measure all four tugs lashed themselves to the crippled ship in an effort to hold her on course and to provide a little extra buoyancy.

Captain Leighton Evans, Royal Canadian Navy Reserve, commanding the *Quesnel,* boarded the tow and directed the movement, steering for the closest port, Neah Bay, Washington. *Fort Camosun's* foredeck was awash, but her cargo of plywood helped keep her afloat. At 8 a.m. on June 23, she was anchored with her keel resting on the mud of Neah Bay.

Quesnel crossed the strait to Esquimalt near Victoria and landed the rescued crew. Word that they were coming had leaked out and reporters with a nose for news moved into the scene. Pathé's noted newsreel photographer, Will E. Hudson, had his camera whirring as the survivors straggled across the dock.

After Navy divers had examined the hull of the *Fort Camosun* at Neah Bay, tugs pulled her out into the strait again. She yawed wildly but

they managed to move her at four knots across to Esquimalt harbor and finally got her home at 4:15 a.m., June 25. Repairs in Victoria and Seattle made her seaworthy again and she lived to survive a second Japanese torpedoing. After an attack by the *I-27* in the Gulf of Aden in the fall of 1943, she limped into port under her own power. She was still afloat in 1959, then owned by the U.S. Department of Commerce, and was later sold for scrap. Commander Tagami's claim that he had sunk her in 1942 was more hopeful than accurate.

Survivors of the *S.S. Fort Camosun* (above) were rescued and returned to British Columbia. A corvette and two tug boats (below) kept the freighter afloat and pulled her back into the safety of the Strait of Juan de Fuca.

The *Camden*

The Operations Report Entry for June 23, 1942, in the *War Diary, Northwest Sea Frontier* reports that at 4:40 a.m. information was received that *S.S. Camden* had been attacked with torpedoes from a submarine at 4:15 that morning less than 50 miles west of Coos Bay, Oregon. Other reports of the *Camden* being struck were received, and the United Press began calling about the tip they had received. But planes sent out to investigate reported that the tanker had been sighted heading north at eight knots apparently undamaged. A crew member of the tanker whom I have contacted does not remember any such attack in June.

Signalman Arnold Lyczewski, a member of the Navy armed guard on the *Camden*, vividly remembers the real attack on October 4, 1942. This 6,600-ton tanker owned by the Charles Kurz Company of Philadelphia and under lease to the Shell Oil Company was en route from San Pedro to Puget Sound with 76,000 barrels of gasoline and oil. She stopped for engine repairs at 43°43'N-124°51'W, close to the same location where the phantom attack had occurred in June.

The *I-25*, having completed a special mission in Oregon in September (Chapters VI and VII), was patrolling for merchant shipping prior to heading home. At about 7 a.m. her lookout sighted a large ship dead in the water. No lights were showing, but the sun was just coming up. The sea was choppy and there was a light northwesterly wind. It was almost ideal weather and the *Camden* made an ideal target. Commander Tagami zeroed in on what he took to be a freighter and fired two torpedoes from a range of 1,000 meters.

On board the *Camden* Captain N. A. Davidson and the mate were on the bridge. Signalman Lyczewski was on watch at the ship's stern near the 4-inch gun. He saw one torpedo miss the ship, and realizing there would probably be another, quickly wrapped himself around a steel ladder. He wrote me many years later:

> The second torpedo hit the starboard bow and the blast was terrible. Fire and smoke and black oil flew higher than our masts. I lost my grip on the ladder and was knocked flat on the steel deck. I immediately got up and turned on the general alarm. The ship's steward, Ray Jones of Laguna Beach, California, was out on deck talking with me when all this started. Right after the blast he jumped overboard and started swimming. I threw him a cork life ring, but he kept right on swimming. We never saw him again.

As the ship settled by the bow with her propeller out of the water, a radioman sent a distress message. At 7:05 Captain Davidson ordered "Abandon ship!" The Navy guard manned the gun until the last minute but did not fire because no target appeared. By 7:20, 47 crew members, in-

U.S. Navy Signalman Arnold Lyczewski.

The *S.S. Camden* after the attack by *I-25* on October 4, 1942, west of Coos Bay, Oregon.

cluding the Navy guard, were off the ship in three lifeboats and a life raft. The Swedish motorship *Kockaburr* picked them up about 11 a.m. and landed them at Port Angeles the following afternoon. Although another ship, the *Victor R. Kelly*, was in sight about seven miles to the north at the time of the attack, it does not appear to have participated in the action.

Commander Tagami's claim of another sinking was only slightly premature this time. A Navy boarding party controlled the fire, the tug *Kemal* took the *Camden* in tow and headed for the Columbia River. Because the tanker was too deep in the water to cross the bar at the mouth of the Columbia, the destination was changed to Seattle. At 6:30 p.m. on October 10, *Camden* suddenly burst into flames and fifteen minutes later went down in 52 fathoms at 46°46'38"N-124°31'15"W, off Grays Harbor, Washington.

The *Larry Doheny*

The day after *I-25's* encounter with the *Camden*, Commander Tagami again sounded battle stations. In late evening on October 5, he had sighted another tanker off Cape Sebastian, five miles south of Gold Beach, Oregon. It was the Richfield Oil Company's *Larry Doheny* (Captain Olaf Brelland) on a northerly course at ten knots, with a cargo of 66,000 barrels of oil. In the previous December, the *Larry Doheny* had been attacked by a submarine about twenty miles north of San Luis Obispo, California, but escaped with minor damage. This time she was not so fortunate.

The weather was clear with good visibility for a moonless night. There were no other ships in sight. The *I-25's* torpedomen depressed the firing button. The first 21-inch torpedo hissed into the sea.

Crew members later reported seeing three torpedo wakes. There may have been a fourth. A strange noise heard at 8 p.m. was later recalled. It may have been a dud striking aft. At 9:20 p.m. the flying bridge lookout shouted out the sighting of what appeared to him as a torpedo track. The forward lookout confirmed the sighting, but the mate on duty considered it to be porpoises and took no action. Suddenly a torpedo slammed into the port side of the tanker six inches below the waterline at No. 2 tank. As No. 2 and No. 3 tanks exploded, flames shot high into the sky. The starboard side buckled and a 14-foot rip up the side opened the hull.

With the blast, all steering gear failed, the engines stopped, and *Larry Doheny* lay dead in the water within two minutes of the attack. Because of flames and fumes, the radioman was unable to send a distress message. A Navy man stayed at the aftergun until ordered into a lifeboat, but he had nothing to shoot at. The *I-25* was never seen.

Within minutes the crew lowered two lifeboats and as many as could get to them piled in. They moved away from the burning ship. A rescue vessel arrived promptly and searched the waters for additional survivors as the ship sank. The lifeboats contained 34 of the 36 crew members and 6 of the 10-man Navy gun crew. Of the six not found, three were known to be dead and three Navy men were listed as missing. Survivors were put ashore at Port Orford on the evening of October 6.

The last American ship to be sunk off the Oregon coast was the *S.S. Larry Doheny*, which fell prey to the *I-25* on October 5, 1942.

The Soviet *L-16*

The *I-25* had one torpedo left. About 800 miles off the Washington coast, as the vessel started back for Japan, two submarines were sighted moving southward on the surface about 800 yards apart. Assuming them to be American submarines, Commander Tagami ordered the last torpedo fired at the leading one from a distance of about 500 yards. It must have hit a vital spot. Witnesses on both the *I-25* and on the submarine that was following the one that was hit describe the resulting explosion as devastating.

Nobuo Fujita, pilot of the *I-25's* reconnaissance plane, calls it "a terrific explosion. The shock was severe, like a near-miss bomb or depth charge" (see Chapter VI). Torpedoman Shoji Aizawa says that the shock broke glass covers on instruments, put out some of the lights, and broke porcelain toilets in the *I-25*.

An officer in the submarine that was following the one that exploded later reported that the man on watch "heard a violent explosion [and] saw a column of water approximately 100 feet high [and] pieces of what appeared to be plating and black smoke" rise from the sea. The stricken submarine sank in about 20 seconds with a loss of all hands on board.

Tagami reported to Japan that he had sunk a U.S. submarine on October 11, 1942 (Tokyo time). It is also listed in the War History Institute of the Defense Agency of Japan as an American submarine. When Mr. Fujita wrote an article for *Today's Topix* in the 1950's he also still assumed that it was an American submarine.

But the U.S. Navy has always claimed—and there appears no reason for doubt—that no American submarine was operating in the area at that time.

Two Russian submarines, however, the *L-15* and *L-16* were in the vicinity. They were crossing the North Pacific from Vladivostok, by way of Dutch Harbor, to San Francisco and the Panama Canal. U.S. officials had offered partial air coverage from Alaska to California, but the Soviet commander refused it, preferring not to follow a definite course.

When the U.S. destroyer *Lawrence* went out through the Golden Gate on the morning of October 15 to meet the Soviet submarines and escort them into port, only the *L-15* appeared. On October 18, Lieutenant Commander Vasily I. Koma-

zov, of the Russian submarine, reported what had happened to representatives of the Western Sea Frontier in San Francisco. He said he had arrived on deck in time to see the bow of the *L-16* disappear and heard two underwater explosions taking place. Two periscopes of a submarine were sighted 1,500 yards to port and the *L-15* fired five rounds at them but without apparent results.

This incident presented a potentially embarrassing international situation. The Soviet Union and Japan were not at war with each other at the time and would not be for nearly three years (until August 1945). Although Western Sea Frontier officers suspected at the time that the Soviet submarine had been sunk by the same submarine (presumably Japanese) that had attacked the *Camden* and *Larry Doheny* within the week, no such announcement was made. The matter continued to be held in secrecy until Mr. Fujita's article mentioned the matter and investigation showed that it was the Russian *L-16*, not an American submarine, that the *I-25* had sunk.

One American was lost along with the 50-member crew of the *L-16*. A U.S. Navy Chief Photographer, Sergi Andreevich Mihailoff, a former resident of Arcadia, California, was traveling with the Russians, serving as a liaison officer and interpreter.

Sergi Andreevich Mihailoff, U.S. Navy liaison officer, who went down with the Soviet *L-16* off the Washington coast. (below) The Soviet submarine *L-15*, sister ship to *L-16*.

Japanese withdrawal

The sinking of the Soviet submarine was the last action by a Japanese submarine off the coast of the Pacific Northwest.

On October 24, 1942, the *I-25* arrived back at its home port at Yokosuka after an 85-day cruise of more than 12,000 miles. There was still fuel in her tanks.

From that time onward the Japanese concentrated their submarine activities in the South Pacific. Not knowing of this change in strategy or not daring to rely on it, the Allies continued to build up defenses along the west coast (Chapters III, IV, VIII), and the U.S. Navy continued to provide escorts at great expense and loss of shipping time for convoys plodding between west coast ports and Alaska and across the Pacific.

All of the plane-carrying submarines listed at the beginning of this chapter were destroyed by March 1945. Two of them, *I-7* and *I-9*, were sunk in the Aleutians in 1943. The others were lost in the central and southwest Pacific. Quite a number of the original crew members of the *I-25* and the *I-26*, however, had been transferred to other duties before their vessels were destroyed. Their memories and diaries have provided an important source of information for this book.

The Japanese had demonstrated the range and versatile capabilities of their submarines, and the subs continued to be a threat throughout the war. We know now that the Japanese never seriously considered invading the United States or the Canadian mainland, but in the early months of the war the possibility of invasion caused considerable apprehension. The Allies prepared, at great expense in manpower, materiel, equipment—and human suffering—to make certain that another Pearl Harbor-type surprise attack did not occur. □

In Seattle, the Boeing plant where B-17 Flying Fortresses were assembled (above) was camouflaged with netting and dummy trees, houses, and streets so that from the air the industrial area gave the appearance of a residential district (left).

II
The War Ashore

IN THE HEAT OF WARTIME EMOTION, rumors fly and panic soars. A country sometimes takes an action for which it is afterwards ashamed. More than 100,000 Americans of Japanese ancestry and their alien parents lived along the Pacific coast at the beginning of World War II. Because of their known ties with the old country in customs, language, and appearance, they fell under a veil of suspicion.

War jitters

In a memorandum on February 14, 1942, to Secretary of War Henry M. Stimson, Lieutenant General John L. DeWitt, Commanding General of the Western Defense Command and Fourth Army, recommended the "evacuation of Japanese and other subversive persons from the Pacific Coast." In part he wrote:

> The area lying to the west of the Cascade and Sierra Nevada Mountains in Washington, Oregon and California, is highly critical not only because of the lines of communications that pass through it, but also because of the vital industrial production therein. Racial affinities are not severed by migration. The Japanese race is an enemy race and while many second and third generation Japanese born on United States soil, possessed of United States citizenship have become "Americanized," the racial strains are undiluted. [There] is no ground for assuming that any Japanese . . . though born and raised in the United States, will not turn against this nation when the final test of loyalty comes.

It took the pressure groups of the west coast about a month to recover enough from the shock of the Pearl Harbor attack to realize their advantage. On December 30, 1941, a chapter of the Military Order of the Purple Heart—mostly World War I veterans—voted to send a letter to President Roosevelt asking that "all Japanese be removed to inland points from California coast counties." These veterans chose to forget that Japanese in California, among other examples of loyalty to the United States, bought nearly $2 million worth of Liberty Bonds during the first world war.

In mid-January, the California State Senate considered restricting civil liberties of the Japanese when a resolution was offered urging special loyalty investigations of *Nisei* state civil service workers. Although President Roosevelt, the Justice Department, newspaper editorials, and influential individuals appealed urgently for racial tolerance of "those fellow-citizens who chance to be descended from natives of the countries with whom we are at war," the snowball was already

General John L. DeWitt

more than 20,000 acres. They specialized in truck crops, orchards, and potatoes. Their work brought in an estimated $4 million annually. In King County (Seattle area) alone, they operated 56 percent of the truck crop acreage, had many fields of carrots and beets, and grew 80 percent of the asparagus, celery, lettuce, snap beans, and cucumbers.

Out on Bayocean peninsula in Oregon's Tillamook County, there lived a handful of Japanese who tended oyster beds. They minded their own business and were in town only often enough to pick up supplies. Soon after the war started some hometown "Americans" became front-line patriots —especially on Saturday nights in local taverns. One particular evening the matter of the Japanese oystermen came up. After several rounds were downed the beer drinkers came to the conclusion it was their patriotic responsibility to chase those .... clean out of the county. The patriots, now more numerous by far than the handful of Japanese, adjourned to their homes for hunting rifles and shotguns. Meeting at rendezvous later that night, the raiders stalked the dimly lit shacks a few miles west of town. On signal they opened fire on the unsuspecting and unarmed Japanese. The Orientals answered with the only means at hand—a package of firecrackers. The beer-bellies were so stunned by the "return fire," they fell all over themselves in a massive retreat. One, careening through the night, fell over a log— breaking a leg.

rolling. While the Sacramento *Union* pleaded for stability, editorializing, "We hope the investigation [which] looks like a plain example of racial persecution . . . will not be a witch hunt . . .," the San Francisco *Examiner* carried more and more anti-resident-Japanese articles, stories, and letters to the editor. The *Examiner* reminded readers of the recent submarine attacks—ships sunk, damaged, or scared back into ports. The newspaper shouted about vague hints of U.S. Navy reports of flares at sea and blinking shore lights. The Los Angeles County supervisors ordered the firing of 56 Japanese-American county employees claiming it was "impossible to distinguish between the loyal and disloyal." The City of Los Angeles let 39 go, but in a gesture of friendliness allowed leaves of absence for the duration of the war rather than outright dismissal.

The California Department of the American Legion demanded *all of California's 93,000 Japanese,* citizen or not, be interned for the duration!

Had the Japanese been a host of troublemakers along the west coast? Immigrant Japanese had shown California how to grow rice, now a substantial part of the state's economy. Japanese-Americans were first to demonstrate that potatoes would be a successful commercial crop in California. A 1921 report to the governor said the Japanese had used barren lands not worth paying taxes on to produce profitable farms, orchards, and vineyards. Japanese eat a lot of fish, so the Japanese-Americans fished along the coast.

In Portland, the Japanese had become a part of the community. By 1938 they had built an import and export trade totaling nearly $1,800,000 a year.

In Washington state, in the spring of 1942, Japanese operated more than 700 farms covering

Businessmen of Japanese ancestry protested that they had no sympathy with Japan's war efforts, but they were forced to close their stores and move to relocation centers.

President Roosevelt issued Executive Order No. 9066 on February 19, 1942, allowing the Secretary of War to define "military areas" and to remove "any and all" persons from those areas.

The United States was at war with Germany and Italy as well as with Japan. Earl Warren, then Attorney General of California, said, "We believe when we are dealing with Caucasians we have methods that will test the loyalty of them and arrive at some fairly sound conclusions. But when we deal with the Japanese we are in an entirely different field. We cannot form any opinion we believe to be sound . . . "

German and Italian aliens—white—were safe, but not Orientals!

With the fall of the Philippines, Wake, Guam, Borneo, Hong Kong, and dozens of other places with names foreign to American ears, the feeling toward the Japanese was not very friendly on city streets on the American west coast. Some Japanese were beaten up. The racists continued their harangue. The military, unprepared and caught short by the declaration of war, felt they had to respond. General DeWitt made speeches and wrote letters.

Since the outbreak of the war there had been no important sabotage on the Pacific coast, and none attributable to a Japanese-American. Even so, columnist Westbrook Pegler wrote on February 16, 1942, "The Japanese in California should be under armed guard to the last man and woman right now and to hell with *habeas corpus* until the danger is over."

Incarceration for Japanese-Americans

Posters suddenly appeared all over the west coast ordering that "all Japanese persons, both alien and non-alien, will be evacuated . . . by 12:00 noon, Tuesday, April 7, 1942." What is a "non-alien," many wondered, if not an American citizen?

The U.S. government uprooted more than 117,000 Japanese, more than 70,000 of them American citizens. Dispossessed and about to be herded behind barbed-wire fences like so many cattle, the Japanese-Americans were forced to sell their belongings for whatever they could get or take the government's offer to store their household and personal items, cars, and trucks. The Army offered to purchase any automobile or truck at *Blue Book* rate through provisions set up with the Federal

Pacific Electric Railway busses loaded and ready to remove Japanese-Americans from a collecting point in Los Angeles. Baggage awaits trucks at curb.

Reserve Bank, should the evacuee elect to sell. In his report to the Secretary of War, General DeWitt wrote, "Evacuee response to the property protection services was most gratifying . . ." Few Japanese agreed.

Farmers, many of whom had spent years developing their farms, had to let the land go for pennies compared to its real value. A few were able to entrust their possessions to non-oriental friends to hold "for the duration."

A Department of Justice report indicates that Japanese property valued at $65,812,000 was handled by the Alien Property Custodian between 1942 and 1954. Most of this property was in California.

Although arrangements had been made between the Department of Agriculture and the Farm Security Administration to undertake property protection, many Japanese fruit and vegetable operations dried up during the summer of 1942. War Department appropriations totaling $1 million were made available for the procurement of substitute farm operators who could take over implements and farm operations. When more money was needed, President Roosevelt came up with an additional $4 million. "Both the evacuees and their communities of residence," General DeWitt declared, "derived much benefit from these loans because many properties otherwise would have remained idle."

Although General DeWitt did not seem to acknowledge it, many sources of fresh produce were soon entirely eliminated, since some new white owners were more interested in making money working in war industries. The consensus was that these owners wanted the land for investment and future gains. Many did not care about farming and did not know how to work the soil.

Japanese-Americans (*Nisei*—born in the United States of parents who had come from Japan) and their parents and other Japanese (*Issei*) were given a chance to leave the coastal areas under a voluntary relocation plan. But because of growing resentment toward Japanese in midwestern and eastern cities, they were not always welcome. Many came back. On the fateful day in April, tens of thousands of Japanese responded *voluntarily* to the call. They went to assembly centers where they were registered, given medical examinations, sent to warehouses for an issue of bedding, and assigned to living quarters. Of the 14 assembly centers, two were in the Pacific Northwest—at Puyallup, Washington, and Portland, Oregon. Living conditions at the assembly centers were tolerable but sometimes rather primitive. Among facilities renovated for quarters were racetrack horse stalls. To the Japanese themselves, great credit is due for the manner in which they, under Army supervision and direction, responded to and complied with the orders of exclusion.

While the civilian-operated War Relocation Authority was taking shape, the Army Engineers built ten relocation centers. Two were located in the Pacific Northwest. One, "Minidoka," was set up in near-desert country in Jerome County, Idaho. To Minidoka went evacuees primarily from the Puget Sound area. The second center was named "Tule Lake," for a nearly dry lake of the same name about 32 miles south of Klamath Falls, Oregon, near Tulelake, California.

Tule Lake acquired the largest number of evacuees of all the relocation centers—between 16,000 and 22,000. Midway through the term of exclusion, a general shuffle of all centers occurred. Many evacuees were dismissed—turned loose. Many were drafted into the Army and Navy to serve as interpreters, while hundreds signed up to later become the backbone of the famous 442nd Regimental Combat Team, which distinguished itself in Italy.

As a result of this shuffle, the peaceful camp at Tule Lake took on a new complexion. Those who acquired a status of being "disloyal," either because of problems in other centers or because they did not fill out a "Loyalty Registration" ques-

Without serious incident, most Japanese-Americans accepted the mandate to leave their homes along the west coast and move to camps inland.

tionnaire to the satisfaction of the War Relocation Authority, were shipped to Tule Lake. Of these, hundreds were *Issei* and *Kibei*. The *Kibei* were those Japanese young people born in America but sent at an early age to Japan for schooling. Now in their late teens, these youths had returned to the United States with freshly implanted Japanese imperialism firmly locked in their brains. "Tule Lake Relocation Center," writes Kitagawa, "became a mass of mentally unbalanced people." Some evacuees, judged by the camp rabble-rousers to be pro-American, were beaten. Later, during a full-fledged riot, a Caucasian doctor was attacked in the relocation center hospital, and a Japanese storekeeper at the center was killed.

The 24,000 Japanese-Canadians, including 7,400 naturalized citizens, did not fare any better than the Japanese-Americans. There were about 22,000 Japanese in British Columbia, all but about 3,000 of them living along the coast or on islands, mainly Vancouver Island. Those within 100 miles of the coast were assembled at Kaslo, B.C., and assigned to resettlement areas in refurbished "ghost towns" in the Kootenay Lake and Slocan Valley areas and in a new settlement called Tashme.

About 2,500 Japanese-Canadians were sent to Lethbridge, Alberta, for a sugar beet farming project aimed at relieving the sugar shortage caused by the war. The heaviest snowfall in years hit the British Columbia mountains and Alberta plains. Accustomed to the milder coastal winters, the Japanese had to spend much of their time just keeping warm. Poor housing was a major complaint.

More than 1,000 evacuees were sent to Manitoba and a few hundred men on to Ontario. Others were placed on special status—42 repatriated to Japan, nearly 1,000 sent to road camp projects, and about 100 to hospital service. In October 1942, 57 were listed as "in detention" in Vancouver.

Mexico moved its Japanese population inland from Baja California. Some of the Japanese in South America, particularly in Peru, were relocated in centers in the United States.

Hindsight from three decades later seems to indicate that the evacuation of Japanese-Americans from the west coast caused a great deal of human misery and an unjustified loss of property and prestige. The equanimity with which the victims accepted their lot, however, the courage they showed in the face of adversity, and the industrious way in which they carved out new lives for themselves proved to be a lesson to the whole nation. After the war, although some evacuees spread out across the country seeking new opportunities, many returned to their previous home areas where they continue to share their rich heritage with their American neighbors.

Meanwhile, in early 1942, while the public and official sentiment that led to evacuation was building up, California came under both actual and imagined enemy attack.

Attack near Santa Barbara

The first Japanese attack on the American mainland occurred at Goleta, a few miles west of Santa Barbara in southern California. The following account is a paraphrase from *Goleta, The Good Land* by Walker A. Tompkins.

At the outbreak of the war, aircraft-spotting stations were built and manned by civilian volunteers. Fishermen on the Goleta pier were alerted to watch for enemy submarines and surface craft, since a Japanese assault on the west coast was feared. The Army emplaced a World War I howitzer near the Barnsdall Oil Company plant at Ellwood, an oilfield west of Santa Barbara, and another artillery piece on the Campbell Ranch at Coal Oil Point. The Coast Guard assigned a patrol boat to the Santa Barbara Channel. The Army spread a few GI's along the coastline for shore patrol.

In their temporary homes, the evacuees used their skills to fill their time as well as to be of service to others.

As the war entered its twelfth week on February 16, 1942, fishermen and shore patrols reported sighting submarines. Lt. George W. Goman, of the Naval Intelligence office in Santa Barbara, reported to his superiors in San Diego that a big sub had surfaced off the Barnsdall pier, with men clustered around a cannon on deck. By the time two patrol planes arrived the sub was gone.

Later in the week Lt. Goman drove out to Ellwood in time to see a submarine in the act of submerging. Again he reported to San Diego and was told, "Stop sending us these submarine-sighting stories—the coast is full of California gray whales. That is what you're seeing, not subs." Goman groaned, "A whale is 20 feet long. This submarine is 300 feet long."

By Washington's birthday, February 22, the Coast Guard had withdrawn its patrol boat. The Army had pulled out all of its men except a sergeant and two privates, had hauled away the two howitzers, and had left the Goleta area without military defense. Civilian volunteers manned the aircraft-spotting stations.

Monday, the 23rd, was a holiday. President Franklin D. Roosevelt was scheduled to deliver one of his intimate "fireside chats" over national radio networks at 7 p.m. Nine out of ten people in the Goleta Valley tuned in to hear the President discuss America's coastal defenses in the event of a Japanese invasion.

A few miles out in the channel the *I-17*, a giant submarine of the Japanese Imperial Navy, surfaced in the twilight. Kozo Nishino, the vessel's commander, had visited Ellwood many times before the war to load crude oil in a Japanese navy tanker. He and his crew had patrolled Hawaiian waters at the time of the Pearl Harbor attack. Within the past two months they had attacked two American tankers off the west coast.

In plain view of shore observers, who were not aware that the sub was an enemy, Nishino steered up the coast a few miles and then reversed course to cruise eastward. No hostile planes were in the sky. The weather was fair, the sea smooth.

On shore, Goleta residents tuned to radio stations KTMS or KFI and heard President Roosevelt's opening words:

My friends . . . Washington's Birthday is a most appropriate time for us to talk with each other about things as they are today and things as we know they shall be. . . .

At 7:07 p.m., seafowl feeding along the beach at Ellwood were scattered by a jolting explosion from seaward. A malignant red flash briefly illumined the sky. A projectile made a low arc over the Barnsdall absorption plant and bored harmlessly into a hill a mile inland without exploding.

People who felt the jolt or heard the concussion hurried out of doors and stood staring in disbelief at the submarine. The superintendent of the Signal Oil and Gas lease herded his employees into the shelter of a railroad cut before starting fire-prevention procedures.

The soldiers stationed at Ellwood were unable to get a telephone message out; the lines were jammed by calls asking the operators what the shooting was about. One telephone message *did* get to the West Los Angeles filter center from a lonely aircraft-spotting tower. The men who made the call settled back to watch American bombers fill the sky and blast the enemy out of the water. No planes came.

The county Civil Defense chief was listening to FDR with friends at a roadside restaurant. He heard the cannonading but dismissed it as coastal defense practice and went home. He did not learn of the attack until he read a newspaper the next day. Soon after he left the restaurant, a newspaper circulation man rushed in, declaring that from the top of a windmill tower he had seen "an enemy submarine shooting at us . . . plain as day!"

A delivery man for the Santa Barbara *News-Press*, from a hilltop vantage point 1,200 feet above sea level, counted 29 muzzle flashes at leisurely intervals. He called the city desk, but the bored night editor told him he was "loco" and hung up in his ear. Before many minutes, however, the *News-Press* became aware that the scoop of the century was taking place at Ellwood.

Traffic on U.S. highway 101 was moving briskly without dimout, let alone blackout. Drivers were listening to the President on their car radios. They were puzzled but not alarmed by the "fireworks" offshore as they approached Ellwood.

The shelling ceased around 7:45 p.m. The submarine did not submerge but vanished into the mists of Dos Pueblos, bound for the open sea. Navy radiomen intercepted a coded report purporting to be from a Japanese submarine to

Emperor Hirohito. It boasted that they had left Santa Barbara "a seething mass of flames, with wild panic visible on shore."

"One question never satisfactorily answered," says George W. Edmonds, night editor of the *News-Press*, "was why the Marine combat pilots at Goleta—stationed on what is now the campus of the Santa Barbara branch of the University of California—were not given the order (or authority) to 'seek out and destroy' the invading sub."

By 8 p.m. a full blackout was in effect from Monterey to San Diego. Radio stations were off the air. Traffic on Highway 101 was halted. Around 10 p.m. a squadron of U.S. planes from Bakersfield began dropping flares over the waters off Ellwood, but by this time the *I-17* was gone.

Experts assessed the damage caused by the bombardment at $500. Many shells were duds, but their casings were inscribed with Japanese ideographs, as if they had been delivered in anger.

The damage included a cracked reduction gear casing on an oil well pump at Luton-Bell No. 17 and a splintered catwalk railing. A sheet-iron-covered shed and the plank decking and timbering of the Bankline pier were peppered with steel fragments. GI's on duty did a land-office business picking up shell fragments and peddling them to the throngs of sightseers who lined Highway 101 for days after the attack.

The United Press recorded and translated a Radio Tokyo broadcast to the Japanese people:

> The U.S. War Department officially announced that Santa Barbara, California, was devastated by enemy bombardment. . . . The U.S. is not publicizing this damage, however, for fear of the impact on the minds of the public.

Retaliation may have played its part in the selection of Ellwood as the site for bombardment.

Captain Bernard E. Hagen, commanding officer of "A" Battery, 143rd Field Artillery, 40th Infantry Division, was wounded while disarming the fuze from one of the shells fired at Goleta by the *I-17*. He was hospitalized for 50 days in Santa Barbara and later received the Purple Heart. He is probably the only U.S. serviceman to receive this medal for wounds received as a direct result of an act of the enemy within the U.S. in World War II.

A splintered catwalk over an oil well and holes in corrugated iron siding were principal damage done by Commander Kozo Nishino at Goleta. Captain Hagen points to holes left by a shell from the *I-17's* deck gun on February 23, 1942.

Kozo Nishino had suffered an embarrassment there in the 1930's when he had come to take on oil. Charles S. Jones, president of the Richfield Oil Company, in 1956 told about the company's custom of meeting the captain of each ship and extending him hospitality. On one occasion they welcomed Captain Nishino and with ceremony escorted him ashore. Along the beach trail, the guest slipped and fell into a patch of prickly pear cactus. "It was an excruciating moment," Jones said. "It cost our Japanese skipper an unbearable loss of face. He left us in a polite but grim mood, but ten years later he returned, and shelled the scene of his humiliation."

"Battle of Los Angeles"

The next night, February 24, 1942, three million people in the Los Angeles area thought the war had come to their front doors. Blackout! About 3 a.m. planes were reported overhead. Antiaircraft guns blazed skyward and shrapnel fell in the streets. Tin-hatted air-raid block wardens roared at everyone whose house emitted even a pinpoint of light. The *Herald Express* rolled presses with a "WAR EXTRA" and printed a two-line block-type headline: "BATTLE ENEMY RAIDERS OVER L.A." A story was headed, "Eyewitness Tells of Air Battle as War Comes to L.A." There were stories headed: "Describe Gunfire Over L.A.," "Intensify Sub Hunt," etc.

The War Department officially said the alarm was real. The Navy stated officially the Los

Night-splitting beams from Coast Artillery searchlights sought aircraft over Los Angeles on the night of February 24/25, 1942.

The front page of this February 25, 1942, issue of the Los Angeles *Times* reported the "Japanese attack."

Angeles "attack" was merely a case of "jittery nerves." A search of Japanese records in 1945 revealed any so-called battle of Los Angeles was a myth—the Japanese did not send planes over that city the night of February 24-25, 1942. "Even so," quipped Leone Arlandson in 1972, recalling the incident, "my husband was a block warden. He took off leaving me and our new baby alone at home. I was scared spitless!"

Coastal alert

All along the west coast of the United States various means of providing warning and protection in case of an enemy attack were put into effect. A few radar stations were installed, but sets were in limited supply and their effectiveness untested. From lookout stations atop buildings, in school belfries and church steeples, in forest lookouts, and other locations, civilian volunteers watched the sky for planes and called in what they saw to filter centers.

In the cities, block wardens were given instructions in how to fight fires caused by incendiaries and how to meet other emergencies. Blackouts and dimouts were decreed for coastal areas, but their effectiveness depended upon the cooperation of the civilian population. In coastal communities of the Pacific Northwest, the electric lights in sawmills could be switched off, but the "wigwam" waste burners still brightened the sky like beacons. Drivers along coast highways at night had to decide which was the greater danger, being arrested for not dimming lights or running the risk of an accident while driving without them.

In response to the reports of suspicious radio transmissions within the coastal area, the Federal Communications Commission monitoring units and the FBI together ran down more than 700 complaints. At KEK, Mackay Radio's Hillsboro, Oregon, commercial overseas radio transmission and receiving station, Coast Guard radiomen maintained surveillance around the clock, while outside the station Coast Guard patrolmen with war dogs watched for prowlers. Japanese-language broadcasts turned out to be from shortwave Japanese stations in Japanese territory. General DeWitt was told by the FCC Radio Intelligence Division there had been no unauthorized radio transmissions or signaling from Japanese or other coastal residents. ☐

III

The War in British Columbia

CANADA, AS PART OF THE BRITISH COMMONWEALTH, had been at war for more than two years when Japan attacked Pearl Harbor. Even before the war, by joint agreement, Canada and the United States had built certain defense installations on Canadian soil for their mutual well-being. In the mid-1930's, a pact with Canada had called for improving defenses on Vancouver Island. It was agreed that a system of forts be built on the north side of the Strait of Juan de Fuca, where the terrain was more favorable than on the U.S. side.

Canadian defenses

When Hitler marched on Poland in 1939, the Vancouver Island fortifications were ready and manned by Victoria's Fifth Regiment. The fortified areas were off-limits to all but the military. Even nearby residents did not know the extent of the armaments. Three 9.2-inch guns were installed at Albert Head along with a labyrinth of tunnels leading to underground quarters and storage areas. The subterranean installations were air conditioned —no small feat in that day—and had an independent electrical system.

At the time of greatest development, there were three 6-inch guns in the rocks of Mary Hill, and two 6-inch guns at Macaulay Point. Two 8-inch railway guns loaned by the United States were installed at Christopher Point at the southern tip of the island. Other fortified locations included Todd Hill, Belmont, Gold Hill, Duntze Head, and Ogden Point dock. Gun crews in training went through their paces with 6-inch weapons in Vancouver's Stanley Park. Gun emplacements near Prince Rupert guarded the north entry into Hecate Strait across from the Queen Charlotte Islands.

When the war with Japan started, Canada was in somewhat the same predicament as the United States when it came to west coast defense. There were not enough ships to patrol offshore waters. The civil population along the coast had to be taught blackout reasons and rules. Classes were held on methods of extinguishing fires caused by incendiary bombs. Soon almost every home had buckets of sand stored in convenient places. Garden hoses were left hooked up, carefully coiled for instant action. Emergency food supplies that could be put away in the face of shortages were hoarded.

The Canadian Navy, as did the U.S. Navy, "requisitioned" large yachts and seagoing fishing boats. They asked the "weekend admirals" to loan their binoculars for "sea duty on fighting ships." An initial squawking of complaint was heard, but quickly disappeared in the spirit of patriotism. There was a general feeling that whatever the government said it needed for the war effort, the government could have.

The Canadian Navy lined up about 15 fishing boats that normally fished the water along the west coast of Vancouver Island. Entire crews were enlisted into the Royal Canadian Navy Fisherman's Reserve. Most of the boats were manned by the vessels' masters, who became Sub-Lieutenants, and the regular crews, who received Navy ratings. By this move, the Navy obtained a fleet of small patrol boats, manned by men with a thorough knowledge of British Columbia's west coast. Fishing boats of Japanese-Canadians were also available, but their skilled crews had been relocated away from the coast.

When the Canadians believed they had something to shoot at, they fired. On January 31, 1942, for example, observers reported a submarine near Gordon Rock off Victoria, and shore batteries opened fire. After investigation the so-called contact proved negative, but the civilian populace had the comforting knowledge that their defenders were alert and active.

Early in 1942, the Canadians as well as the Americans feared Japanese landings. This was especially true among inhabitants of the sparsely settled west coast of Vancouver Island and the Queen Charlotte Islands. One suggestion was made to train the Fisherman's Reserve in commando fighting, but the idea did not go very far. Eventually, a joint Army-Navy plan was developed which did not involve the Reservists. By the time the plan was ready, the defense of the area was becoming less urgent because of the successful turn of the war in the Pacific.

Amos Wood, who beachcombed the west coast of Vancouver Island after the war and who has written a book on Japanese glass fishnet floats, discovered one means the Canadians had taken to thwart any Japanese invasion plans. He found thousands of what looked like telephone poles (pilings) implanted in the sands of the broad beaches. He was told that they had been placed at intervals to prevent enemy airplanes from landing. In time, many of these poles rotted out. Those remaining were finally removed in the late 1960's.

Pilings along beaches on the west coast of Vancouver Island created a hazard for landing of enemy planes.

Not until after the war when Japanese records were studied was it learned that the Japanese had not envisioned landing farther east than Adak. Order No. 106, (Japanese) Naval General Staff, 23 June 1942, directed that Kiska and Attu be "securely occupied and the capture of Adak shall not be carried out." After the Battle of Midway in June 1942 the strategic initiative shifted to the Allies and the Japanese lost most of their ability to move eastward.

In Victoria the pace of life quickened as shipbuilding facilities expanded. Yarrows, Ltd., had nearly 500 women on its payroll of 2,500 during the peak years of the war. The yard turned out five corvettes, two 10,000-ton cargo liners, five LST's, and 17 frigates. The Victoria Machinery Depot Company, Ltd., produced twenty 10,000-ton Victory ships and two 8,000-ton steel ships.

The *Queen* arrives

If people living in and around Victoria ever felt that enemy air attacks might be imminent, it was early on the morning of February 23, 1942. Through the sinews of every living thing in the area, the demand of a mighty ruler was felt—the *Queen Elizabeth* sounded her contra-basso trumpet. "England's age-old sea power," gushed a Victoria resident. "It was thrilling. It was primrose. It was hope!"

The world's largest ship had arrived from Sydney, Australia, for servicing and additional armament. She steamed into the Royal Roads amid a small fleet of antisubmarine patrol boats and anchored to await docking.

This *Queen* had a price on her head! Adolf Hitler had pledged huge rewards to the German U-boat captain who could sink the giant Cunarder.

Would Herr Hitler have paid a Japanese skipper for sinking her? The world lost a chance to find out. The *I-8*, skippered by Mochitsura Hashimoto, was in the eastern Pacific about this time. In early February, this Japanese submarine had been west of San Francisco for the purpose of disrupting coastal communications. Sending its GLEN floatplane to reconnoiter the San Francisco Bay area had been contemplated, but the flight could not be made because of bad weather. The *I-8* patrolled as far north as the Strait of Juan de Fuca. In his postwar book, *Sunk!*, Hashimoto says he "had no opportunities for attack" and that he headed back toward Japan, arriving at Kure on March 2.

The *Queen Elizabeth* in graving dock at Esquimalt, British Columbia.

In British Columbia waters, the *Queen's* very presence brought chills of wonder, relief—and fear that she might draw a Japanese attack. She had been launched in 1939 for trans-Atlantic luxury service but was immediately used as a troop transport. In her 1,031-foot-long hull with eleven decks, she could carry up to 20,000 fully equipped troops. It was easy to see why the British Commonwealth took such pride in her—and why the enemy was so eager to destroy her.

With a beam of 118 1/2 feet and drawing 39 feet of water, the *Queen Elizabeth* was so big that the Esquimalt harbor near Victoria had to be dredged before she arrived. The twin-stacked mammoth towered above dockside buildings. Viewing her anchored in the harbor, one man shook his head and exclaimed, "You know, with that ship in here, I'd swear the water comes up on the shore a couple of more inches!"

Thrilled to see her but also eager to see her leave, workers lost no time in getting her back to sea again. "Fix it and get rid of it" became the watchword.

With repairs completed, the *Queen Elizabeth* sailed out into the Strait of Juan de Fuca silently under cover of darkness in the early morning hours of March 11, 1942. Her next business, in a kind of reverse lend-lease, was to load U.S. troops at Los Angeles bound for Australia. Throughout the war she made dozens of transoceanic trips—all solo because with her speed she could outdistance all submarines yet developed.

Estevan Point attack

Three months after the *Queen Elizabeth* excitement in Victoria, British Columbia came under actual attack at Estevan Point. Midway up the west coast of Vancouver Island, Estevan Point has several claims to historic fame. The Spaniard, Juan Perez, and his navigator, Estevan Martinez, anchored near there in 1774 and traded with the Indians. Four years later the English Captain James Cook rounded the point and sailed into Nootka Sound, where he repaired his ships. His crew members purchased furs for clothing and bedding. Sales of these same furs a year later for immense profit in China touched off the "fur rush" to the Pacific Northwest. This trade centered for more than a decade in the vicinity of Estevan Point. For this story, Estevan's moment in history came one evening in June 1942, when it became the only place in Canada to come under enemy shellfire in World War II.

In 1907 the Canadian government had built an important lighthouse that rose 125 feet above the water at Estevan Point. Even though the west coast generally maintained a blackout during the war, the Estevan Point light continued to operate as a safeguard to navigation because it marked a dangerous area of coastline.

At 9:25 p.m. on June 20, the lightkeeper sighted what appeared to be a smokescreen coming toward the point from the southwest. Beneath the screen was the big Japanese submarine *I-26*. It stopped opposite the lighthouse and at about 10:15 began firing its deck gun.

Minoru Hasegawa (formerly Commander Yokoda of the *I-26*) has these recollections of the attack:

It was evening when I shelled the area with about 17 shots. Because of the dark, our gun-crew had difficulty in making the shots effective. At first the shells were not reaching the shore. I remember ordering the men to shoot at a higher angle. Then the shells went too far over the town toward the hilly area.

As I watched from *I-26*, the townspeople were very quick to put the lights out, but the lighthouse was very slow, the last to turn the light off.

Witnesses on shore claim that the submarine was plainly visible about two miles offshore and that they could hear the throb of the diesel engines. The weather was "unlimited, clear." There was a moderately strong northwest to west wind, a moderately choppy sea with rollers on the horizon.

Edward T. Redford, Officer-in-Charge at the wireless station, Brian Harrison, senior operator, and their wives were playing bridge. Redford recalls:

When the first shell exploded on the beach about 150 yards from our house, I ran to the door and looked out, thinking it was our fuel tanks, down about halfway to the beach, which had gone up. I saw the sub quite clearly about a mile offshore. I shipped my wife and the Harrisons with their baby in arms out the back way and down a trail to the beach, then took off for the office. I sent out the general call of C.Q. along with the information that we were being shelled by an enemy submarine and that we were shutting down and going off the air temporarily.

I shut down our diesel generating power plant, then made sure all were off the site, women and children especially, took them about half a mile up the beach, got them all settled as comfortably as possible, then started back for the station.

The lighthouse at Estevan Point on the west coast of Vancouver Island.

The *I-26* (above), like other type B-1 Japanese submarines had a seaplane hangar and catapult forward of the conning tower, but on its 1942 voyage to Vancouver Island it carried extra supplies in the cylindrical hangar instead of a floatplane. View looking forward (right); note hangar and catapult. View aft (below right); its 14-cm deck gun sank the *Cynthia Olson* and shelled the Estevan Point lighthouse.

Residents at Estevan Point in June 1942 included (left) Edward T. Redford, officer-in-charge of the radio station, who lost his left arm in World War I; (center) R. M. Lally, lightkeeper; and (right) Audrey, wife of Brian Harrison, senior radio operator, and their daughter Sandra (8 months).

When R. M. "Mike" Lally, the lightkeeper, who had only minutes earlier lit the light, heard the first shot, he ran back up the steep, circular steps to the light chamber. He remained there during the entire engagement. IIe took bearings of the submarine and entered them in his log. He noted that the vessel had only one gun. At 10:17—two and a half minutes after the first shot—Lally put out the light. While he was doing these things, the sub's gunners were adjusting their aim, but their next shots went high. Lally said he saw flashes from the gun, heard shells whistling, saw some of them explode, and counted two duds. He thought that about 25 rounds were fired. The concussion broke glass in the lighthouse and slammed the iron doors shut.

Other than concussion damage and a few pockmarks from fragments hitting the side of the tower, the lighthouse and radio station were untouched. As Commander Yokoda (Hasegawa) summed up the results of the attack, "There was not a single effective hit that night."

The message Redford sent on the International Distress Frequency of 500 KHZ was heard over a wide area. Former U.S. Coast Guard radioman Otto Freytag said:

We at Westport, Washington, intercepted the broadcast from VAE on the coast of Vancouver Island stating that they were being shelled, presumably by a Japanese submarine, and that they were securing the station post haste. The information was passed to the Seattle District Office and down the coast by land line telephone to Tatoosh, to the Radio Direction Finder at Klipson Beach, and to the Direction Finders at Fort Stevens and Empire, Oregon. Fort Stevens Radio D/F "NZR" relayed the flash to the Commanding Officer of the Coast Artillery at Fort Stevens, then to all Coast Guard lifeboat stations along the line.

At the Central Filter Center in Portland, Mrs. Clarence C. Evans was attending the Seattle open line when the word came. "I turned the line over to the duty officer. He listened, made no comment, and left the room in a hurry."

The shelling stopped at 10:45 p.m., about half an hour after it started. Redford says:

The submarine pulled out on the surface where everyone could see and hear her. While naturally there was some nervousness, almost everyone, including the women and children, took the whole incident in stride. The shells that exploded near the Hesquiat Indian Village, three miles behind the lighthouse, scared the hell out of the Indians. Some of them took to their boats for safer points until late the next morning.

Later that night, Redford reported, one of the airplanes which responded to his call came directly overhead. He could not see it in the darkness but could hear it. The following morning, official parties from two Canadian Navy ships landed. (H.M.C.S. Santa Maria, Capt. David Ritchie; H.M.C.S. San Tomas, Capt. James L. Detwiler.) The station was inspected and residents interviewed. Captain Detwiler reported on the questioning of a native woman:

She was sincere and tried to make me understand that she knew the difference between a whale and a boat. She said that she first thought it was a whale, but when it didn't splash or "blow" she knew it was a boat.

The only loss associated with *I-26*'s raid was an RCAF patrol bomber that crashed on takeoff. But any landing one can walk away from is a good one. The crew walked away.

In response to the radioed flash message of the attack, Redford recalled,

The first boat to arrive was one of our Fisherman's Navy Reserve craft, which had been patrolling the Vancouver Island coast. This boat was on her way to the base at Esquimalt for refueling and getting fresh supplies and had tied up at Ucluelet for the night. When they got word that we were being shelled by a Jap sub, she immediately left Ucluelet and headed back for Estevan, a distance of about forty miles. The boat landing for Estevan Point is at Hesquiat, about five miles by plank road from the lighthouse. We picked those up who came ashore up there, and took them over to the light station in our truck. When they were through looking around and picking up pieces of shell casings, etc., we took them back.

The next day just about everybody not on duty went souvenir hunting while planes from Ucluelet and Coal Harbor R.C.A.F. bases looked for the sub. The planes didn't find it but the souvenir hunting was pretty good.

Though there is some mention that the women and children were taken off the station because of fear of future attacks, this appears to be "an exaggeration," Redford recalls.

I endeavored to have the Department take the women and children off the station, but [the Department] took a rather lax-a-dazical view of the whole thing and I had no luck. Fortunately, it never happened again. It is true two or three [of the dependents] left the station on their own volition a few days after the shelling.

As the shells whizzed over, Audrey Harrison went with the women and children to a secluded spot that her family had found on an outing earlier in the day.

It was plenty dark [Mrs. Harrison says] and we stumbled over rocks and driftwood. At times when the trail took a sharp turn we were breathless because of what we might find around the bend. The ship that was firing at us might have landed a beach party and we might meet them coming along that single trail. I did have a bit of luck: I was wearing my only pair of nylons and they didn't get a single snag.

Mrs. Lally, wife of the lightkeeper, recalling these events in 1966, said:

Canadian warships passed the lighthouse almost daily. I saw two early in the morning of the shelling, so the sound of gunfire that night didn't bother me. I thought it was target practice. I was just putting the youngest of the children to bed when the first shell exploded on the beach. "That's pretty poor shooting! It came pretty close," I yelled to my husband who had just come down from turning on the lighthouse for the night.

"Get the hell out of here! It's a Jap sub and they are shelling the lighthouse!" my husband Mike shouted back. More shells sailed overhead. But that wasn't our only scare. Later, while we huddled together behind a fallen tree, we heard a strange ticking—much louder than our pounding hearts. We wondered if the Japs were firing delayed-action shells? The "time-bomb" turned out to be an alarm clock my 12-year-old daughter had brought along for some unknown reason.

The next morning's edition of the Victoria newspapers carried brief dispatches with an Ottawa dateline. The *Daily Times* headlined "Two Japanese Subs Off Coast"! The Canadian government acknowledged that the attack was the first enemy activity on Canadian soil since Confederation. In Portland, *The Oregonian* gave front-page space to the same dispatch from Ottawa under the headline: "Sub Shells Vancouver Island: Oregon Coast Dims Out."

As a precaution against similar attacks, the vehicle-carrying Victoria-Vancouver-Seattle ferry ships were reinforced and their wheelhouses were enclosed in concrete and heavy timbers.

About two weeks after the Estevan Point shelling, wireless operator Redford came upon an unexploded Japanese shell about 100 yards south of the wireless station. "Having had a bit of experience with these things in the first world war in 1915," he says, "I took care it was left strictly

An unexploded shell from *I-26*, which Ed Redford found and photographed in a pile of driftwood two weeks after the attack.

alone." With his folding size-116 camera, he shot most of a roll of film showing the shell as he found it in a maze of driftwood. He called his head office, and the next day a Navy boat came and took it away. The shell is now on display in Ottawa, and one of Redford's snapshots has become the official photo of the Estevan dud.

This attack was the *I-26's* last business in Pacific Northwest waters. She sailed for the home islands via the Aleutians and arrived at Yokosuka Navy Yard on July 7, 1942.

International neighborliness

The traditional friendship between Canada and the United States really paid dividends. The two peoples helped each other as good neighbors do. The governments aided each other with harbor defenses. Vessels and aircraft of both countries worked together when ships, regardless of registry, were attacked by the common enemy. The international communications link was efficient.

The seriousness of the war situation to Canada came into focus when it was realized that Estevan

Point was shelled on the same day as the fall of Tobruk. If the Germans drove on across North Africa and took control of Egypt and the Middle East, the United Kingdom would become ever more dependent on her Allies across the Atlantic. In this world-circling conflict, Canada was coming more and more into the zone of immediate concern and danger.

But all was not wartime jitters. A Hollywood movie studio sent crews to Victoria to film parts of *Commandos Raid at Dawn*. With John Farrow as director and stars including Paul Muni, Lillian Gish, and Robert Coote, assisted by the Canadian Scottish and Royal Rifles battalions and the auxiliary cruiser *H.M.C.S. Prince Henry*, cameras rolled on a mock invasion of Saanich Inlet.

At the same time, plans went quietly forward for the evacuation of all residents on Vancouver Island should there be a Japanese invasion. Acknowledging the British lessons at Dunkerque, arrangements were made for everything that floated — motorboats, yachts, barges, and ferry boats from as far south as Tacoma and Olympia— to be available "just in case." □

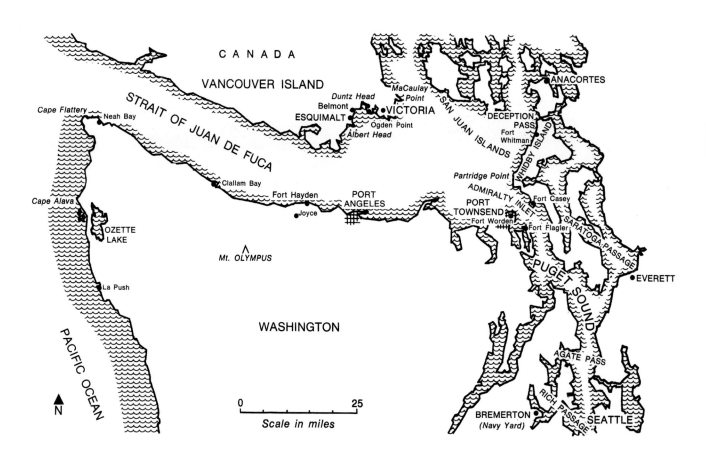

IV
Pacific Northwest Harbor Defenses

THE TWO PRINCIPAL INLETS from the sea into the Pacific Northwest are through the Strait of Juan de Fuca and up the Columbia River. The Strait leads to the ports of Victoria and Vancouver and the Canadian naval base at Esquimalt in British Columbia and to the ports of Seattle and Tacoma and the U.S. naval base at Bremerton on Puget Sound in the state of Washington. The Columbia River provides access to the ports of Longview and Vancouver, Washington, and Portland, Oregon, and during the war, to three large shipbuilding yards in the Vancouver-Portland area. Defense of these two inlets from possible enemy attack from the sea has therefore long been a concern of the U.S. and Canadian governments. As indicated in the previous chapter, Canada had prepared for the defense of the north shore of the Strait of Juan de Fuca.

Puget Sound defenses

On the U.S. side of the Strait, defenses of the entrances into Admiralty Inlet and Puget Sound were based primarily on a trio of coast defense forts that had been built between 1890 and 1910. They included Fort Casey on the west coast of Whidby Island, Fort Flagler on the north tip of Marrowstone Island, and Fort Worden at Port Townsend.

During World War I, these forts and some smaller and more temporary installations had been manned by regular Army troops and twelve units of the Washington National Guard. In addition to guarding the inland waterways from possible attack from German U-boats or surface vessels, they served as training camps. Seven overseas regiments of the Coast Artillery Corps were formed and trained either wholly or in part in the Puget Sound defenses.

At that time (1917), Fort Worden had 11 batteries with a total of 38 guns, ranging in size from 12-inch rifles on barbette carriages, 10-inch rifles on disappearing carriages, and 12-inch mortars to 6-inch rifles on disappearing carriages and 5-inch guns on pedestal mounts. Fort Casey had 10 batteries with a total of 35 guns; Fort Flagler had 9 batteries with a total of 26 guns.

After World War I, Fort Worden continued as the main post and furnished caretaker personnel for Forts Casey and Flagler and a few smaller installations. In 1924 the 14th Coast Artillery Regiment was formed and was based at Fort

Worden. The facilities and personnel were used, especially in the summer months, in various peacetime training programs such as the ROTC (Reserve Officers Training Corps), the CMTC (Civilian Military Training Corps), the Washington National Guard, and the U.S. Army Reserves.

In the 1930's some improvements in facilities were made, such as installing underwater listening devices, antiaircraft batteries, and hangars to house captive balloons used for observation work.

In 1940, before mobilization began and a program of modernization was started, the garrison consisted of four companies (batteries) of the 14th Coast Artillery—about 30 officers and 600 enlisted men, all stationed at Fort Worden. On September 23, 1940, the 248th Coast Artillery Regiment (Washington National Guard) was federalized and assigned to the harbor defenses to provide additional manpower.

One phase of the 1940 modernization program was installation of bigger and longer-range guns. In 1922 at the time of the Limitations of Armaments Conference in Washington, D.C., the United States had agreed to suspend construction of 12 capital ships, which were to have been armed with a new-model 16-inch rifle. At the time of the cancellation most of the guns had already been manufactured. Since the Navy did not need them, they were made available to the Army. These huge guns, 45 feet long and 5 feet thick at the breech, could throw a one-ton projectile as far as 26 miles.

Army Ordnance officers agreed that these guns would be excellent for coastal defense, so the Army made plans to use them. A new type of barbette mount was designed to provide maximum elevation for the guns. The earliest models were open to the air, but with development of air power these mounts were enclosed in concrete and steel casemates to give protection from aerial bombing. Overhead they had a thick roof of reinforced concrete supplemented by several feet of earth. Each battery was composed of two guns mounted 500 to 1,000 feet apart, plus underground ammunition storage areas, shops, and living quarters. The entire installation was protected on all sides from enemy attack. The first of the casemate batteries of the Navy-type 16-inchers was constructed at San Francisco (Battery Davis) between 1937 and 1940. Others of similar design were installed

at the Panama Canal, at Dutch Harbor in Alaska, and in Hawaii.

Three 16-inch gun installations were planned for the Strait of Juan de Fuca, two of them on Cape Flattery at the entrance to the Strait and one 15 miles west of Port Angeles. Construction started on the emplacements in May 1942 and continued for more than a year on Cape Flattery before the project was discontinued at that location. Work on the third continued, however, at the Striped Peak military reservation near the village of Joyce,

Coast artillery on the Strait of Juan de Fuca, installed during World War II, included a 6-inch gun in a metal turret at "Fort" Hayden near Joyce, Washington; an 8-inch railway gun in Port Angeles; and two 16-inch guns emplaced at "Fort" Hayden.

42

at a site named *Camp* Hayden but more popularly known as *Fort* Hayden. This installation, completed in 1944, was the last of the 16-inch gun batteries to be built in the continental United States.

Col. Floyd D. Robbins was the officer in charge of proof firing for the Ordnance Department in March 1945. Under the extreme test conditions of proof firing, using extra powder, he says, "at 50,000 yards range on the 16-inch guns, shells were dropped within 100 yards of the predicted point." According to Robbins, "This same 16-inch battery was the first to be fired using a *computer*." The Fort Hayden 16-inch guns proved that they could do what they were supposed to do, but were never fired again. They were scrapped at the conclusion of the war.

As another part of the modernization program, a new installation, Fort Ebey, was completed in August 1943 at Partridge Point on Whidby Island. It was armed with a battery of new-model 6-inch guns mounted in steel turrets. These guns could shoot a 105-pound projectile 15 miles. In addition to the 16-inch battery, Fort Hayden also had a battery of these 6-inch guns, but their installation was not completed until March 1945. Although they were test fired they were never manned.

In addition to these major fixed installations, other defense measures were taken. Some of the antiaircraft weapons were relocated so that they could fire upon fast-moving surface craft, such as motor torpedo boats, as well as at aircraft. Temporary batteries of 90-mm and 37-mm guns were emplaced at Deception Pass, Saratoga Pass, and other locations in. Puget Sound to defend the harbor cities and the Bremerton Navy Yard from possible attack by high-speed surface craft. Searchlights were installed where they could illuminate any surface vessel that passed through Admiralty Inlet. Provision was made for laying mines and a mine-planting vessel was stationed at Fort Worden, but mining the entrance to Admiralty Inlet was not very feasible because of the depth of the water and shape of the sea floor. The Navy installed underwater detection devices and established a system of antisubmarine nets in Admiralty Inlet, Rich Passage, and Agate Pass.

In the early 1940's the Puget Sound Defenses were commanded by Brig. Gen. James H. "Jittery Jim" Cunningham, an officer with a reputation for worrying about details and possibilities. He had

an intense interest in the installation of the big 16-inch casemate guns at Fort Hayden. With these in operation, it was his opinion that the defenses of the Strait of Juan de Fuca could carry out their mission, which included guarding against hostile ships, defending against naval bombardment of the harbors and ships in the area, providing supporting artillery fire to defend against enemy landings on either side of the Strait, and denying enemy ships access to the Canadian naval base at Esquimalt and Victoria Harbor.

Sperry searchlights, model 1937, stored in daytime at Grayland, Washington, ready to roll out to positions along the coast for nighttime duty. The beam of these 60-inch arc lights could illuminate a target many miles at sea.

Brigadier General
James H. Cunningham

43

The *Octopus* of the Columbia

On the Columbia River, the task of establishing and maintaining minefields between Astoria and the bar at the river's mouth fell upon the shoulders of Lt. Col. Claude B. Washburne of the 249th Coast Artillery (Oregon National Guard). About mines, the colonel knew little, but he was a past master at getting jobs done and cutting red tape. This happy trait did not endear him to the higher echelons of command, but it did get the river mined. The Columbia River defenses were supposed to include a mine-planting vessel, and a ship designed for this job was dispatched from the east coast to Astoria via the Panama Canal. It did not get past Panama. The Army authorities there "requisitioned" it.

Faced with the job of laying mines without a minelayer, Washburne used his initiative. He either bought or rented a ferry boat (the records of this transaction are not clear), changed its name from *Tourist #2* to the *Octopus,* and went to work. In some ways, the vessel made an excellent minelayer for river operations, being of shallow draft and capable of traveling forward or backward. The ferry also had an exceptionally large carrying capacity on the car deck. The only thing it lacked was General Accounting Office approval. But after an abortive effort to withhold the colonel's pay to force settlement for the boat, the GAO abandoned thoughts of winning any argument with Claude Washburne.

In time, the mine-laying operations accumulated a sizable flotilla: the former ferry boat *Octopus* under the command of Lt. Col. Kenneth "Admiral" Rowntree, two Army Corps of Engineers boats (the *Paul Hemus* and the *B. F. Stone*), and several gill-net fishing boats. With dedication to duty and disregard of danger, this ragtag fleet sowed mines along the lower Columbia and won a big "E" award for efficiency. In some ways it was an incredible operation. It made military purists shudder, but it worked.

And, of course, as soon as the operation was completed, what should come steaming over the Columbia bar and up to the dock at Hammond but the *Major General Wallace F. Randolph*—USAMP No. 7, 182 feet of gleaming, mine-planting efficiency, accompanied by two smaller vessels, the *L-64* and *L-75!*

It would be logical for the mine-laying episode to die here, but it does not. All of the mines the

Tourist No. 2 (top) carried passengers and vehicles across the Columbia River at Astoria before being converted to plant mines. The 249th Coast Artillery called her *Octopus* (center).

USAMP No. 7, the *Major General Wallace F. Randolph*

44

Octopus and her cohorts sowed were not recovered at the end of the war. This is not particularly unusual, but it does lead to some speculation. What has happened to those missing mines? Are they tucked away in odd corners waiting for some incautious boater or adventurous skin diver? There are charts in the files of the Corps of Engineers showing where the Columbia River mines were planted. Officials say they *think* they know where the missing mines are located. But chains and cables rust and the oceans are wide and their currents travel around the earth.

In the three years following World War II, 14 mines and a depth charge were recovered by the U.S. Navy along the Oregon and Washington coast.

In 1953 a contact mine of Russian manufacture washed ashore near Cape Meares, Oregon, causing excitement among beachcombers. Coast Guardsmen cleared the beach of people just before the mine, rolling about like a toy in the running tide, struck a rock and let go with all its deadly strength. Windowglass salesmen had a field day, and Bob Watkins' house a quarter of a mile inland still has a cracked beam as a result of the explosion.

In 1974 a Japanese mine was brought up in a fish net from a depth of 1,800 feet 22 miles offshore from Brookings, Oregon. A demolition team put it on a derelict skiff, towed it away a safe distance, and detonated it. Navy officials estimated it contained 220 pounds of explosives.

Mines lost from the Columbia River might still make their way to almost any place in the Pacific Basin.

Two of the mines that have been found along the northwest coast since World War II. (right) The Soviet mine that exploded on Cape Meares beach in 1953. (below) The Japanese mine recovered from deep water in a fishing net off Brookings, Oregon, in 1974.

Columbia River defenses

The fixed defenses of the Columbia River were centered in three Coast Artillery installations: Fort Stevens on the Oregon side of the river and Fort Canby and Fort Columbia on the Washington side. These forts, like those on Puget Sound, had been in existence for many years, some of them having been established during the Civil War. Most of the armament, like that in the Puget Sound area, had been installed in the two decades from 1890 to 1910. The armament consisted of 6-inch and 10-inch disappearing rifles and 12-inch mortars. Field pieces of 75-mm caliber and machine guns were emplaced· early in the war for beach defense. The heaviest guns were located at Fort Stevens, with Forts Canby and Columbia operating in secondary roles.

Fort Canby on the Washington side of the mouth of the Columbia River, 1941.

Guarding the beach against invasion at Fort Stevens were machine guns, French 75's, and a lookout post called While Evelyn in an old water tower.

46

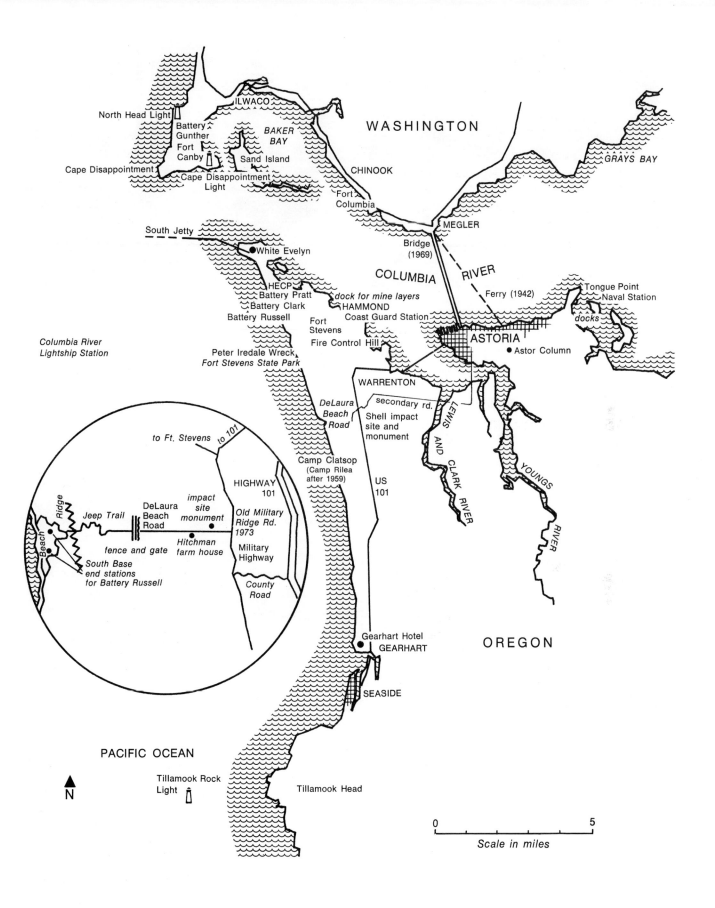

North Head Light

Battery
Gunther
Fort
Canby

ILWACO

BAKER
BAY

WASHINGTON

GRAYS BAY

Cape Disappointment

Cape Disappointment
Light

Sand Island

CHINOOK

Fort
Columbia

MEGLER

South Jetty

Bridge
(1969)

COLUMBIA

RIVER

Ferry (1942)

Tongue Point
Naval Station

White Evelyn

Columbia River
Lightship Station

HECP
Battery Pratt
Battery Clark
Battery Russell

dock for mine layers
HAMMOND

Fort
Stevens

Coast Guard Station

docks

ASTORIA

Fire Control Hill

Astor Column

Peter Iredale Wreck
Fort Stevens State Park

WARRENTON

secondary rd.

LEWIS

to Ft. Stevens

to 101

DeLaura
Beach
Road

Shell impact
site and
monument

Camp Clatsop
(Camp Rilea
after 1959)

AND

YOUNGS

CLARK

RIVER

Ridge

Jeep Trail

DeLaura
Beach
Road

impact
site
monument

HIGHWAY
101

Old Military
Ridge Rd.
1973

US
101

RIVER

Beach

fence and gate

Hitchman
farm house

Military
Highway

South Base
end stations
for Battery Russell

County
Road

OREGON

Gearhart Hotel
GEARHART

SEASIDE

PACIFIC OCEAN

▲
N

Tillamook Rock
Light

Tillamook Head

0   5

Scale in miles

The entrance to Fort Stevens in 1939

Fort Stevens

At one time Fort Stevens had eight 10-inch disappearing carriage (DC) rifles, but when World War II started only two of the guns were still operational. They fired projectiles that weighed 500 to 600 pounds, depending on whether they were high-explosive or armor-piercing shells. The guns were accurate; they could place a shell inside a 30-foot-square target eight to nine miles away. With a good gun crew and proper fire control data each gun could fire a well-aimed shell every 32 seconds.

The Buffington-Crozier DC mount was designed for the period when there were no aircraft. Gunners on an enemy battleship could not aim at a weapon that disappeared behind a concrete-reinforced earthwork and only showed itself long enough to fire. The carriage was designed so that the recoil of the weapon drove the gun backward and downward behind a parapet against the resistance of a counterweight. A locking device held the gun in the depressed position while it was sponged out and reloaded. When the gun was armed and ready, a lever tripped the counterweight mechanism, which raised the gun into firing position ready to fire. The Buffington-Crozier mount was made in different models to accommodate guns from 6 to 14 inches in caliber and was extensively used in coast defense fortifications in the continental United States, the Panama Canal zone, the Philippine Islands, Hawaii, and Canada.

The 12-inch mortars, like those installed at Fort Stevens, were short-barreled, large-caliber weapons that delivered plunging fire nearly vertically on a target. The 700-pound projectiles were designed to penetrate the relatively light deck armor of warships and cause severe damage to the hull and interior. The guns were emplaced in batteries of four (later two) that were set in deep pits. Their range was surprisingly long, about 15,200 yards (9 miles), and the guns themselves were virtually immune to naval gunfire.

The 12-inch mortars at Battery Clark, Fort Stevens

48

Battery Russell

In 1942, Battery Russell contained the only operational 10-inch guns at Fort Stevens. They were model 1900. Although installed in 1904 they were in good condition and competently manned.

Were Battery Russell's guns ready? Photographs of the period attest that the guns were in excellent condition. Old residents in the area tell of numerous practice firings and gun drills that were increased considerably after the 249th was called into federal service. In the fall of 1940 and thereafter, the big guns were an annoyance to local residents, who complained of broken windows, damaged dishes, disturbed pets, and noisy nuisance as the guns fired during a stepped-up training schedule.

Like most National Guard units, the 248th and the 249th Coast Artillery were principally composed of men from their local areas. In the days of partial mobilization before Pearl Harbor the hometown ranks were thinned to form cadres for new units, but the essential neighborliness was not lost even though draftees replaced many of the original men. Most knew each other well and brought to the service skills, crafts, and enthusiasm

One of the 10-inch disappearing carriage guns at Battery Russell about to fire a practice round (above). Towed targets (below) were used in practice by Coast Artillery batteries at Fort Stevens. Observers recorded photographically the results of each round fired so that the date, unit firing, and shot number could be identified.

not ordinarily found in the conventional Regular Army unit of that time.

Success in practice, if properly carried out as nearly as possible under service conditions, is by far the best evidence of the state of training. The final objective of target practice is to develop ability to score a *hit!* Artillerymen of the 249th believed the old saw: "Practice makes perfect!" They knew their guns. They knew their range-finding equipment. They regularly shattered the target with direct hits. (Of course there is also the tale of the shot that took off the top of the funnel of a tugboat!) The 249th, insofar as drill and practice could make it, was a battle-ready unit.

The forts were manned 24 hours a day. There was a "ready" battery at all times, theoretically capable of returning fire within 60 seconds, and the other gun positions had men and ammunition ready to fire within minutes after an alert was ordered.

Colonel Clifton M. Irwin, commander of the 249th Coast Artillery, a thin, intense disciplinarian, was not generous with overnight passes from the post. Vardel Nelson of Junction City, Oregon, who served with the unit, recalls that Colonel Irwin was convinced as early as 1937 that the United States would eventually be at war with Japan. Nelson says:

We called him Jap-Happy Irwin. During all our drills we never saw a flashboard silhouette of a German ship. But we saw plenty of Japanese ships. The colonel was getting us ready. When we were federalized in 1940 and sent to the Columbia River forts, Colonel Irwin would only allow 15 to 20 percent of the men to be on pass at any one time. He insisted that we were on duty and must be ready.

During the last week of November 1941, the Inspector General visited the post. The I. G. listens to all the gripes of the men and has wide discretionary powers to settle personnel problems. Just about everybody cried on his shoulder about the limited number of passes.

Lieutenant Colonel
Clifton M. Irwin

Since it was peacetime, the I. G. ordered Colonel Irwin to issue weekend passes to 50 percent of the command. Staff sergeants and higher ranks who lived in nearby houses and towns were to be allowed to go home every night unless they were on duty. This was usual peacetime procedure.

The first Saturday after the I. G. inspection, Colonel Irwin issued the first big batch of passes. Right after Saturday morning inspection we pulled switches on everything in the communications room and took off. It was a Grand Exodus! That was on December 6, 1941. Next morning Pearl Harbor got shot up. I called Fort Canby from Fort Columbia and no one answered. The switchboard was closed and the garrison was either in town or fishing on the jetty. I finally contacted the post electrician and gave him step-by-step instructions about how to activate the fire control phones, the time interval machines, and the other instruments necessary to get the gun batteries into action. It was about 5 p.m. before there was any rank in that control room.

Colonel Irwin, now vindicated, reestablished the previous duty schedule and the 24-hour alert. The Harbor Entrance Command Post (HECP) was manned at all times. Field grade (major and above) officers were daily assigned as duty officers.

Barracks life at Fort Stevens interspersed alert duty with periods of relaxation: at Battery B headquarters (left); at "H" Station, Fire Control Hill near Battery Russell (center); and in underground bunkers at White Evelyn (right).

Introduction of RADAR

A little-known instrument for defense was coming into limited use when the war started, but it was not talked about. Actually it was not new. For many years, the U.S. Navy had been investigating an electronic device for RAdio Detecting And Ranging (hence the name RADAR). The original continuous wave or "beat" radar had by 1935 developed into "pulse" radar which could accurately determine range. The technique of using radar as a ranging device was improved by the British who developed an efficient multicavity magnetron tube to generate the microwave pulses. The U.S. Navy successfully tested radar on the destroyer *Leary* in 1937 and equipped the battleship *New York* with the device in 1938. By 1942 all major nations involved in World War II had radar, but its operational use was initially limited to Great Britain and the United States.

There were two families of radar. One was for air defense and included model SCR-268—a searchlight director—and SCR-270 and 271 for long-range aircraft detection. The first two SCR-270 sets were set up in June 1940 for the defense of the Panama Canal, No. 1 on the Atlantic side and No. 2 on the Pacific side. The antenna for the early SCR-270 set took a great deal of room—four dipoles horizontally polarized with a 6-by-6-foot screen reflector 4 feet deep—a king-sized set of bedsprings, as some people called it.

The other family of early radar included SCR-296, designed for seacoast artillery fire control. Unrelated to the air defense models, this type had been requested by the Coast Artillery Corps as early as 1937. Development was delayed, however, because the air defense models were considered more urgent. Nevertheless, some work, including testing, continued on the SCR-296. By December 1941 an order had been placed for twenty sets. Delivery probably commenced in early 1942 with the first set delivered in April and the second in July. Just where these sets were installed has not been determined.

By early January 1942, however, four early warning radar sets (SCR-270-B) were in operation along the Washington and Oregon coasts. They were located at Neah Bay on Cape Flattery, at Pacific Beach north of Grays Harbor, near Ilwaco (North Head) north of the mouth of the Columbia River, and near Yachats, Oregon.

On alert at the Coast Guard Radio Direction Finder station near Battery Russell at Fort Stevens.

The defense of the Columbia apparently did not have high enough priority to receive one of the earliest SCR-296 sets. This appears to squelch rumors that in 1942 radar was used to spy on the mouth of the river from a perch atop Astoria's Astor Column. Also, the Signal Corps wanted the antenna out of sight and would not have placed it in such an exposed position. They sometimes hid the bedsprings in a mock water tower.

One of the Fort Stevens outposts was near the foot of the jetty that extends into the ocean from the south bank of the Columbia. A rickety old water tower which once served the narrow-gauge railroad that hauled rock to build the jetty had been cleaned out for an observation post called "White Evelyn." It could have contained a radar antenna but it did not. Ben Loftsgaard says no—and he was there. Colonel Carl S. Doney, commander of the Columbia River Defenses, says he was aware that there was radar around, but he did not know what kind or where it was.

A check of available sources indicates that there was an SCR-270 radar at North Head in June 1942, but there was no SCR-296 radar in the Columbia River defense area.

Command posts

At Fort Stevens, as in other coast defense complexes, there were several different headquarters. The Commander, Columbia River Defenses, had one headquarters which included all three forts on both sides of the Columbia as well as Camp Clatsop, about five miles south of Fort Stevens. Each organization within the Columbia River De-

Before radar came into general use, the M-2 Sound Locator helped ground observers at night or under other conditions of poor visibility to detect the presence, determine the position, and follow the flight of aircraft. Sounds picked up by the horns were amplified for the operators. Data collected could be transmitted electrically to a searchlight control station or plotting board.

fenses had its own command. The Harbor Entrance Control Post (HECP) was manned by representatives of all services who had any interest in the area. The purpose of the conglomeration of Army, Army Air Force, Navy, Marines, and foreign representatives at HECP was to leave no agency concerned out of the action. The HECP was situated underground in the old Battery Mishler complex on the main post at Fort Stevens and was principally staffed by Coast Artillery people.

The Navy had a seaplane base at Tongue Point on the river east of Astoria. The Coast Guard operated a permanent lifesaving establishment at nearby Hammond and a radio direction-finder station just north of Battery Russell.

The Coast Artillery forward observation and command post was built partly underground into a hill a little southeast of Battery Russell. This installation was called Fire Control Hill or "H" Station. A headquarters unit was stationed in the Hill to operate communications equipment. The unit had a small barracks, officers' quarters, mess hall, and target-plotting room.

So, it would seem, all was in readiness for any sort of emergency that might arise in defending the mouth of the Columbia from enemy action. In June 1942, the Portland *Oregonian* editorialized:

The waters that ripple and gleam off the Oregon coast can shelter the enemy. We're not panicked, nor greatly disturbed, but they won't catch us napping. □

V
Uninvited Visitor at Fort Stevens

SUNDAY, JUNE 21, 1942, was a pleasant day at the mouth of the Columbia River. Weather observer Fred Andrus recorded a temperature of 72° F, clear sky, and wind from the northwest at 4 knots. Captain Jack R. Wood, commander of Battery Russell at Fort Stevens, did not leave the post, but his wife came from their apartment in Warrenton for a visit. At a resort hotel in Gearhart, 15 miles south, U.S. Supreme Court Justice William O. Douglas had addressed the Oregon Newspaper Publishers Association the night before. Most of his audience had left for home, but he had stayed to enjoy the weekend and thus was on hand to witness the unusual offshore fireworks that Sunday night.

As night came on, the air cooled but the skies stayed clear. Although there was supposed to be a dimout along the coast because a submarine had shelled the Estevan Point lighthouse on Vancouver Island the night before, lights blazed in Seaside, a resort town on the beach two miles south of Gearhart. Many people followed their normal patterns of activity, apparently unaware that a war had been under way for the past six months.

As reconstructed by Jack Fink, planetarium astronomer at Medford, Oregon, Senior High School, sunset was at 7:54 p.m. This was the longest day of the year, and evening twilight lasted until 10:30 p.m. The moon, just past the first quarter, was due to set at 12:16 a.m. The Tongue Point Naval Air Station reported at 11:30 p.m.: "Light clouds, less than .3 cover at 40,000 feet, temperature 57° F, wind north 3 knots, barometer pressure 30.20."

At Fort Stevens on Fire Control Hill, Major Robert Huston, Senior Duty Officer, and a Corporal "Tully" were on duty. Technical Sergeant Vernon Greig and Sergeant Gil Mather were getting ready for bed in a room of the small noncoms' barracks in a gully behind the plotting room. In "B" Battery, at the 249th headquarters in the main cantonment, Ken Evans, a battery cook, was CQ (Charge-of-Quarters).

Battery Pratt was the "ready" battery and Lieutenant Lynn Neeley was the duty officer. Back from his visit with his wife, Captain Wood was still in uniform in his quarters under the big guns of Battery Russell.

At "White Evelyn," the South Jetty outpost, the men on duty slept with their clothes on in

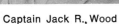
Captain Jack R. Wood   Corporal Ken Evans

their underground bunker to be ready at a moment's notice to strafe the beach south of the jetty if the enemy attempted a landing.

Mr. and Mrs. Cliff Hitchman, who lived on a farm close to the post, had gone to a movie in Seaside, but their daughter Ardith, 12, and her brothers had gone to bed.

Two Coast Guard vessels, the *USCGC 402* and *Mañana II*—a converted private yacht formerly owned by Aaron Frank, a Portland department store executive—were in position inside the bar at the mouth of the Columbia. They were to meet

White Evelyn, an observation post on the beach. It was in an old water tower which once served the narrow-gauge railway used in constructing the South Jetty.

two freighters at 4:30 the next morning and escort them through the minefields.

Across the Columbia, the lighthouse on Cape Disappointment was sending out alternating beams of red and white light powerful enough to be seen 21 miles at sea. At Fort Canby, Captain Zed Harris had put the 12-inch mortars of Battery Gunther to bed; his unit was not on alert that night. He had notified duty officer Neeley at Battery Pratt and was getting ready for sleep himself. At nearby McKenzie Head, Richard Ebi, Private Joe Campbell, and another member of a searchlight unit were playing cards to pass the time during their nighttime duty shift.

A Portland business executive transferred his yacht, *Mañana II*, to the Coast Guard for patrol duty in the estuary of the Columbia River.

Panic—submarine!

Into this tranquil scene rose the long black hull of a submarine. The Japanese *I-25* came in through a fishing fleet because its commander, Meiji Tagami, knew there would be no mines where these boats were. The deck lookouts scrambled up and out of the hatch to their battle stations. The submarine swung around with its stern toward the shore so that the deck gun would have a clear field of fire and the submarine could leave for the open sea in a hurry if necessary.

As Sensuke Tao (formerly Sensuke Izutu) took his position as chief gunner at the brace of 25-mm machine guns he could see the lights of a city on shore. He also noted that the preparations for the firing of the deck gun were not going smoothly. He joined Commander Tagami, Air Officer Fujita, and the gun crew on the aft deck to give advice about adjustments and to help pass

The lighthouse on Cape Disappointment, 1941

ammunition. "We elevated the gun to 30-40 degrees," Tao says. "I myself fired some shells."

Commander Tagami had the impression that there was a submarine base on the Columbia River and ordered firing in that direction. Sadao Iijima, a gunnery officer, was alert for possible response by the Americans. "I shot the gun with my right hand," he says, "keeping the optical rangefinder ready at my left hand. Should we be air attacked, then I would snap on the rangefinder and elevate the gun to attack the plane. In shooting at the land I did not use any gunsight at all—just shot."

On shore the sound of the gun brought an immediate reaction. Captain Wood recalls:

When the first shot echoed across the harbor, I jumped off the cot and ran up to the command post. Battery Russell wasn't the "ready" battery; in fact, most of the men in "F" Battery had chicken pox and some were gone on pass. But when the first shot came, everyone who could started running to their stations from their tents behind the battery. Most weren't dressed. Chris Murphy, my sergeant down in the ammunition room under the guns, was in shorts and T shirt. We looked like hell, but we were ready to shoot back in a couple of minutes.

Lights came on in the tents when the first alert sounded—then just as quickly went off again. Each tent had a Presto-log-burning stove in the center of the floor. In the darkness, soldiers crashed into these Sibley stoves, knocking some of them over while trying to get out to the guns.

At the Harbor Defense headquarters, Major Frederick C. Dahlquist was Senior Duty Officer. Lt. Wilbur T. Cooney was the Junior Duty Officer. They were dressed in field service uniforms and were in adjoining rooms in their quarters when they heard the first shot. They immediately rushed to the underground Harbor Defense Command Post. Colonel Carl S. Doney arrived soon thereafter and assumed full command of the Harbor Defenses, releasing Dahlquist and Cooney to take command of their units.

At the main garrison Lawrence Rude, First Sergeant of "B" Battery, was awakened by confusion in the barracks:

I opened the door of my room and stood there in my drawers cussing at the guys to shut up. Some nut yells back that the Japs are shooting at us and then tore out of the barracks. It was a real madhouse. The men were going in and out like a herd of elephants.

A 3/4-ton Dodge recon car was parked nearby. Somebody was grinding the starter, then revving the engine, but the vehicle did not move. The regular driver stuck his head out of an upstairs window. "You stupid SOB," he swore at the man (who turned out to be an officer) in the open-topped car, "Release the emergency brake!"

One man ran out the barracks door into the dark and smacked his head on a parked truck. He cut his forehead a little and by the time he had regained his feet and staggered back into the building, his face was covered with blood. "The guys who saw him," Sergeant Rude says, "knew for sure he had been shot and that there must be Japs all over the place! The whole place jumped. It's a wonder somebody wasn't killed with all the itchy trigger fingers around."

"B" Battery, the outpost unit, had a string of machine gun emplacements along the beach equipped with World War I .30-caliber Browning water-cooled machine guns. Cliff Moriarity was in a nest near the wrecked *Peter Iredale*, a land-

Colonel Carl S. Doney

Sergeant Laurence Rude

mark on the Clatsop Beach since 1906. With one hand on his gun and the other cranking his EE-5 field telephone, he started calling headquarters where Ken Evans was the CQ: "I wanna shoot. I wanna shoot. He's right out in front of me!"

Ernest Fieguth, the duty sergeant at the South Jetty outpost, says, "Hell, we couldn't give him permission. All I could do was keep talking to him so he wouldn't shoot. Besides, that Browning wouldn't reach the sub anyway."

The telephone circuits from Fire Control Hill to the outposts along the beach were made of Signal Corps W110-B wire—three strands of steel and three of copper, but a fragment from one of the bursting shells cut a line running to three outposts. "The beach boys were out there alone," says Greig. "It was dark. Shells were whistling overhead. When their phone went dead they thought they'd had it. A patrol from the command post worked its way down to the dugouts to relieve tensions if for nothing else."

At outpost White Evelyn, Bennett Loftsgaard recalls:

We were awakened in the underground bunker by Bud Neal screaming, "Get out of the sack, you guys. The Japs are here!" As we ran to the water tower, we saw a flash of gunfire out to the sea on our left. I got upstairs and swung the telescope around to the flash, read the azimuth off the dial, and had one of the men phone it to headquarters. A little later we got reports on the location of the target and began plotting its course. None of us realized exactly what was going on. We were closer to the sub than anyone else, but we couldn't see it; yet some guy in headquarters was telling us where the Jap was and we were plotting his course. Later when I knew a bit more, I realized we were getting radar reports, but at that time even the word "radar" was top secret.

Out in the bay a bit north of White Evelyn, the Coast Guard's converted yacht *Mañana II* had been drifting toward the south shore inside the bar. The skipper, Chief Motor Machinist's Mate George W. Cooper, had barely gotten into his bunk when his bosun's mate called, "Mr. Cooper, Fort Stevens is shooting at us!" Cooper recalls:

I was on the deck in a second. All was quiet on shore when suddenly from the sea I saw a flash and a few seconds later heard a "whup." The outline of a conning tower was seen in the flash; then all was dark again. A submarine was firing on Fort Stevens! I raced to the radio room and called Coast Guard radio at Grays Harbor in clear language—no time for messing with any code. I said, "Submarine bearing south west, distance 2-3 miles south of South Jetty, firing at Fort Stevens." As far as I have been able to learn, this radio report was the first news of the attack flashed to anyone.

By this time our crews were alerted by the shooting— we didn't have to sound Battle Stations.

William Gaither, commanding the *USCGC 402*, put his ship alongside the *Mañana II* and we talked to each other from about ten feet. His armament was greater than mine. He had a Lewis .30-caliber air-cooled machine gun and a 37-mm gun mounted on the deck. Gaither asked, "Do you think I ought to ram the sub?" I said, "No, because our ships will never survive the ramming against the steel hull of the submarine."

On the north side of the Columbia, Battery Commander Zed Harris had just put his head on his pillow when he heard a shot followed by several others. He says:

About the fourth shot, the siren at Fort Canby went off. I thought Battery Pratt was firing at something in the harbor. I dressed and went to the Battery Command post. I saw flashes out to sea; it wasn't Pratt doing the shooting after all.

The First Sergeant of Harris' battery, Henry K. Scott, rushed to his duty station in the command post. He recalls:

Although the flashes of the Japanese gun were visible, the submarine was completely out of range and off the edge of our plotting board. Captain Harris was deeply concerned that no return fire had been opened. Finally unable to contain himself, he turned to me and asked, "Sergeant, if I made sure all phones were open, then lit a piece of paper and yelled *Fire!* would I be court-martialed if my guns went into action?" I could only reply, "*Yes sir!*"

As Harris recalls, the Army Air Force radar at North Head first plotted a submarine close to the South Jetty and a little later near the North Jetty. The radar plot then indicated that a submarine had turned west and headed seaward past the Columbia River lightship station. Captain Harris says:

I could have dropped mortar shells down his hatch if we had visibility, but it was too dark. The radar operator had only a 1,000-yard-square grid system to work with—not accurate enough for big guns or mortars.

On each rotation the beam of the lighthouse was splashing across the face of the command post. I called the chief of the Coast Guard and told him to turn off the light—quick—we were being fired on. He argued. He said he didn't have authority to turn off a lighthouse in the middle of the night. I snatched up an M-1 rifle, shoved in a clip, and barked at the chief over the telephone, "I have a loaded M-1, and if you don't douse that light in 60 seconds, I'll shoot it out!" The light blinked out.

Meanwhile, back on Fire Control Hill, Tech. Sergeant Greig and Sergeant Mather jumped out of their bunks and dashed up the stairs to the command post in time to hear Corporal "Tully" on the field telephone trying to convince a major at HECP that they were being fired on. Greig says:

It's probably the only time that a corporal cussed out a major and got away with it. Although we had people on duty it appears nobody saw the submarine until they spotted the flash and heard the explosion of the first shell.

In our plotting room we had a large, lighted, glass-top table. Under the glass was a map of the Columbia River entrance and all the shores around the river. The radar up on North Head told us where the submarine was, but according to our plotting board, the gun flashes were never within range of our guns. The original tracking was by gun flashes computed by triangulation methods from various observation stations. This data was plotted on our operations board mostly from data originating in the Harbor Entrance Control Post. Since the sub plots continued to come in to our board for some time after the firing stopped, it could have been more assumption on our part than fact that the plots we were receiving were from radar sources. The flashes of the gun shots were all southwest of our Command Post, between us and Tillamook Rock.

At the Battery Russell Command station on top of the parapet Captain Wood bent over the rangefinder in order to start taking readings. Years later Wood recalled:

Getting the range with a DPF [Depression Position Finder] is pretty rough with just gun flashes to sight on. When the sub's guns would fire out there I'd crank the dog-gone thing and try to get the crosshairs on the flash and try to read the range from them. But, by golly, the range drum went clear off the scale, which indicated to me that the range was probably 18 to 20 thousand yards. Our old guns at Battery Russell were good for only 16,000 yards with armor-piercing ammo and only a little bit more with high explosive shells.

The guns at Battery Russell had been sitting out in Oregon-coast weather since 1904 with only a plug in the muzzle and a canvas cover over the breech for protection. When Captain Wood was asked if this long exposure would have affected their range and accuracy, he roared:

No! That wouldn't make any difference. I had the boys load the guns with armor-piercing shells and trip them into battery. I had both guns ready to fire. Hanson, gunpointer on No. 1 gun, was trying to pick up the flashes on his gunsight. I thought if worst came to worst, I'd just fire the guns like field pieces. Zero in on the flashes and start firing over and short as the field artillery does. But the sub was down-range from our guns. If we'd been able to get a definite location on him he still would have been beyond our range.

I don't think the sub skipper had any idea he was shelling Battery Russell. He was just dropping a string of shots across the place. It was just an accident that he came close to us. We just happened to be there.

I asked for clearance to fire. I asked the Field-Officer-of-the-Day up on Fire Control Hill if I could have the searchlights turned on. We had searchlight units all along the beach—one only about 300 yards away. They could have picked up anything out there without any trouble.

The searchlight units had arc lamps noted for their brilliance and ability to split the night with

The best photo this newspaper could find was that of *I-3* a submarine built for the Japanese Navy at Quincy, Massachusetts, in 1905. The editors presumed—incorrectly—that the same sub attacked both Estevan Point and Fort Stevens only 27 hours apart. Two submarines, *I-25* and *I-26*, were involved.

WAR EXTRA

The San Francisco News

FINAL
Complete N. Y. Stocks

Vol. 40   SAN FRANCISCO, MONDAY, JUNE 22, 1942   No. 148

PRICE FIVE CENTS

ORE. COAST SHELLED!

Japanese sub like this, 331 feet long, capable of 15,000 miles without refueling, presumed to be one that shelled Vancouver Island, then coast near Astoria, Ore. Arrow points to 4.7-inch gun.

2nd Alaska Landing
Battle On for Egypt!

COLOR MAP
A map of Alaska to clip and save, showing where Japanese have landed, vital American sectors, resources and strategic importance.
[SEE PAGE 8]

RAIDER HUNTED

TARGETS   Sub Fires 6 to 9 Times at Beach Near Mouth of Columbia River in 2nd Attack

a terrifying splash of blue-white light. At least one of the searchlight crews was as eager as Captain Wood to get the lights into action. At McKenzie Head, Richard Ebi and his card-playing crew members heard the first shot and immediately got busy. In a couple of minutes they had the light ready. Private Campbell telephoned the Harbor Entrance Control Post and asked permission to turn the light on the submarine. Captain Wood called from Battery Russell about the same time requesting permission to fire on the sub. They were told that such permission would have to come from Colonel Doney.

Ebi says that from his high vantage point on McKenzie Head he watched the submarine travel in a northerly direction across the track of the setting moon, firing as she went. He distinctly heard 14 rounds fired. He knew that his light "could reach a phenomenal distance" and that he could have easily illuminated the submarine so the batteries could have seen it. But permission to flip the switch did not come, and the unique moment of opportunity slipped by.

In Battery Clark at Fort Stevens, Captain Platt Davis had four 12-inch mortars ready. He says:

> My, did we ever want to fire! The men were so excited about this chance to put our weapons into action and so disappointed at not being permitted to use them that twenty-two of them went over the hill that night. Letting them pull the trigger just once against an enemy target would have been like having a boil lanced. It would have released tension and anxiety—even if they didn't hit anything.

What happened?

The next day, June 22, 1942, a great clamor arose from both military and civilian authorities to find out exactly what had happened. As might be expected in a time of surprise and confusion, ear-witnesses to the shelling had many estimates of the number of rounds fired. Captain Wood thought that there were "around a dozen." His wife said that when she heard the first shot she thought the President had died and it was the beginning of a 21-gun salute, but not that many were fired. She said there were more than nine—the number painted on a sign at the entrance to Battery Russell a few days later. From the searchlight station on McKenzie Head, Richard Ebi counted 14 rounds fired. We now have authentic reports from across the Pacific that the *I-25* fired 17 rounds that night. This is the number given by Mr. Fujita, and by

58

The sign posted at the entrance to Battery Russell a few days after the June 1942 attack.

Fragment of a Japanese 14-cm shell fired from *I-25*. Actual size: 4½ inches tip to tip.

A hole blasted out by a shell from *I-25* near DeLaura Beach Road.

members of the gun crew who were on deck with Commander Tagami.

Some of the 17 rounds, of course, may have been duds. Some burst and left craters in the beach or among the skunk cabbages in the marsh behind Battery Russell. Some which may not have exploded may still lie buried in swamp or sand.

One shell, the closest one to Battery Russell, smashed the backstop of the baseball diamond, about 70 or 80 yards in front of the big guns. Captain Wood says a jagged, circular plate from the base and a fragment from the nose of the shell were recovered. Other fragments were found in the camouflage net that covered Battery Russell.

When Mr. and Mrs. Hitchman returned to their home three miles south of the post after the shelling, they found their sons and daughter huddled together in one bed for mutual security. Daughter Ardith (now Mrs. Wayne Severson) said in 1972 that they had been frightened by an explosion and she had bribed her brothers by offering them 25 cents of her potato-hoeing money if she could snuggle in bed with them until their parents came home. Army investigators next morning found remains of an exploded shell along DeLaura Beach Road 125 yards inland from the Hitchman house. The shell's trajectory apparently had been parallel with the road and about 12 yards in front of the bedrooms where the children slept. It had hissed over an ammunition dump just inside the north fence of Camp Clatsop. When it exploded it shattered a tree and blasted a big hole in the edge of the swamp.

One fragment from this shell caused damage

DeLaura Beach Road monument

HISTORICAL LANDMARK

ON JUNE 21, 1942 A 5.5" SHELL EXPLODED HERE, ONE OF 17 FIRED AT COLUMBIA RIVER HARBOR DEFENSE INSTALLATIONS BY THE JAPANESE SUBMARINE I-25. THE ONLY HOSTILE SHELLING OF A MILITARY BASE ON THE U.S. MAINLAND DURING WORLD WAR II AND THE FIRST SINCE THE WAR OF 1812.

59

that was not discovered until 16 months later. A power outage caused maintenance men of the Pacific Power and Light Company to wonder why a breakdown had occurred in a low-risk area. The break was on DeLaura Beach Road within sight of the Hitchman farmhouse. Pacific Power men found that a shell fragment had nicked the power line's copper cladding, exposing the steel core to the corrosive effects of the salt air. Eventually the steel wire had rusted through and broken the circuit. Pacific Power thus became one of the few stateside American firms to sustain damage from an enemy attack in World War II.

Fragments of this shell and others that exploded were found in the following weeks by souvenir hunters who tramped through the marshes and along the beach, but the number carried away greatly exceeded the actual number of pieces of Japanese shells. The Hitchman sons and other boys of the neighborhood made a little money by selling to eager tourists broken pieces of cast iron stove lids, fire-pot doors, and other scrap from the city dump as "genuine Japanese shrapnel."

Rumors of men getting hit—denied at the time —have persisted through the years, but none of them have held up under close scrutiny.

Observers who claim to have "seen" the *I-25* have it going in various directions. Some claim it was headed south, others say it was going north. One man from a high vantage point saw it sailing "in a wide arc—firing as she went." If some reports are to be believed, it made a 360 degree turn before retiring. Tales of how long the submarine stayed and how it maneuvered are undoubtedly exaggerated by time and retelling. Many people saw the muzzle flashes, but it is doubtful if anyone actually saw the submarine— a long, low black hull seven to ten miles at sea.

Sources in Japan (see Notes) indicate that no track for the firing run for this attack has been found. Perhaps one reason there is none is that the submarine was not moving, other than from the swells of the sea. When the sub left about midnight, it ran on the surface to the west, passing several fishing boats and the blacked-out lightship *Relief* on the Columbia River Lightship station.

At the Columbia River Light Station, the *Relief* was the ship on duty the night of June 21/22, 1942.

The decision

For more than three decades there have been rumors, speculation, myth, and just plain lies about why the defenses of the Columbia did not strike back when fired on by a Japanese submarine.

Captain Wood at Battery Russell estimated that the flashes came from a distance of 18,000 to 20,000 yards. He knew his guns were good for only about 16,000 yards with the armor-piercing shells with which they were loaded. But that is not the reason he did not fire. He asked for searchlight support and permission to fire, but authorization never came. Captain Harris at Fort Canby also wanted to fire, but did not receive permission.

Bennett Loftsgaard, who saw the flashes from near the South Jetty, declared, "We were closer to the submarine than anyone else and we couldn't see it." Sergeant Ernest Fieguth said, "I could see the gun flashes, but our old 75's wouldn't shoot that far, but we were sure in the front row to see the action."

The specifications for 10-inch guns like those at Battery Russell give the maximum range as 16,200 yards. The men who were using these particular guns estimated their range from 14,000 to 16,000 yards. Some evidence has come from Japan that tends to negate the claims that the *I-25* was actually beyond the range of these guns.

In his letter to Admiral Russell, Admiral Samejima wrote, "Commander Meiji Tagami told that the firing had been made where the water was thirty meters deep and with the gunsight range at 13,000 meters [14,217 yards]." Tatsuo Tsukudo, former executive officer of the *I-25*, describes the 14-cm (5.5-inch) deck gun as being a 1922 model which had a maximum range of 14,000 meters (15,310 yards). Another crew member, Sadao Iijima, a gunner who did some of the firing, confirms the fact that it was a 1922-model gun that had been manufactured in 1936. He says the gun had a range of 14,000 meters but that he fired from 10,000 meters (10,936 yards). Sensuke Tao, who also fired some of the shells, says that the gun was set "dead center—zero degrees, firing range 14,000 meters."

If these men who were on the submarine are to be credited, the *I-25* was *probably within range of Fort Stevens' guns* when it lobbed the shells that landed on the baseball field close to Battery Russell and nearly a mile inland on the DeLaura Beach Road.

Regardless, whether or not the submarine was within range, those in authority believed that it was not and made the decision not to fire. An arsenal of weapons—machine guns, French 75's, mortars, and heavy coast artillery guns were manned. Searchlight crews were at the ready. But no one gave an order to pull a trigger or pressed a button to activate the carefully prepared systems.

What was the reasoning behind the decision not to fire? Replies to inquiries came from many places—Hong Kong, Ottawa, Florida, Victoria, South Carolina, Virginia—but the probable answer came from Saipan in the Mariana Islands. In a letter written on Christmas Day 1972, former Major Robert M. Huston wrote:

I was the Senior Duty Officer on duty at the Group Fire Control Station at Fire Control Hill the night that the Japanese submarine fired on the beach area. As Senior Duty Officer I represented Colonel Kenneth Rowntree, the Group Commander. I asked all stations to report the range of the flashes . . . we determined that the submarine was about 2,000 to 3,000 yards out of range of the nearest battery—Battery Russell. Captain Wood requested permission to open fire. I refused permission on the basis:

1. The submarine was not in range and was very likely firing a reconnaissance mission to spot location of our batteries.

2. The submarine outranged us by about 4,000 yards, being a modern 5-inch (approximately) gun on a barbette carriage. Our old disappearing guns were limited in range. Due to the disappearing carriage they could only be elevated a little over 14°. Battery Russell had a maximum range of about 14,000 yards, having been designed for use against 1900 vintage cruisers and battleships.

3. We had no radar at that time and we had to depend on visual observation of the flashes, or use searchlights, which certainly wasn't advisable when you are outranged and the target is out of range.

Jack Wood wanted very much to open fire. I made a decision [not to fire] which I thought was tactically sound and later supported (I was told) by the Commanding General, 9th Coast Artillery District, in San Francisco. . . . I wish I could have gone along with Jack because of the effect on morale.

The Harbor Defense Commander came to similar conclusions. Without consulting his superior officer, General Cunningham at Fort Worden, Colonel Doney made the ultimate decision not to use the searchlights and not to return fire. As he cryptically described the situation years later:

They were out of our range and there was no reason to fire—give our position away. We had them tracked all the time and they were from 500 to 1,000 yards out of our maximum range. A big flash from shore would have given them a pinpoint and been absolutely useless.

This is the answer. These are the men who made the decisions, which are clear enough and logical enough once one knows the basis for them. Zed Harris, a long-time loyal member of the Coast Artillery Corps, has his own opinion of the major result of the events of June 21, 1942:

> The death blow to the Harbor Defense units was dealt the night of the Japanese attack on Fort Stevens. There was no return fire. Whether the fire would have hit anything or not wasn't the point. With hundreds of guns and mortars along both Atlantic and Pacific shores, and thousands of men at the ready, we blew it for our Corps when we had a chance to shoot—and didn't.

Harris exaggerates, of course, but in a way what he says is true. At this turning point in coast defense history, it became obvious to all concerned than an enemy could always build weapons that could outrange the old-style shore installations. Because of momentum, construction of some new batteries already in progress continued. Work on three 16-inch gun emplacements on the Strait of Juan de Fuca, for example (Chapter IV), continued, but two were discontinued in 1943 and the third, although completed, never became fully operational. All coast defense installations of the traditional pattern have long since been abandoned. Almost every one of the big guns was cut up for scrap during or soon after the war, and only the huge concrete emplacements remain as mute reminders of this period in our military history. □

Stripped of its armament and equipment, the casemate of Battery Russell is now part of Fort Stevens State Park. The only disappearing carriage coast artillery guns remaining in the Pacific Northwest are at Fort Casey State Park, Whidby Island, Wash.

VI
Mission: Retaliation

In war, there is a time for caution and a time for boldness
—John Toland

I TRANSFERRED to the submarine *I-25* as chief flying officer six weeks prior to the war with the United States. With Lieutenant Commander Meiji Tagami in command of the submarine, we left Yokosuka Naval Base on November 21, 1941. Our sealed orders sent us to Pearl Harbor as part of the Japanese Navy strike force that was to attack Oahu 30 minutes after our envoys in Washington, D.C., handed a declaration of war to the American government. Our orders were to attack and sink any U.S. warships that survived the air attack and tried to leave Pearl Harbor.

My only duties during the attack were to stand control room and conning tower watches. Later we chased the carrier *U.S.S. Enterprise* and other American ships but could not get into position for an attack.

At sea after the Pearl Harbor attack, we were ordered to patrol the west coast of the United States. We maneuvered between Seattle and San Francisco. On this mission we were directed to fire on a coastal target near the mouth of the Columbia River about Christmastime, but a few days before the attack was to occur, the *I-25* was ordered south to intercept vessels reported heading north from the Panama Canal. By Christmas, we were in the vicinity of Monterey Bay, California.

It was after the Pearl Harbor episode that I had the idea our reconnaissance airplane could have more value as an attack aircraft under certain conditions. The aircraft could be armed with bombs and could search far ahead of the submarine. It would greatly increase the effectiveness of the mother ship as a commerce raider or as part of the fleet.

I discussed the idea with Lieutenant Tatsuo Tsukudo, the *I-25's* executive officer. Then I wrote it out and submitted it to Commander Tagami through Mr. Tsukudo. Specifically, my idea was that Japanese submarines could attack such targets as the Panama Canal, west coast naval bases, aircraft industries, and shipping. I was firmly convinced that submarine-based planes could do this sort of work. The submarines had a very large operational range, including the entire western coast of the American mainland. There were such targets as Seattle, Portland, San Francisco, Los Angeles, and San Diego. My only concern about pos-

Nubuo Fujita
Chief Flying Officer

Tatsuo Tsukudo
Executive Officer

sible rejection of my plan was the reaction of the submarine commanders. We all knew how long it took to handle the aircraft. I was afraid they would call the plan impractical because of the risk of having the submarine on the surface too long for assembly, launching, and retrieval of the airplane.

What if we were intercepted by a destroyer or some other American warship? I thought how useful our aircraft could be in this situation. It could bomb a warship, causing distraction long enough for the submarine either to make a torpedo attack or get away. But again we received a change of orders and returned toward our base in the Marshall Islands. Near Johnston Island we fired torpedoes at a ship that looked like the *U.S.S. Langley.* We went on to Kwajalein and spent some time refitting and repainting our ship and enjoying the luxuries of fresh fruits, vegetables, and baths.

At Kwajalein one of our officers was killed by accident. The water-tight door on the aircraft hangar was jammed shut. When he forced it, the pressure released, and he was struck by the door as it flew open.

While we were in the lagoon, we were attacked by American aircraft, but we quickly submerged and lay on the bottom until the attack was over. When we surfaced, I was certain that some of our vessels would be damaged or destroyed. Those Americans had a lot to learn about how to attack ships. With all their zooming and bombing I did not hear of any of our submarines being hit but there was damage to some surface ships.

Later I flew reconnaissance missions over Sydney and Melbourne, Australia; Wellington and Auckland, New Zealand; Hobart, Tasmania; Suva in the Fiji Islands; and Noumea, New Caledonia.

Although my observer and I were in constant fear of discovery, we were never attacked and we got a great deal of useful information. Our ZERO-type small reconnaissance seaplane would have been a sitting duck to any fighter. Top speed was only 150 miles per hour and we carried only one machine gun. I suppose no one expected to see a Japanese aircraft in this area.

We were not the only ones who worried. Members of the crew were always anxious during our takeoffs and landings as the airplane had to be assembled before it could be launched, and taken apart and stored in the deck hangar before the *I-25* could submerge. These things took time and no submariner likes to get caught on the surface in enemy waters. It is like asking to commit suicide.

Petty Officer Second Class Shoji Okuda, who was my observer, and I told the crew that if we

Meiji Tagami
Commander

Shoji Okuda
navigator/observer

were sighted by an enemy plane that we would crash into it if our light machine gun could not down it. If at any time we could not locate the submarine, we would keep trying to find it as long as gasoline was available. When low on fuel, we would land on the sea at the first rendezvous point, then the second, then the third point. If the submarine failed to appear and we were endangered by the enemy, we would sink the secret code documents, destroy the airplane, then kill ourselves.

Shortly after the Battle of Midway, the *I-25* was again on station off the west coast of the United States. During this time we attacked a large merchant ship [Fort Camosun] off the coast of Washington, then shelled the coastal defense base west of Astoria, Oregon [Fort Stevens]. We came in through a fishing fleet because we knew there would be no mines where these boats were. With our gun pointing over the stern—so we could leave for the open sea in a hurry if need be—we fired 17 rounds at the shore installations. Both Commander Tagami and I were on deck during the firing. After we had fired the seventeenth shell, we left the area at flank speed.

We returned to Yokosuka Naval Base in Japan by way of the Aleutian Islands. In port, I was surprised and puzzled when Commander Tagami handed me a telegram from Imperial Navy Headquarters. It ordered me to come to Naval Headquarters, 3rd Division (submarines) immediately. The message did not divulge any reason for my summons. I was to report to Commander Iura in Tokyo.

I was very nervous as I went into the Navy building, and the large number of senior officers in the halls and offices did not make me feel any better. I located the 3rd Division offices and went in.

Everyone was busy so I approached a sub-lieutenant, introduced myself, and asked for Commander Iura. The junior officer said, "Thank you for coming—wait awhile," and showed me a chair. I stood. In a few minutes Prince Takamatsu, the Emperor's younger brother, came into the office. The Prince and I were acquainted as he had previously visited my flying field.

Another man joined us. "I am Iura," he said.

"I am Warrant Officer Fujita, sir," I said, "Flying Officer of the I-25."

"Fujita," he said, "you are going to bomb the American mainland. I'll bring the ex-Vice Consul from Seattle. He will explain the mission to you." He went out.

I was speechless. My mind considered Seattle, Portland, San Francisco, Los Angeles. Perhaps I could hit a vital target like a carrier. I did not consider for a moment that my quite small reconnaissance plane could carry only two 76-kilogram bombs. The whole thing seemed like a dream.

As I was pondering Commander Iura's pronouncement, he re-entered the room with the former diplomat, who was now in Naval uniform. He had four or five charts which he spread out on a table. "We took these at Wake Island," he said. "They should be useful." He pointed to the American coast about 75 miles north of the California border. "Here," he said, "you will bomb these forests for us."

Forests? My dreams came to earth! Any cadet could bomb a forest! A thing like that would be impossible to miss. What did they need me for? My disappointment must have shown because the officer with the maps began to explain.

"The northwest United States is full of trees," he said. "Once a fire gets started in the deep woods it is very hard to put out. Sometimes whole towns are burned. If we could start some big fires it would cause the Americans much trouble. It might even cause panic if the people knew Japan could bomb their country, their factories, and their homes."

I felt a little better, and the feeling improved when I learned that my bombing mission was considered a very important and urgent duty. The officers said that my bombs would force the Americans to defend their homeland after seeing that Japan was capable of bombing their land by aircraft. I was enjoined to secrecy.

I remembered that I had promised my wife, Ayako, that I would take our son, Yasuyoshi, for an outing that day. This would now have to be delayed because I had to return to the submarine and report to Commander Tagami.

Yokosuka, where I-25 was docked, was some distance from Tokyo, and even farther from my native town. My wife had rented a room for us near the Naval base, and I had planned on spending my time there unless needed on the submarine. With the charts in my packet, I headed back to my ship but stopped to see my wife and son on the way. I told Ayako, "I am too busy now, but I will be back in two hours." On the submarine I gave the charts to Commander Tagami, who locked them in the wall safe.

We sailed from Yokosuka on August 15, 1942, and crossed the Pacific in calm weather without incident. As we neared the mainland, however, the ocean became very rough. On a morning early in September, the lookout sighted the Cape Blanco lighthouse. Because of the rough seas, there was no hope of getting the aircraft assembled and making a launch. We were forced to wait.

I was usually the first man up (other than the night-duty men) and went into the control center each morning to check the weather. I was anxious to fly my mission. For days the weather was bad.

To pass the time away, five of us, Commander Tagami; our navigator, Mr. Tanabe; Lt. Fukumoto; the ship's physician, Dr. Hoshi, and I, played bridge.

One morning while I was cleaning my pistol, Commander Tagami asked me to come to the control center. He nodded toward the periscope. "Take a look, Fujita," he said, "The view is fairly good today." I looked. The Oregon coast was plainly visible in the pre-dawn grayness. The Cape Blanco light flashed by us as it swept the sky. Today the sky was clear except for a light coastal fog, but when *I-25* surfaced I was disappointed again—the sea was still too rough for launching the aircraft.

I had made my final preparations while awaiting my mission. I had placed a clip of my hair and my will in a small box in the bottom of my desk drawer. If I were to die and my body could not be recovered, these "remains" would go back to Japan and be presented to my wife in a small container of *kari* (paulownia) wood.

On September 9, 1942, (U.S. time) the sea was almost calm. As I put on my flying clothes,

I was excited with the thought that at long last I was going to bomb America.

The *I-25* surfaced at about 42°N-125°W. The aircraft was taken out of its hangar and assembled and armed. In a few minutes, Okuda and I and two 76-kg (170-pound) incendiary bombs were airborne. Behind us the *I-25* submerged to move to our rendezvous point to await our return. I flew toward Cape Blanco light, crossed the coastline, and went inland on a southeast course about 50 miles.

The sun was rising at this time and it was like a gigantic Chinese lantern. We flew at about 100 knots over the coastal mountains. The plane was a little above 2,500 meters (about 8,200 feet) altitude after climbing through the coastal fog. Over a heavily wooded area [east of Brookings] I yelled to Okuda through the voice tube, "The bombs are to be dropped here." With my left hand I reached for the bomb-release knob, called to Okuda, "Ready—fire!" and pulled the knob.

Nothing would disappoint me more than the bombs not exploding after being carried all the way from Japan. With this thought in mind, Okuda and I watched carefully. Moments later we saw the scattering of flickering fires through the trees [on Wheeler Ridge about eight miles east of Brookings]. Each bomb contained 520 firing elements which would spread over 100 meters in diameter at the time of explosion and start to burn at the high temperature of 1500°C.

The float plane Fujita and Okuda flew over Oregon forests to drop fire bombs was launched by catapult from the deck of *I-25*. Upon return, it landed on the sea and taxied up to the side of the submarine. A derrick hoisted it aboard. With wings, fins, and floats detached and tailplane folded, it was returned to its hangar forward of the conning tower.

The lighthouse on Cape Blanco, the westmost place in Oregon, was the reference point for Fujita and Okuda on both of their bomb-dropping flights.

The aircraft was quickly disassembled and stored while the navigator laid out a course to intercept the two merchant vessels. We were maneuvering for an attack when one of the duty officers sighted an enemy airplane coming out of the sun. It looked like a dive bomber. We dove and were 18 meters under the surface when the first bomb exploded. The submarine rolled sharply and the lights went out. About a minute later they came on again. There was some damage in the radio room and the submarine was taking water. Fortunately for us, the other bombs dropped by the Americans missed. Fortunate also was the fact that our damage was minor and could be repaired while we were at sea.

The lookout told us later, "It was a quick action. At the instant I sighted the plane, it was already diving on us. I really thought this was the end of us."

At first I did not know that the attack was going on. I was in my quarters taking off my flying suit. Mr. Tagami was in the conning tower. I made my way to the tower to find out what happened. Commander Tagami was saying, "What a rascal! His action was close and speedy. Ha! Hmmmm!"

A little at a time the color came back on the crew's faces as their Commander made his way

It gave me great satisfaction to get some revenge for the bombing of my homeland by Doolittle's raiders. I felt that it partially evened the score. We flew a few more miles and dropped the second bomb.

Although the area was mountainous I took the plane down to treetop level and hedgehopped back to the sea. As I passed over Cape Blanco I saw two merchant vessels southwest of the cape. I skimmed along about 40 feet above the waves and passed midway between the two ships, hoping that they would not see me, or if they did, that they would not recognize my airplane as Japanese.

The *I-25* was waiting. I landed and reported to Commander Tagami. "Mission completed, sir," I said. "Fires were started. The plane is in good shape, and I saw two merchant ships east of us heading north at an estimated 12 knots."

Kou Maki, an *I-25* crew member, drew this impression of the attack by a U.S. patrol bomber.

through the damaged submarine reassuring everyone in a quiet but cheerful voice.

Our orders were to keep perfectly quiet and to remain at a depth between 60 and 70 meters until surface sounds disappeared. When all was quiet above we crept in toward the shore and lay on the bottom until nighttime.

A few days later we received a radio message from Tokyo that quoted a San Francisco broadcast about a Japanese airplane that had dropped incendiary bombs on forest areas of Oregon. The broadcast said the plane probably came from a submarine. This made us cautious. We ran submerged during the day and surfaced at night to recharge our batteries and search for targets.

A second flight was not planned originally, but we had brought along from Yokosuka six incendiary bombs, the two that we had dropped and four extras. Commander Tagami proposed that we fly again. He and I decided to do this second flight at night. We believed that it was too dangerous to fly in day time because of expected severe air patrol.

We surfaced on September 29 about 50 miles west of Cape Blanco and assembled and armed the plane. Okuda and I took off in the dark, flew inland for about half an hour, and dropped our bombs [in the Grassy Knob area east of Port Orford]. We saw the explosions of red fire in the forest.

On the return flight, I was very careful to avoid being seen. I turned off the engine when we reached the coast, passed north of the Cape Blanco light, and glided well out to sea before starting the engine. I reached the rendezvous point safely, but I could not see the *I-25*. Then I suddenly remembered the faculty compass in the airplane which had given me trouble on previous reconnaissance flights over Australia and New Zealand. Our rendezvous point should be 50 to 60 kilometers offshore on a compass heading of 270° from the Cape Blanco light. I turned back toward the lighthouse and called to Okuda, "Get the aircraft position and obtain the return course."

Okuda answered quickly, "The heading is 250° for this attempt."

I flew back out to sea on a new course of 245° and presently we saw a streak of something that gleamed on the surface of the water. It looked like oil on the sea, and I followed the track until it narrowed to the black outline of a surfaced submarine running dead slow. I directed Okuda to radio the recognition signal and within a few seconds the answer came back from the ship. I landed on the water and taxied up to the starboard side to the derrick. We were hoisted aboard immediately.

I reported the success of the mission to Commander Tagami and told him of the leakage of oil. We surmised that the leak occurred during the difficult night launching. He thought it was lucky for me, but even more lucky that American ships or planes did not find us. The floating oil would have given away our location.

Any additional flights were not considered because of bad weather and rough seas. We spent the rest of the patrol time attacking merchant shipping. We sank two tankers, one on October 5th [*Camden*] and another [*Larry Doheny*] on October 6th. We were down to our last torpedo so Commander Tagami decided to return home. On October 11th we fired our last torpedo at two submarines traveling on the surface about 800 miles off the Washington coast. One of the submarines [Soviet *L-16*] blew up in a terrific explosion. The shock was severe, like a near-miss bomb or depth charge.

We were greatly relieved when we sailed into our home waters and neared our dock at Yokosuka because our skipper had insisted that we maintain full war-alert duties right up to the time we entered the bay. I did not realize that I was suffering from beriberi, a common ailment among submariners on long cruises, until I saw the home port. Then I felt heavy in my legs.

It was then that I realized for the first time that indeed, a small submarine-borne reconnaissance plane could be turned into a bomber and could raid enemy lands. As the submarine proceeded slowly through the bay I looked about my ship. Its color, like the red ball and gray paint on my airplane, was faded, and its paint was peeling after the 70-day struggle with the seas.

Our voyage had been long and our mission successful. Okuda and I had bombed America twice! Our crew had sunk two enemy ships and a submarine! Our *I-25* had been damaged by enemy bombs yet we lost no lives! I wanted to thank everybody in the world. I wept. I tried to hold back my tears with binoculars, pretending to be a lookout as we tied up at our dock. □

VII
Air Strikes on Oregon

HOWARD GARDNER arose and dressed at dawn on Wednesday, September 9, 1942. From the windows of his lookout tower on Mt. Emily (elevation 2,926 feet) in the southwest corner of Oregon he had a view like that of a captain on the bridge of a ship. He looked out over a sea of billowy fog. Other peaks, ridges, and treetops formed islands jutting out of the fluffy foam.

In the depths of this 2,000-foot ocean of fog, he knew that the twigs and branches were dripping (as a result of fog and an unseasonal rain the previous day). The dense forest of Port Orford cedar, hemlock, spruce, Douglas-fir, shore pine, tanoak, and myrtlewood was soaked. The town of Brookings eight miles southwest was dank, wet, and grey. Along the rocky beach sea gulls skimmed through the morning mist.

But up in Gardner's heaven, the sun brightened by the minute. Bob Larson, a relief lookout and fire guard who had spent the night with Gardner, was still in his sack and sound asleep. As Howard started preparations for breakfast he heard a strange sound, like a Model-A Ford backfiring—strange in this location a quarter of a mile from the nearest road. Scanning the panorama, he saw a small airplane circling above the fog. He shouted to Bob Larson, "Come quick—have a look!" They could not distinguish the plane's color in the early light but could see it clearly enough to note its odd shape and to tell that it was a model with which they were not familiar.

Howard's call by radio crackled into the Gold Beach ranger station, 35 miles north of Brookings, at 6:24 a.m. "GOLD-56 reporting one plane. Type unknown. Flying low. Seen east, two miles, circling."

Rita Ganong, the radio relay operator on duty, forwarded the message to the Roseburg Filter Center. No particular significance was attached to the report. Patrol craft flew up and down the coast every once in a while.

Bob Larson, now fully awake, fixed himself a breakfast and then left to go to Harbor, a village across the Chetco River south of Brookings, to pick up supplies. As a roving guard in the Chetco District of the Siskiyou National Forest, Larson did a wide variety of jobs, filling in wherever needed.

Seven miles east of Mt. Emily, at the Bear Wallow lookout (elevation 2,385 feet), 18-year-old Keith V. Johnson awoke under the surface of the fog sea. Because he could not see anything but misty white around him, he notified the ranger's office (as was customary on such occasions) that he was leaving his lookout to clear trail and do other routine chores.

By noon the fog had cleared out of the canyons, but Howard Gardner at Mt. Emily noticed that one thin patch of white remained about five miles southeast. He put his glasses on it. Smoke! He called the ranger's office.

Ed Marshall, the District Ranger, had been on duty all morning at Gold Beach. He was getting ready to go home for lunch at about 12:20 when Howard Gardner's second report came in. Marshall called Snow Camp lookout for a cross shot and located the area of the fire on his map in Township 40 South, Range 12 West, Section 22. Marshall later recalled:

It puzzled me considerably, why we should have a fire in this remote location, because ordinarily there would be no reason for anyone to be in that part of the forest. Howard and I talked over the situation and concluded

From the lookout tower on Mt. Emily in Curry County, Oregon, two Forest Service men saw the Japanese plane on its first bomb-dropping mission in September 1942.

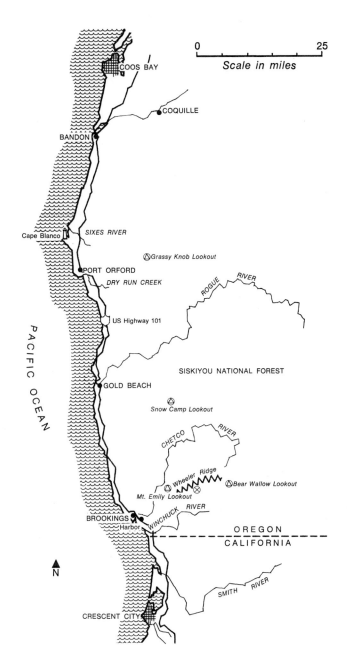

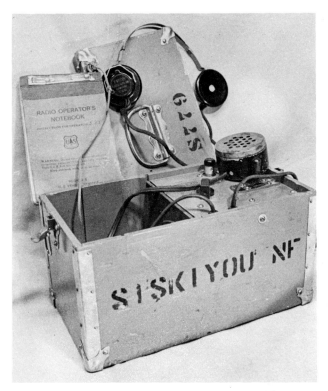

Radiophone Type S Model A 1937, a set widely used in World War II by Forest Service men throughout the Pacific Northwest. Keith Johnson used one of these 9-pound "S" radios to announce the discovery of the Japanese bomb on Wheeler Ridge.

it could possibly have been a "sleeper" fire from a lightning storm the night before in that vicinity. At 12:25 p.m., I dispatched Gardner to the fire with a one-man outfit. He was to travel a distance of about four and a half miles cross-country. There were no trails.

Marshall called Snow Camp again and asked that the Bear Wallow lookout, Keith Johnson, be sent to the fire. As soon as Keith returned from trail work, in early afternoon, he called in and learned that Howard Gardner had sighted a fire and had started down toward it. "After some real hard looking," Keith says, "I detected a wisp of smoke, thus confirming Howard's observation. After reporting azimuth and angle of elevation, I packed my portable "S" radio, rations, and a fire-

fighting kit and was off for the trail that led along the Wheeler Ridge hogback." He had an eight-and-a-half-mile hike on rough trail ahead of him.

At about 2 p.m. Ranger Marshall got in touch with Bob Larson, the roving guard, at Hanscom's store in Harbor. He told Larson to pick up another man and go to Wheeler Ridge. With Fred Flynn, Larson packed a two-man outfit, an "S" radio, and extra rations. They drove up the Winchuck River Road to the Wheeler Creek Trail where they parked and started a three-mile hike to the fire site.

Keith Johnson from Bear Wallow had made good time on the rough trail, which was mostly downgrade. After almost eight miles and two hours, he came to a small tree that had been recently cut and dropped across the trail. He recognized that this was Howard Gardner's sign he had crossed the trail at this point. Down the ridge through heavy brush, Gardner had blazed his trail by cutting small notches in the bark of trees every few yards. Keith followed the marks easily and soon began to shout for Howard. Just as he ran out of blazes, Howard answered—from

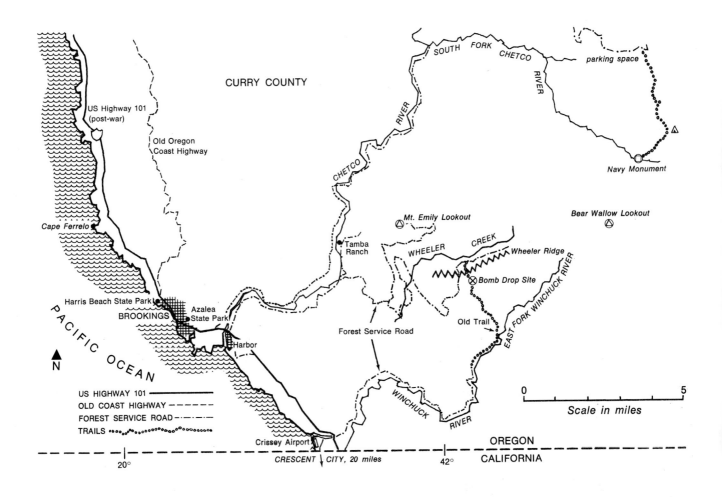

CURRY COUNTY

US Highway 101 (post-war)

Old Oregon Coast Highway

Cape Ferrelo

Harris Beach State Park
BROOKINGS
Azalea State Park
Harbor

PACIFIC OCEAN

N

US HIGHWAY 101 ——————
OLD COAST HIGHWAY — — — —
FOREST SERVICE ROAD — · — · —
TRAILS ••••••••••••••••••••

Crissey Airport

20°

SOUTH FORK CHETCO RIVER
parking space

CHETCO RIVER

Navy Monument

Mt. Emily Lookout
Bear Wallow Lookout

Tamba Ranch

WHEELER CREEK
Wheeler Ridge

Bomb Drop Site

EAST FORK WINCHUCK RIVER

Old Trail

Forest Service Road

WINCHUCK RIVER

0   5
Scale in miles

CRESCENT CITY, 20 miles   42°

OREGON
CALIFORNIA

30 feet up in a fir tree, where he had climbed to get a visual fix on the smoke.

In less than 500 yards they came upon a broad circle of smoldering fires scattered over an area 50 to 75 feet across. None of the fires needed emergency attention. Howard and Keith probed around a little and found a small crater in the center of the area and noted sliced branches and split tree trunks. They came to the conclusion that a bomb must have started the fires and they should report immediately.

Keith went back up to the top of the ridge to rig an antenna for his radio. On his way down from Bear Wallow, he had taken a tumble and landed on his radio. He was worried now that the set would not work, but after climbing a tree and attaching the antenna he energized the set and raised Gold Beach on the first try.

Ranger Marshall noted in his diary:
4:20 p.m. Johnson reported via "S" radio from ridge above fire that fire was started by bomb. He said fire under control.

At 5:40 p.m., Johnson called again to tell Marshall that he and Gardner had found fragments of a metal casing and thermite pellets scattered in the vicinity of the fire. Marshall's immediate assumption was that a bomb might have been dropped accidentally by a U.S. military aircraft or that the plane had been in trouble and had jettisoned its bombload to reduce weight. He called the Roseburg Filter Center to inquire if any military aircraft had been reported in the vicinity of Mt. Emily that morning.

Roseburg answered negative and asked Marshall to go to the fire site to get more details. He replied that he would not have time to get there before dark that night but would go the next morning. He had men at the site and assured the filter center that nothing would be removed.

At 8:10 p.m., the FBI called Marshall from Portland asking for information on the fire and complete details on the bomb. Marshall called Les Colvill, Assistant Supervisor of the Siskiyou National Forest, who was at Long Ridge lookout on an inspection trip, and alerted him to the situation. They agreed to meet in Brookings the next morning and go to the site of the fire together.

72

Meanwhile, Larson and Flynn had joined Johnson and Gardner at the fire. They found scattered pieces of phosphorus still burning and several small trees that had been sheared off. Because Howard Gardner had regular reporting schedules to meet on the aircraft warning network, he departed. Keith Johnson made the last radio contact at 8:30 p.m. and reported that Larson and Flynn were returning and that he (Johnson) would continue mopping up the fire and stay with it overnight. Keith remembers that night well:

There was a small stream less than 200 yards down the ridge, so in addition to isolating each little fire and trying to extinguish it with wet earth and duff, I transported many gallons of water up the hill. By dark, I felt certain that there was no danger of the fires spreading. I built a campfire and cooked my supper. Several sets of glowing eyes in the surrounding darkness joined me in observing what we little realized at the time was a unique historical scene.

A Japanese bomb in an Oregon forest!

Late the next morning Ed Marshall, Les Colvill, Fred Flynn, and Bob Larson climbed to Wheeler Ridge and found Johnson still mopping up a few remnants of the fire. Together they gathered a pile of fragments and incendiary pellets that had not ignited. Flynn and Johnson dug up part of a blue-gray bomb casing and found what appeared to be *Japanese* markings on it. At the bottom of the 3-foot crater in the center of the area they dug up the nose cone of the bomb. It too had Japanese markings on it!

They came to the conclusion that the bomb must have been dropped from a low altitude and had not had time to straighten out. It had tumbled as it fell and the tail fin must have hit first. A tanoak tree had been split—slivered like so many pieces of split bamboo. When the bomb hit, it had broken open like an egg with the contents tumbling out. The fact that they found numerous unexploded incendiary pellets indicated that the bomb had not completely detonated.

At 3:40 p.m. Marshall radioed a statement to Gold Beach about the inscriptions and asked that the Roseburg Filter Center be notified. In reply, Army officials asked him to bring all the pieces that could be found and to meet the officials in Brookings that night.

Although more than thirty hours had elapsed since the bomb dropped, some of the fires it started continued to smolder. The most difficult one to put out, Keith Johnson recalls, was in a large

The nose cone from one of Fujita's bombs

Forester Fred W. Flynn holds fragments from a Fujita bomb beside the tree it shattered.

73

old fir stump where the thermite pellets had started deeply embedded fires. Realizing by this time that this was not an ordinary occasion, Keith brought out his No. 116 folding camera and he and others took pictures with it. Some time during the day Bob Larson brought the commander of the coastal infantry detachment to the site.

About 65 pounds of one of the 170-pound bombs Nobuo Fujita had dropped the previous morning were loaded into a Trapper Nelson packsack and Colvill and Marshall packed it down the trail to their pickup. Johnson and Larson remained at the site. The others returned to Brookings.

Ed Marshall and Les Colvill arrived in Brookings about 8:30 and went to the Army detachment where an Army officer and an FBI man named Kennedy were waiting for them.

Army alerted

"G" Company of the 174th Infantry, 44th Division, composed mostly of men from the New York National Guard, had the mission at this time of guarding the southern Oregon coast against enemy landings. The company commander, Captain Claude E. "Eddy" Waldrop, had about 200 men spread out in detachments from Coos Bay to California. He well remembers this duty:

We would have had one hell of a time if the enemy had been serious about any landing. Each man was limited to five to ten rounds of ball ammunition. We had mostly Springfield rifles and a few Garand M-1's. Bandon's American Legion Building was our company headquarters. We had our own telephone lines to the several outposts and a teletype for communication with higher headquarters.

In addition to the rifle company, we had a mobile machine-gun squad—two jeeps, each mounting a .50 caliber air-cooled machine gun. We also had three .30-caliber water-cooled machine guns. This equipment was based in Bandon. I could dispatch it to any point needed, but there was a problem. Any attack would probably be a surprise, commando-type raid, either by a suicide force or a strike-and-withdraw force. It would take us hours to move the jeeps by the up-and-down, over-and-around coastal highway US 101 from Bandon to Brookings. By the time we could get to Brookings, should there be a landing, the attackers would have either done their damage and gone away or would have been so strongly entrenched that my fifty men would have been ineffective. We did do one thing to confuse the enemy. Soon after the war started we took down all the highways markers to prevent an attacking group from knowing where the roads went.

A soldier coming off duty from an observation post on September 9 reported seeing a plane come in from the sea at about 6 a.m. PWT and heard one going out to sea at 6:30. Waldrop says:

Fred Flynn ignited an incendiary pellet for the benefit of *Oregonian* photographer Frank Sterrett on the day following the bombing raid.

Captain Claude E. Waldrop

When the report of an unidentified airplane in the Cape Blanco area reached me in Bandon, I got on the teletype and reported to the Roseburg Filter Center. The Roseburg people were to get fighter planes over to Bandon. I don't remember where the planes were supposed to come from, but they were P-38's. I heard rumors that somebody at the filter center goofed and scrambled the planes to Bend, in the opposite direction from Bandon!

On Thursday night, September 10, while Colvill and Marshall were reporting to the FBI and Army representatives, the Brookings Army unit was getting into the action. Following instructions from Captain Waldrop, Platoon Sergeant John Zlock was preparing his detachment of "G" Company for a trip into the forest. When Howard Gardner first radioed his sighting to the Gold Beach Ranger office, no one had thought about calling the Army at Brookings—despite the fact it was their mission to repulse all enemy attacks from the sea. Zlock recalls:

The newspaper in the town knew about it before we did. They called us. I understand that Army Headquarters at Corvallis was more than slightly enraged about not being notified first; so they clamped a security lid on all information. All hell broke loose the next couple of days. The brass never got tired of chewing. I have never saluted so much or seen so much Army and Navy brass congregated in one place before or since.

Young Keith Johnson, the lookout from Bear Wallow, who subsequently joined the Navy and eventually rose to the rank of captain, wrote from Hong Kong about the experiences he had the next day. It was the end of the annual fire season and his summer work contract was about to expire. When the fires were extinguished, he and Bob Larson returned to the Bear Wallow lookout station to close it for the winter, since with the rains and fogs, fire danger was nil. Larson departed from the station for the long hike to town with a pack of official materials and personal belongings weighing about 120 pounds.

Johnson set out for a final check of Wheeler Ridge. He was to examine the bomb-drop site and make sure the fires were actually out. He says:

Before I reached the site—it was midafternoon—I heard several rifle shots and shouting voices. My own yelling failed to bring responses, so I went on down the ridge, verified that the fire area was cold, then tried to catch up to the shouts that continued to reach me from lower on the mountain. At the point where the trail met the road, I met a slightly crippled man, who identified himself as an FBI agent. He told me the voices I had been following were U. S. Army troops who had been ordered to the site but had not found it.

We drove into Brookings in the FBI car and went to Army headquarters. I was taken in tow by a young officer. After several hours of questioning, it was decided that "at the convenience of the government" I would not terminate my job but would stay on to escort Army officials to the site.

The next day, we left the Army trucks where the trail started and we proceeded at a snail's pace up the mountain. It wasn't long before most of the troops who started the climb gave up. They were in no condition for this sort of hiking. When we arrived at the fire site three hours later, only the Intelligence Officer and his two assistants were left. After a short rest, we spread out and collected what fragments and thermite clusters we could find. We were there about two hours before starting back to Brookings.

Later Lt. Ron Cameron and a large contingent of soldiers combed the area on the chance there might have been another bomb. Even though they did not know Fujita had dropped a second bomb, they thought it was a possibility. No trace of the

Keith Johnson, 18, was one of the first two men to reach the fires started by Fujita's bomb.

second bomb has ever been found. No one knows whether it exploded or still lies buried in the duff on a Curry County mountainside.

The authorities admonished Captain Waldrop to order his men not to talk about the attack, which was now agreed to be of Japanese origin. Waldrop said:

We were sworn to secrecy but one of my officers (not Ron Cameron) talked too much and was later court-martialed. The Japanese plane was lucky not to have been shot down. If the Filter Center hadn't messed up the information and sent our planes in the wrong direction, it would have been the end of the Japanese bomber.

Consternation

The town of Brookings, with so many people coming and going, was buzzing with rumors. Some of the townspeople had heard of the bombing. There was a lot of talk about what kind of airplane it was, where it came from, where it went, and who saw it. So far as is known, only Howard Gardner, Bob Larson, and an unidentified soldier on duty at an observation post on Cape Blanco actually saw the plane.

Many people claim they heard the plane, but few can actually relate the sound to some experience that would fix the time. Allen Ettinger, who later became the Brookings postmaster, says:

I heard it. I was a teenager and a senior in high school. Only I wasn't in school that morning. I was out doing a little early morning hunting when there was a "putt-putt-kaputt" sound in the air. It sounded like a Model-A Ford hitting on three cylinders. I couldn't imagine what a Ford would be doing up in the sky. At the time, I didn't think of it as an airplane and went on hunting, but I didn't see anything to shoot at.

It is really not surprising so few people saw the plane nor that its incendiary missiles did so little damage. According to the weather records in the National Climatic Center at Asheville, N. C., the six-hour synoptic observations for September 8, 9, and 10, 1942, were consistently "Morning rain and fog."

The weather helps explain why Fujita's especially designed incendiary bombs did not cause more damage, why they caused no large fires such as the Japanese envisioned when planning this venture. The strict ban in force on the broadcast of weather information, both along the coast and inland, denied Commander Tagami data on which to base the time of the attack. If it had occurred a few weeks earlier or if this had been a dry September in Curry County, he might have found the forests tinder dry.

Although government officials tried to keep the attack secret, so many people knew about it that the effort was futile. The Grants Pass *Courier*, forty miles from the blast, gave picture coverage and was especially complimentary to Les Colvill and other Forest Service people. The Seattle *Post-Intelligencer* ran a WAR EXTRA with a two-line block-type headline, JAP AIR RAIDER DROPS FIRE BOMB IN OREGON. The New York *Times* relegated the story to Section Three with an account supplied by the Western Defense Command. An Associated Press wirephoto showed an incendiary pellet alongside a folder of matches to illustrate its size.

The newspaper and radio accounts of the episode caused a good deal of consternation and demands in high places for more protection on the western frontier. General DeWitt sent staff officers to Washington, D. C., to seek priorities that would enable him to obtain additional equipment. A four-plane flight of P-38's from the 55th Fighter Group at McChord Field was sent to Moon Island on the coast near Hoquiam, Washington. From this mile-long, 300-foot-wide strip of sand, pilots were frequently sent aloft to chase reported targets. But with no real targets to shoot at, this exercise was soon discontinued.

The FBI decided to make a search of southwest Oregon and adjoining regions of California. They reasoned that since the Japanese aircraft was a floatplane, it could conceivably be operating from one of the small, hidden mountain lakes. The Pacific Northwest coast was extremely vulnerable to clandestine landings (see Chapter VIII), and the FBI sent special agents into the area in droves. One agent was ordered to base himself in a motel in Crescent City. From there he was to inspect a marked-out map area. His mission was to look for lakes and ponds large enough to accommodate small, float-equipped planes. Thinking in officialdom was that the Japanese might have landed prefabricated aircraft parts on the coast and assembled a plane on one of the lakes, which need only be large enough for takeoff on a suicide flight. If anything was discovered, the FBI's responsibility was to document the location and leave the follow-up to the military.

Weeks of trudging passed into limbo. As the ground was covered, the agents were withdrawn. "We found beautiful mountains, beautiful lakes, good fishing, tall wonderful trees, and mosquitoes and sore, wet feet," my source revealed. "We didn't find any Japs."

In the post-attack period there was a crack-down on motorists driving at night near the ocean with their lights on. In the Crescent City area, nine motorists were cited for failure to heed warnings during the week of September 13. One man, George A. Argus of Seattle, was picked up for "driving with a flashlight in a dimout zone."

Fujita's flight did shake the military wide awake. America had been bombed. It worried the civilian population. The public knew attempts were being made to keep the attack secret, and they did not know how many other events had occurred that were being kept from them. A statement from a Salem, Oregon, resident reflects the psychological effect of the Curry County bombing:

As a small child living near Sweet Home (75 miles inland from the coast) I detected the fear in adults that we might be bombed. It was a very real feeling. I've remembered it for thirty years.

A narrow escape

After their bombing run on September 9, Fujita and Okuda flew back out to sea, avoided being seen by two merchant ships they sighted, located the *I-25*, and landed beside it. The long arm of the submarine's derrick reached out, picked up the

U.S. Army Air Force Hudson bomber (A-29) of the type piloted by Captain Jean H. Daugherty (right) for the attack on *I-25* on September 9, 1942.

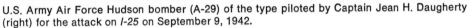

little GLEN aircraft, and set it down on the deck. In 15 or 20 minutes, the efficient crew had folded the wings and rudder and tucked the plane back into its hangar.

Commander Tagami was preparing to attack the two merchantmen when a lookout reported an enemy airplane coming at them from out of the sun. Tagami gave orders to dive. The *I-25* was submerged by the time the plane was overhead.

The attacking plane was a Lockheed Hudson A-29 from McChord Field near Tacoma. On routine antisubmarine patrol, Captain Jean H. Daugherty and his three-man crew were flying low over the sea, under broken clouds and through patches of fog. West of Gold Beach, southwest of Cape Blanco (at approximately 42°22′N-125°12′W), they saw something dark in the water straight ahead. Daugherty made a tight left turn through a fog bank and came out into the sunshine with bomb bay doors open. He dropped three 300-pound bombs, the first two straddling the rapidly disappearing object and the third a few moments later. "Under the circumstances," Daugherty says, "I wasn't sure whether I'd made contact with anything—particularly with an enemy submarine." (See Notes pages 165-166.)

Shoji Aizawa, a torpedoman on the *I-25*, recalls, "There was a big explosion above our heads at the depth of about 25 meters. A second explosion at 30 meters. Big shock. Went down to 70 meters to escape."

Another crew member, Sensuke Tao, remembers that lights went out, the switchboard room and the auxiliary transmitter and receiver were flooded, and the wave guard for the deck gun was broken. He adds that all except the last-mentioned damage were "smoothly mended." From the engine room, Chief Petty Officer Morikazu Kikuchi, a machinist, reported, "No damage here."

For awhile the damaged submarine lay submerged with engines off. Tao recalls:

Commander Tagami quietly worked his way throughout the ship giving stirring remarks to the crew because we were all plenty scared. When our sound men could no longer detect engines of surface craft, *I-25* was carefully trimmed for balance, then with slowest underwater speed moved nearer to the coast with great care and stayed underwater for a long time.

On the surface during daylight hours, Coast Guard cutter *265* and three additional aircraft searched the area. One plane dropped a 300-pound demolition bomb on an oil slick without noticeable results. The U.S. Navy Operations Letter of 9 September 1942 concludes, "There was no further evidence of the submarine and the oil slick had disappeared by about 1700."

Second attack

Twenty days after the first mission, the weather appeared favorable for another attack but a radio message from Tokyo quoting a San Francisco broadcast about the first bombing caused Tagami to be cautious. In the pre-dawn hours of September 29, 1942, the GLEN plane was taken out of its deck hangar, assembled, and armed. It was shot off its catapult in darkness because the defense forces were presumed to be more alert than three weeks before. Again, Fujita and Okuda used the Cape Blanco light as their reference point.

For nearly 30 years the Curry County site where the Japanese bomb started several small fires lay untouched and unmarked. On August 10, 1972, this party of six men and a boy, following old blazes on trees and using photographs taken in September 1942, found the spot near the 1,500-foot elevation on 1,700-foot-high Wheeler Ridge. The old charred snag in the background was one means of identification. Thermite pellets found in 1973 further identified the spot. Members of the party (left to right) were: C. E. "Eddy" Waldrop, Bandon; Leslie L. Colvill, Portland; Jack Valentine, Brookings; Leslie R. Colvill, 14, grandson of Les Colvill; Bert Webber, Medford; M. "Gus" Nichols and Russell Kahre, Brookings. In 1942 Waldrop was captain of an Army defense unit on the southern Oregon coast and Colvill was Assistant Supervisor of the Siskiyou National Forest. Nichols, who was the first to spot the site on this expedition, Valentine, and Kahre were employees on the Siskiyou National Forest in 1972. A well marked trail now leads to this historic location (see map page 72).

The following excerpt is from the report of the incident by Ed Marshall, the Gold Beach District Forest Ranger:

The Grassy Knob lookout [seven miles east of Port Orford] was in process of being remodeled for winter occupation. Because of this activity, a large work crew was there.

The Japanese plane was reported at 5:22 a.m., when a flash message was sent to the Gold Beach Ranger Station from Grassy Knob. Robert Ruth was the Forest Service radio operator on duty at Gold Beach. The reports that followed, sometimes only minutes apart, described the aircraft and reports of people having seen "flashes falling from the plane." Ranchers in the Sixes River area said they had seen the plane. One said it "sounded like a Model T with a rod out."

Les Colvill, the area supervisor, arranged to have a crew of loggers stand by to fight fire if need be. When Associated Press reporter Floyd Lausen called Gold Beach for a story, Bob Ruth told him he would have to clear it with the regional office in Portland or the Siskiyou National Forest office in Grants Pass.

A firefighting patrol headed by Marshall left the Grassy Knob lookout, plotting a compass course as they went in order to be precise about locations. The forest was dense, and the going was much more difficult than on Wheeler Ridge twenty days earlier. They scouted for fires and bomb fragments until 7:30 that night and found nothing.

They camped overnight on a ridge above the main fork of Dry Creek. The next morning, they continued the search but with no results. By afternoon the men were tiring and they were out of food. No smoke or debris had been found. They returned to Grassy Knob.

Fujita says that his second flight was in the same vicinity as the first, but he does not know exactly where he went, only that he flew inland a short distance, dropped his load, then flew back out to sea, and after a worrisome bit of searching, found the I-25 waiting for him. Like the second bomb dropped on September 9, those released on the 29th have never been found.

Although the I-25 had brought six bombs and had dropped only four of them, Commander Tagami was increasingly apprehensive about the threat of patrolling U.S. planes and worried about the rough sea and weather conditions that had already prolonged the mission. He canceled any further aerial activity and prepared to return to Japan. His prime mission, the bombing of the U.S. mainland in retaliation for the Doolittle raid, had been accomplished. □

VIII
Patrolling Northwest Beaches

THE COMMANDER IN CHIEF U.S. FLEET AND CHIEF OF NAVAL OPERATIONS DESIRES THAT THE BEACHES AND INLETS ALONG THE ATLANTIC GULF AND PACIFIC COASTS OF THE UNITED STATES BE PATROLLED BY THE COAST GUARD WHENEVER AND WHEREVER PRACTICABLE.

THE ABOVE DISPATCH arrived at District Coast Guard Headquarters, 13th Naval District, Seattle, Washington, on August 6, 1942. It signaled the start of a two-year operation that combined courage, foolhardiness, dedication, incompetence, ingenuity, and heroism—all glued together.

The Coast Guard embarked upon a "learn on the job" operation that was taught in the ferocious and grisly School of Experience. It was surprising that the job was done so well with so few casualties. Virtually no one from the Commander in Chief on down had the slightest idea of the magnitude of the assignment. The task of patrolling the hundreds of miles of beaches and estuaries was enormously difficult, but it would have been next to impossible if the Coast Guard had not already been operating a string of lighthouses and surf-boat patrols.

Coast Guard lookouts

Actually, the Coast Guard was not caught completely unprepared, for as early as November 1941, at the request of the Navy, it had begun to establish lookout posts at ten lighthouse stations along the Oregon and Washington coasts. The stations were equipped with 12-inch signaling lights and a crew of four signalmen to operate them on a 24-hour basis. The primary tasks of these groups were to prevent or mark the landing of enemy agents, to sight and report submarines, unidentified ships, and aircraft, and to observe and report attacks on coastal shipping. Later, after the war began, the directive was hardened to cover enemy activities and retaliatory efforts by the U.S. Armed Forces.

The ten original stations designated by the Navy were subsequently augmented by others and by August 6, 1942, there was a loose but fairly effective observation network along the coastline of the Pacific Northwest. Locations which appeared to be ideal on maps sometimes did not turn out so well on the ground. One feasibility report indicates some of the problems facing the Coast

Guard in establishing observation stations along the Oregon coast:

> It was found impracticable to locate a lookout on Cape Lookout, as the nearest approach by road is five miles from the cape; two miles across sand dunes, and three miles of ocean beach and trails. However, an excellent lookout can be obtained at Cape Kiwanda . . . The road approaches to within one mile of the cape, and from the end of the road a broad flat beach extends to the foot of [Cape Lookout] . . . Board and room for personnel can be obtained at the Nestucca Hotel at Pacific City for $35.00 per month.

Independent units like this were common. Many units encountered worse situations, because places like the Nestucca Hotel were not available in their areas. Prefabricated shelters housing a signaling light and a pelorus were established wherever practical, but some areas were characterized by camping out until almost the end of the operation.

By April 29, 1942, there were 13 lifeboat stations and 26 coastal lookout stations keeping watch over the coastline. Each station maintained a 24-hour lookout and was equipped with a radio or

The coasts of Oregon and Washington have many wide beaches and protected coves where landings by an invading force would be possible. The task of patrolling the shoreline in World War II was assigned to the U.S. Coast Guard.

telephone. Guardsmen were armed with pistols, rifles, and occasionally machine guns. By May, certain stations with continual fog and restricted visibility established beach patrols in order to do their job. By June 20, the coastal lookout system was virtually complete and was augmented by Army coast defense troops and civilian volunteers. In favorable weather, the entire coastline could be kept under observation. On June 22, a submarine was reported 8 miles off Siletz Bay (Lincoln City) headed south.

Observation and patrol were two different things. As early as March, disrupted telephone communications plagued the observers and caused a certain amount of alarm because of the possibility of sabotage. Most of the lines were Army field telephone wire hastily installed and not designed for continuous service. Failures were bound to occur, and patrols had to be sent to check and maintain the lines. People on the coast still talk of night activity and ship-to-shore signal lights. Rumors of this sort were far more common during the war, and even though none were substantiated, all required investigation.

One early defense plan envisioned fencing the coast! Seven hundred miles of fence! The plan was quickly abandoned. The observation posts and beach patrols were augmented by a small boat division and in late 1943 by Navy blimps, based at the newly created Tillamook Naval Air Station. Control stations were established at twenty harbor mouths and estuaries large enough to serve as harbors (see map). These stations checked every vessel entering and leaving, together with passengers, crew, and ship's officers, and examined the vessel for radio equipment and unusually large supplies of fuel and cargo. This was an incredibly detailed task as every boat, regardless of size, was checked. Lists of arrivals and departures were phoned twice daily to the Navy Intelligence Center in Seattle.

The Coast Guard vessels *Mañana II* and *402* convoyed entering vessels through the minefields at the mouth of the Columbia, and all vessels except those in convoy entering the Strait of Juan de Fuca were stopped at Neah Bay to await passage to Port Angeles or Williams Head where they were boarded and examined. Convoys went directly to Port Angeles and were checked in and disbanded at that point. Inlet patrol boats covered the minor inlets and estuaries and acted as control stations where no shore stations existed. These inlet patrol boats were independent commands, which gives some idea of how thinly the Coast Guard spread its ships and men.

General John L. DeWitt, Commanding General, Western Defense Command, was, in addition to being uncomfortable about resident Japanese, quite concerned over the possibility of Japanese attacks in force along the coast. German saboteurs had been landed from submarines on the U.S. east coast. Something similar might happen on this side of the continent. After the shellings of Goleta, California, and Fort Stevens, Oregon, the general ordered a survey to be made of the west coast. It was by far the most meticulous and accurate survey of the Northwest coastline during the

The Coast Guard established lookout towers and had many stations along the coast equipped with surf boats to conduct patrols and to provide aid wherever needed.

Patrolling beaches took sailors out of their boats and put them on foot. Dogs assisted the Coast Guard in making effective use of manpower.

entire beach patrol period and was important not only for easing General DeWitt's mind about the vulnerability of the Pacific coast, but also for keeping the beach patrols working efficiently and effectively.

Beach surveys were made to determine which control areas were most vulnerable to attack and infiltration. In general, the surveys indicated that certain portions of the Oregon and Washington coastline were peculiarly susceptible to penetration due to a combination of accessible beaches or bays, low population density, and available roads.

Three sectors

To facilitate control, the coastline was divided into three sectors with headquarters at Port Angeles, Washington, and Astoria and Coos Bay, Oregon.

In the COOS BAY SECTOR, the areas pinpointed as extremely vulnerable included the beaches north and south of the Winchuck River (near the Oregon-California border) and an area near Cape Ferrelo and north to Crook Point where a series of small coastal bays could provide ideal landing spots for agents or small groups of infiltrators. Extending northward along the Oregon coast were other beaches interspersed with bays and estuaries, some of which could be considered vulnerable, but most of them were interdicted by surf and shallow water. Although boats could land here, the locations were not ideal. North of Cape Blanco to Bandon is an area consisting mainly of dunes and broad beaches which was classed as extremely vulnerable.

From Coos Bay to Heceta Head there are about fifty miles of accessible beach backed by sand dunes and marshes which could be classed as vulnerable in good weather. A similar area extends north from Cape Perpetua to the Yaquina River mouth. North of this area to Cascade Head are a number of good beaches and bays, but the population density was great enough to make the area a relatively high-risk landing site.

The Oregon coast is as notoriously treacherous as it is beautiful, and is subject to quick storms that give little warning and develop high winds that frequently cause dangerous seas. The currents along the beachline vary, moving from north to south in the summer and in the opposite direction in the winter. The winter storms are particularly

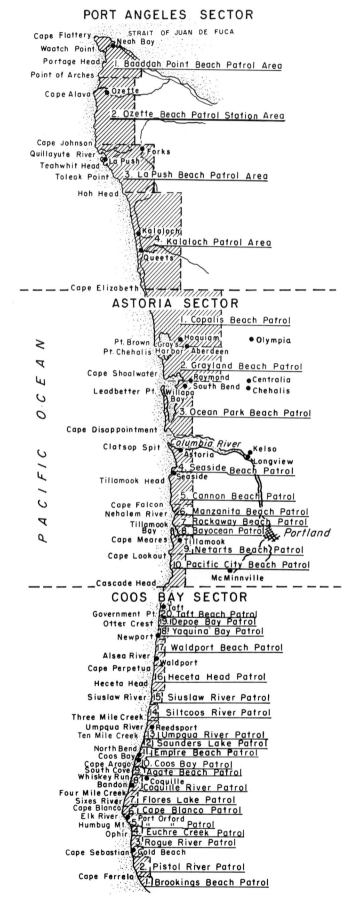

severe. In summer, usually after periods of easterly winds, the ocean may be as calm as a lake, but these periods are never prolonged. Fog may be encountered at any time, but is prevalent from July through September, as the moist, warm sea air strikes the cool, forested coastal hills. Fog often forms in late morning and may persist into the next day. These characteristics would be advantageous to troops who wished to land undetected.

Access to the interior of the Pacific Northwest states was not too difficult in 1942. A number of all-weather highways led inland and a large number of Forest Service roads and trails could be used by a determined man or group of men who knew the country. In the Coos Bay Sector there were six good highways through the Coast Range.

One of the first actions of the Coast Guard in this sector was to dynamite the entrance to an 1890 mining tunnel near the mouth of Lone Ranch Creek south of Cape Ferello so that it could not become a fortification for Japanese invaders.

The ASTORIA SECTOR extended from the Salmon River in Oregon north 160 miles to Cape Elizabeth in Washington and was divided by the Columbia River. The coastline is composed of long, wide, sandy beaches interspersed with rocky headlands. Two areas were considered vulnerable: Smuggler's Cove south of Cape Falcon and the beach south of Cape Lookout. The former, which got its name because of its history as a site for illicit landings, probably would not have been used by an enemy because it was under the nose of the Cape Falcon lookout. The beaches north of the Columbia River are open and vulnerable but are subjected to heavy surf and can only be utilized during good weather.

Weather conditions are generally the same in the entire Astoria Sector. The prevailing winds are from the southwest and occasionally increase to gale force with little warning. Rain is frequent, and coastal fogs are common, particularly in the summer and early fall months. Storms with driving on-shore rain are characteristic of the winter months. In the summer, northwesterly winds are frequent. These tend to rise late in the morning and die by evening. Evening fogs and relatively calm weather will generally follow a northwest wind. East winds tend to flatten the surf and give excellent landing conditions.

The PORT ANGELES SECTOR, extending approximately 75 miles from Cape Elizabeth north to Cape Flattery at the mouth of the Strait of Juan de Fuca, is composed of rocky promontories separated by short, sandy beaches. In the south, there is a fairly long stretch of open beach. Around Cape Flattery the coastline is rugged and unsuitable for landings, but from Hoh Head north to Waatch Point, three miles southeast of Cape Flattery, there are several vulnerable beaches. One in particular, south of Cape Alava, called Yellow Bank, was intensively worked by the Japanese in 1932, ostensibly for mining gold from beach sand. At that time the beach was visited by well-dressed Japanese, and an aircraft is reported to have landed on it. A narrow, rough road was cut through the woods to Lake Ozette, but by 1942 this road was completely overgrown. Between Cape Elizabeth and Hoh Head is a long, narrow beach paralleled by a good highway ashore. This area is the only one which afforded good access to the interior in 1942.

The weather in this sector differs from that in the southern sectors. In summer the prevailing winds are northwest and westerly. In winter the winds come from the southeast and southwest, with an occasional short northerly gale. Fog is most frequent from July through September, and may be very dense and persist for several weeks without clearing. Offshore currents are southerly most of the year but may be easterly during the fall months.

Along this variable coastline with its densely forested areas and sparse settlement, the Coast Guard proceeded to establish a series of beach patrols. In some places the task was relatively easy, in others incredibly difficult. As mentioned before, quarters were available in some areas, but in many places there was nothing. The original plan called for the establishment of temporary quarters in Army pyramidal tents. These were requested, using the highest priorities, from the nearest Army posts.

The chief survey officer for each of the three coastal sectors was instructed to canvass the various localities along the beach for persons who knew the local terrain and conditions and could effectively patrol the beach in periods of darkness or low visibility. Minor physical defects were no handicap. These people were inducted into the Coast Guard Reserve and placed on active service patrolling the area. A lot of good old-fashioned

exhortation and arm twisting went into the recruitment program, and as a result a small cadre of hard-bitten old-timers were brought into the Coast Guard, theoretically releasing younger and more active men for combat duty.

Implementation

Considerable planning was done while the surveys and recruitment were in progress. On August 19, 1942, General DeWitt called a conference at the Presidio of San Francisco. The Assistant District Coast Guard Officer and a representative of the 13th Naval District were present. It was decided that whenever the Coast Guard established a patrol it would be correlated with Army activities in the area.

One of the first moves was the takeover by the Coast Guard of the Army's responsibility in the Lake Ozette region. Lake Ozette is a long, narrow coastal freshwater lake on the northwest

end of the Olympic Peninsula in Washington. The Army's 44th Division, which was supporting the patrols in the area, happily turned over its responsibilities to the Coast Guard and evacuated the area. They knew what the Coast Guard was getting into and were delighted to let them have it.

The Coast Guard had three days in which to make the changeover. With the establishment of the Lake Ozette patrol it became apparent that the idea of recruiting local talent with minor disabilities was not going to work. The locals knew the Lake Ozette region well enough to want no part of it. Therefore it was necessary to use regular Coast Guardsmen.

No other area in the United States offered more disadvantages from a viewpoint of accessibility, terrain, and weather. It had the highest rainfall, the most wind, the coldest summers, the most persistent fogs, the most impenetrable forests, the rockiest coast, and the narrowest beaches bounded by the steepest cliffs. In 1942, this was one of the last true wilderness areas in the continental United States, and its rugged inhospitable terrain was incredibly hard to traverse. In some places mountaineering techniques were required.

Many of the difficulties were known and the men who were selected for the Lake Ozette station were carefully chosen from volunteers for their physical stamina, psychological stability, and knowledge of the woods. Workdays were estimated to be 14 hours long with no time off for Sundays or holidays for the first few months. Interestingly enough, there was no lack of volunteers.

On September 1, 1942, an aggressive, adventurous crew left Seattle for Lake Ozette in two trucks, a carryall, and four private cars. The Army party at Lake Ozette was relieved as soon as the Coast Guard arrived and departed with a cheerful "You'll be sorry." Immediately two parties of four men each, heavily burdened with food, water, cooking utensils, rifles, ammunition, compasses, and sleeping bags, were dispatched to the beach, three and a half miles away. They didn't have the least idea of what was waiting for them.

An infantryman, carrying full field equipment, can march across good country at about three miles per hour. The Coast Guardsmen made it to the beach in two hours over the easy part of the trail. They made camp on the uninhabited beach. There were no facilities. Small rodents and skunks were abundant and there were signs of bear. Fortunately, it did not rain. Late in the evening of September 1 the first patrol was made. The Army had stood only fixed guard duty at the ends of trails. The first patrolmen covered about twelve miles of coast by day, cooked their meals over an open fire, and slept on wet ground at night. Two more patrols were added within three days, providing twice-a-day coverage for the 26 miles of the Lake Ozette section. The patrols remained on the beach from 2 to 16 days, depending on the availability of relief.

After three weeks of patrolling, trails had been cut through the forest and tents erected at five beach camps. For another three months, the patrols cooked over open fires or on stoves made from oil drums. The tents had neither frames nor floors, but they provided limited shelter from winter storms. Everything was damp.

The construction of patrol routes was harder than anyone expected. Cutting trails through the rain forest was extremely difficult. The thickly matted undergrowth, fallen trees, ferns, and mosses made cutting trail a miserable task, and continually moist soil made the best routes treacherously slippery once they were finished. Whole areas of the forest floor were swamps over which the patrolmen built split-log causeways and "corduroy" roads.

A story is told of a colonel with experience in Panamanian and Philippine jungle operations who was sent to the Olympic rain forest to apply his experience in trail building. He claimed that pack mules were the answer to the transportation problem and that he could take a string of mules from Lake Ozette to Quillayute in ten days. The natives tried to talk him out of it, but the colonel insisted that he knew mules. He set out for Quillayute with ten mules and disappeared into the forest. Ten days later he reached the beach, but he did not come out at Quillayute and he had only one mule left. The story may not be true, but the conditions are. Man is about the only animal that can carry a pack through the Olympic rain forest.

Life at the Ozette Beach Patrol Station at the north end of the lake was more civilized than it was at the tent camps on the beach. There were five one-room shacks and an old houseboat. The lake provided a landing site for seaplanes and a road at the north end of the lake connected with the state highway. Thirty men lived in the shacks and houseboat. An old service station building provided space for a mess hall and a galley that boasted a constantly smoking stove. Conditions were primitive and crowded. The office, storerooms, armory, radio room, and repair shop were sardine-packed into a 9-by-18-foot shack. But the men were resourceful. By Christmas 1942 they had built a 150-by-20-foot barracks, a storeroom and armory, several other service buildings, a shower room, and 18 miles of forest trails.

Later, permanent camps were constructed along the beaches of the Ozette patrol area with lumber floated in by rafts from Neah Bay. Equipment not floated in by sea was packed to the sites on the men's backs. One man, unfortunately nameless in the official Coast Guard history, earned a giant's reputation by packing a 100-pound kitchen stove nonstop from Lake Ozette to the beach!

In the meantime the primary duties were not neglected. The patrols went on, two a day, every day over the 26 rugged miles of coastline. Training in cover, concealment, observation, and patrol technique was continuous, and answers were found to new problems as they arose.

The outstanding problem was clothing and equipment. Nothing in the Coast Guard experience was quite like the Olympic rain forest. Army issue was insufficient and impractical. Rainwear ripped and tore with constant snagging along the narrow forest trails. Shoes and boots were inadequate; uniforms were improperly designed and tailored. What was needed was loggers' clothing—calked boots, tin pants, wool shirts, canvas ponchos or oilskins, and blanket coats. The men spent their own money for these things and quickly lost virtually all visual relationship to the tidy, uniformly dressed Coast Guardsmen. They became timber beasts as far as outward appearance was concerned. This state of affairs lasted for months until the Coast Guard approved and authorized issuance of proper clothing and suitable rainwear. Actually, the problem was not unique, because the global war demanded abandonment of traditional uniforms and materials. Places like the Southwest Pacific, the Arctic, the African desert, and the Olympic rain forest all offered special problems.

As the patrols developed, the Navy brought in two boats for Coast Guard use on Lake Ozette. Since the lake was nine miles long and parallel to the patrol route, the boats saved a lot of back-breaking and leg-wearing labor in moving personnel and supplies.

The Lake Ozette station quickly became one of major importance. Ancillary personnel were screened and sent to the station as quickly as possible. War dogs were trained and sent. The unit had more dogs (40) and handlers (10) than any other beach patrol on the Washington or Oregon coast. When the Lake Ozette station was finally decommissioned on March 29, 1944, a genuine saga in Coast Guard history came to an end, and one of the most colorful units that ever served in the armed forces of the United States was disbanded.

Meanwhile, other things were brewing and foaming between Cape Flattery and the California border. By the end of 1942, beach patrols in Washington were operating from Baaddah Point (Neah Bay) and La Push. In Oregon, patrols combed the beaches and climbed the sea cliffs at Nelscott (Lincoln City), Depoe Bay, and Port Orford. By early 1943 a complete linkup of shore and offshore patrols was established, and the entire vulnerable coastline was put under periodic inspection and continuous observation.

One of the offshore patrols, in a 36-foot motor lifeboat, was en route from Tillamook Bay to the Point Adams Coast Guard station when, for some unknown reason, the boat (traveling at full speed of 8 knots at night) piled up on the South Jetty at the entrance to the Columbia River. The crew leaped for their lives. Wet, bruised, and battered, on a pitch-black night, they crawled slowly over the jagged rocks of the jetty to the shore. They passed the 75-mm artillery challenge gun at the base of the jetty, went by the machine gun emplacements near "White Evelyn," the 249th Coast Artillery lookout, and walked into the middle of Fort Stevens—*unchallenged!*

At first communications were a problem. It soon became apparent that patrols would have to be supplied with portable radios as there was no practical way to set up a field telephone system. The Forest Service "S"-type Model A radios were tried and adopted. They were small and easy to use and could be carried with one hand. The "S" radio had been developed in the Pacific Northwest for northwest conditions and was less cumbersome and more dependable than the heavy, backpack Signal Corps radio.

The Coast Guard beach patrols had their problems with the Army coast defense units, especially with problems of authority and jurisdiction. Although there was reasonable cooperation between the two services, the cooperation failed to hold up well on Saturday nights in town when traditional interservice rivalries erupted into barroom brawls. Guardsmen of the Lake Ozette stripe did not take kindly to being pushed around by Army and Navy garrison personnel, and it quickly became policy for Coast Guard and Navy Shore Patrols and Army Military Police to work together to keep order. Thus combined operations are born!

Organizational problems

In a way the Coast Guard Beach Patrol was like the tail of a dog. Which way it wagged depended on what was going on. During noninvasion, it came under Navy jurisdiction. If invasion occurred, the Coast Guard was to give early warning and come under Army jurisdiction. The Coast Guardsmen were to form an outpost line of resistance to delay landing operations as much as possible while the heavy units of the Army and Navy brought their might to bear. By late September 1942, the Army and Coast Guard had exchanged enough information that the two services could coordinate patrols.

The original lookout system and the beach patrols, formed at different times with different roles, caused administrative tension within the Coast Guard. Although men of both units were often stationed together, they were under separate administrations. The situation was further complicated by the fact that the Coast Guard patrols did not in any way release the Army from the responsibility for beach defense. The Navy placed all Coast Guard coastal units in the Naval Local Defense Forces but under the command of the District Coast Guard officer. While the Coast Guard was to assist the Army in preventing landings, they were in all other ways an arm of the Navy. The administrative jungle became so dense that a special conference had to be called to iron out the details. A "Joint Army-Navy Standard Operating Procedure, in Cases of Landings or Suspected Landings of Enemy Spies, Saboteurs," November 28, 1942, was the result. It helped bring order out of chaos and with slight modifications was the policy under which the Coast Guard functioned as a tail which could be wagged by either the Army or Navy big dogs, depending on the situation. Fortunately for the Coast Guard, the Japanese never did land.

Problems have a way of proliferating. The beach patrols could shoot enemy infiltrators, but they could not legally detain or arrest civilians who were on the beaches at night. This lack of authority continued until August 9, 1943, when Oregon's governor finally issued a proclamation making it a misdemeanor to loiter on the beaches between sunset and sunrise. Washington's governor had issued a similar proclamation on March 7, 1942, nearly a year and a half earlier. The proclamations remained in force until August 1944.

By August 1943 the entire Oregon and Washington seacoast with the exception of the Fort Stevens and Fort Canby area was under close patrol and observation by the Coast Guard. There were 463 guard dogs working with the beach patrols. The dogs were valuable particularly in making more effective use of manpower, but they caused some apprehension among the civilians living along the beaches. The dogs were well trained and vicious, as a few people had reason to remember, but on the whole they were more helpful than detrimental to the operation.

By August 1943, the war was going so well elsewhere that official opinion was that a saving in troop strength could be made in the beach patrol. Strength was cut from 3,132 to 1,450. The Army and Navy were advised of the reduction and also of a new plan of operation soon to be established.

Join the Coast Guard—ride a horse!

Back in October 1942, the Commanding Officer of the 13th Naval District made an inspection of the beach patrol operations from Cape Flattery to California. He must have been a frustrated cavalryman. After days of trudging through beach sand on foot, he arranged a meeting with the Army Remount Service. As a result, arrangements were made for the Coast Guard to acquire horses. There were some snide comments about "horse marines" that the Coast Guardsmen pointedly ignored. The mounted patrols promised to be quite effective and sparing of manpower under certain conditions of weather and terrain. A new operation plan came down from on high on September 11, 1943, indicating that even though troop strength had been cut, the critical areas would continue to be patrolled—on horseback!

War brings odd situations. The Army had disbanded a highly trained horse cavalry. Now the Coast Guard, with no mounted tradition or training, was to become equestrian.

The horse patrols, however, proved to be an effective method of covering accessible beach areas. The surprising thing is that they were not established prior to March 10, 1943, when the first mounted patrols went on duty at Ocean Park, Washington. Interservice protocol had some part in the delay. The Army Remount Service was not eager to have its cherished horses entrusted to greenhorns like the Coast Guard, but agreed to the plan with the proviso that Army remount officers be placed on detached service with the Coast Guard to ensure that the animals received proper care and the riders were properly trained. Actually, green hands were preferred for training in horse-

The U.S. Cavalry had little need for horses in World War II. The Army Remount Service made a large number of their prized animals available to the Coast Guard and helped supervise the conversion of sailors into horsemen.

manship and stable management. Any man can be taught to ride, but it takes an act of God to change a horseman's habits. The Army did not want to see its generations of expertise disrupted by amateurs who happened to be enlisted in the Coast Guard.

Quantities of saddles, blankets, halters, bridles, blacksmith tools, horseshoes, veterinary supplies, and training manuals arrived from Fort Robinson, Nebraska, at the Coast Guard warehouse at Tongue Point near Astoria. On February 23, 1943, the first shipment of 48 horses arrived from Nebraska. Railroad freight handlers had apparently forgotten how to ship horses, and some arrived in poor condition. But with good feed and care the sick animals quickly recovered and went on duty. The men and horses worked well together. Once trained,

they were kept together and personnel shifts were discouraged. Rapidly, the horse patrol took on the air of an elite group. It was not long before many riders were sporting cowboy hats, and in town on Saturday one didn't hassle the wearers of pointed-toe, undercut-heel, high-topped boots.

By January 12, 1944, the Army coast defense installations were virtually disbanded. By June 30, 1944, most of the troops from the mobile installations had been transferred to staging areas en route to the combat zones. Only two mechanized cavalry detachments, one at Fort Lewis and one in Portland, were left. Coast Artillery personnel from Fort Stevens, Fort Canby, and elsewhere had been transferred to other duties. The war was winding down along the beaches.

But the horse buildup continued! By early 1944, stables at Ocean Park in Washington and Gearhart, Manzanita, the Siuslaw River, and the Umpqua River in Oregon were built, manned, and put into operation. Three more were built at Rockaway, Sand Lake, and the Coquille River, Oregon. Six more were under construction and two others were planned but not started.

In areas that Coast Guard personnel had abandoned, civilians were hired by the Army. If they found anything they were to report to the State Police, the Forest Service, or the Coast Guard. The Coast Guard would ultimately get the news and pass it on to the Army.

By April 1944, twelve Coast Guard beach patrol stations had been replaced by horse patrols. By late July that year the beach patrols were discontinued altogether and became a part of history.

Accomplishments

In retrospect, one can find indications that the beach patrols served a useful purpose. Fortunately, they never had to report an enemy landing. For security, they provided a force in being in case of emergency, and in the course of their duties they engaged in a number of ancillary activities.

In the fall of 1943 they reported what they thought was a submarine conning tower in the fog a mile and a half offshore in the vicinity of Port Orford; strange lights on the beach and at sea; and unidentified persons walking on the beach late at night. In some instances there was an exchange of gunfire and pursuit, although none of the suspects was caught.

Patrols examined and reported odd objects cast up on the beaches. Occasionally bodies of drowned persons were discovered. Patrols cooperated in rescue operations, helped salvage planes and vessels, set and manned highway barriers to stop fleeing criminals. In at least one instance a Coast Guardsman apprehended a suspect unaided. Patrols helped the Forest Service detect and fight forest fires.

The Coast Guard cooperated with a blimp squadron at the Tillamook Naval Air Station by providing surface support and in retrieving floating offshore objects sighted from the airships. On one occasion, on April 2, 1945, blimp *K-87* sighted a floating mine four miles off the entrance to Grays Harbor. The blimp reported the find and stood by, awaiting arrival of surface craft. A Coast Guard vessel arrived and attempted unsuccessfully to

The Tillamook Naval Air Station on the Oregon coast

To provide an additional means of patrolling the coast, especially in scouting for submarines off shore, the Navy assigned a squadron of blimps to the Tillamook Naval Air Station. Because of the wartime shortage of steel, the huge hangars were framed with lumber. They still stand in 1975, one of them housing an entire saw mill.

detonate the mine. The airship then poured 250 rounds of .50-caliber ammunition against the sides of the bobbing sphere but was unable to explode it. Another blimp, the *K-119,* gave it a try and after firing about fifty rounds hit a vital spot and caused the mine to explode. A mine disposal officer identified it as a Japanese Type 93 Model mine which had floated in from somewhere in the Pacific just as glass fishnet floats have been doing for many decades.

Stanley Janowski of Tillamook found a mine on the beach at South Rockaway and was chiseling off the barnacles when stopped by the Coast Guard before he struck a detonator.

In March 1944, a Navy PBY flying boat was forced down into Lake Ozette by engine failure. CGR Vessel *1310* was on lake patrol at the time and towed the crippled aircraft six miles to the mooring buoys at the north end of the lake. After a replacement engine had been trucked in, Coast Guardsmen helped the Navy mechanics install it.

A more serious airplane crash involving B-17F No. 230236 occurred at Cape Lookout and brought the Coast Guard from Pacific City. Three beach patrolmen searched the wreckage in the dark but failed to find any trace of the crew members. The following day a fishing boat reported a survivor on the cape. Near the top of the ridge, Coast Guard and Army parties found five bodies and one survivor, 2nd Lt. Wilbur L. Perez, the bombardier, who was in fairly good condition. He said there had been ten men aboard the plane. Searching

parties eventually found the other bodies but found no survivors other than Perez.

For sheer drama of men against the sea, the rescue of the crew of the USSR freighter *Lamut* off Teahwhit Head near La Push, Washington, is an outstanding feat in the annals of the Coast Guard. The ship ran aground at 11 p.m. on April 1, 1943, on a shoreline studded with towers of rock jutting upward like skyscrapers from the sea. A 75-knot wind whipped the sea into a froth of pounding surf. Heavy rain restricted visibility to a few hundred yards. The Soviet ship lodged between a 100-foot-high cliff jutting out from the shore and a small rocky island.

In the initial excitement of the crash, the crew —unaware of the rocks around them—attempted to lower a lifeboat. The effort was a disaster. A davit cable broke, dropping the bow of the boat into the water and critically injuring 19-year-old Antonia Shmeliova. Koshova Alexandra, also 19, was killed when a rolling oil drum struck her on the head and knocked her overboard. (Her body was found in the surf farther up the beach by a patrol unit.)

A Coast Guard surf boat from the La Push Beach Patrol station attempted to reach the *Lamut* during the night but was unsuccessful, so stood by until dawn. Meanwhile a shore party hacked a

When a B-17 Flying Fortress crashed on Cape Lookout in 1943, Coast Guardsmen rescued Lt. Wilbur L. Perez (left), but nine other crew members, including Roy J. Lee (center) and Victor A. Lowenfeldt (right), died in the crash.

Survivors from the Soviet freighter *Lamut* were brought up the cliff to safety by Coast Guardsmen. The rescuers and rescued can be seen on a shelf midway up the cliff and on the ridge at the top of the rock.

trail through the swampy rain forest to the beach. Two miles south of the wreck the Coast Guardsmen broke through and began a hard and dangerous climb over wet, slippery, spray-swept rocks to the top of the cliff against which the ship was pinned.

From a narrow ledge near the summit the shore party could look down on the slanting deck and huddled survivors of the storm-wracked ship. On the other side of the towering barricade of rock on which they were perched, they could see a sandy beach and a calm bay. The beach patrolmen did not have rescue equipment and could not wait for the rescue group that was following overland with ropes and other equipment. The patrolmen had to improvise. They tied together rolls of gauze bandage from their first-aid packets, and managed to drop the weighted end of the light line onto the ship. A heavier line was tied to it below and soon a cable strong enough to carry one man at a time was stretched between ship and

cliff. One by one the survivors were pulled to safety on a ledge halfway up the cliff, from where they made the climb to the top and down the other side. The injured girl had been placed in a stretcher. Pulling her from the ship to the ledge and on over the top was especially difficult, but the patrolmen finally got her to the beach.

By this time additional helpers had gathered on the shore. First aid to the injured was administered by a surgeon from the U.S. Public Health Service and an Army medical detail. The Russian crew of forty men and nine women, obviously happy to be alive, trudged through the swamp with their rescuers to waiting Coast Guard trucks and ambulances. The elapsed time between wreck and rescue was 24 hours.

This incident illustrates the dedication of the men who made up the Pacific Northwest Beach Patrol. They were tough, courageous, and smart—proper men for a task that was difficult even on the best of days. ☐

IX
River of Death

THE PREVAILING WESTERLIES blow from Japan toward North America in a great S-shaped double arc that swings northeastward and then southeast and finally eastward across the United States and Canada. The winds in the lower regions are variable and often stormy, but high above the storms a vast current of air flows smoothly across the earth at speeds as high as three hundred miles per hour. This is the jet stream, the river of air that carried death and fiery destruction, for into this river was launched a weapon which claimed the only lives lost in the United States as a direct result of enemy action in World War II.

During the war the existence of this vast river of air was virtually unknown to the Americans and their Allies, but was fairly well recognized by the Japanese. The utilization of this natural force was a work of imagination and intelligence. A free balloon might seem primitive to those who were accustomed to radar and bombsights and flying fortresses, but in reality the balloons that carried bombs to North America were highly sophisticated, economical, and potentially deadly devices prepared by a clever people who understood Nature and used her to aid their ends. That the weapon did not work quite as its inventors hoped was more the fault of bad luck and poor choice of time rather than any technical defect in the concept. In its way, the balloon slowed the total war effort of the Allies and possibly contributed a little to the prolongation of the war.

Tragedy in the mountains

Saturday morning, May 5, 1945, dawned bright and clear in the uplands of south-central Oregon. The sun came up over Gearhart Mountain, brightening the green freshness of the Sprague River valley and arousing the 750 or so people of Bly, a lumbering and ranching community about halfway between Klamath Falls and Lakeview.

Archie Mitchell, the pastor of the Christian and Missionary Alliance (C&MA) church in Bly, and his wife were getting ready to take a fishing trip with five children. Archie was in his early thirties. Mrs. Mitchell, the former Elsye Winters of Port Angeles, Washington, was 26. Both of them were graduates of Simpson Bible College, Seattle (now Simpson College, San Francisco). They had taken special training for missionary work with the Christian and Missionary Alliance church school in Nyack, New York. Archie's predecessor, the

The Reverend Archie Mitchell and Elsye Winters were married at Port Angeles, Washington, on August 28, 1943.

On their cross-country honeymoon trip, Elsye posed for a snapshot in front of their tourist cabin in Bryon, Illinois.

Reverend Floyd Pollock, had left for a new pastorate in the Willamette Valley, and the Mitchells had been in Bly for about two weeks. They were eager to make a success in the new community, especially with the young people in the Sunday School classes.

The day before the outing, Elsye Mitchell, who was five months along in her first pregnancy, had written to her sister, Thelma Winters, in Port Angeles:

I feel swell today. Have my house cleaned up . . . Archie is taking his boys' S.S. class out tomorrow so I baked a *chocolate cake* for the occasion. They wanted me to go along but since I'm still pretty weak I won't be able to keep up with a bunch of boys. They wouldn't have any fun with an old woman—in my circumstances—tagging

along. One of the boys . . . Dick Patzke, just couldn't understand why I was sick so much. He was telling me all kinds of things to take and I just laughed up my sleeve. He is almost 15. I just about up & told him but thought I wouldn't. He'll find out some day. . . .

While Elsye took care of household chores and visited with the neighbors, Archie worked on his sermon for Sunday and then made arrangements for the Saturday trip. The next day the Mitchells awakened to a beautiful spring morning. Archie's enthusiasm and the eagerness of the excited children caused Elsye to change her mind about joining the expedition.

Archie loaded his 16-year-old sedan with fishing gear, picnic lunches, the freshly baked chocolate cake, four boys, one girl, and Mrs. Mitchell. The children were:

Jay Gifford, 13, son of Mr. and Mrs. J. N. Gifford

Edward Engen, 13, son of Mr. and Mrs. Einar Engen

Sherman Shoemaker, 11, son of Mr. and Mrs. J. L. Shoemaker

Joan Patzke, 13, and Dick Patzke, 14, daughter and son of Mr. and Mrs. Frank Patzke.

Mitchell drove a mile east of Bly and three miles north to a Forest Service road that took them eastward through a grove of large juniper trees and then into a pine and fir forest on land owned by the Weyerhaeuser Timber Company. As they climbed upward toward the south flank of Gearhart Mountain (elevation 8,364 feet), they crossed Dutchman Flat and for four more miles wound eastward through the park-like forest. The road was rough and filled with soft spots and slippery areas. A mile after they passed from Klamath into Lake county, the road dipped slightly toward Leonard Creek. Fifty yards from the creek, their progress was blocked by a Forest Service road grader, a pickup truck, and three men who had just managed to pull the grader out of a mudhole where it had been stuck.

Richard R. Barnhouse, the foreman of the road crew, and his two helpers, George Donathan and John Peterson, shrugged when Archie asked about road conditions and fishing possibilities. Barnhouse told him the road was impassable and that the creek at this point might not be clear enough for fishing.

The rough road had made Elsye a bit carsick. She was glad to go with the youngsters to inspect

Victims of the Bly balloon bomb included (above left to right) Jay Gifford, Edward Engen, Sherman Shoemaker, and Joan Patzke; and (right) Dick Patzke with his sister Betty, his mother, and sister Joyce.

the creek while Archie took the car back to park it at Salt Spring, about 250 yards west of Leonard Creek. Barnhouse started the grader and followed Mitchell. It was about 10:20 a.m.

Archie heard Elsye call twice, "Look what I found, dear." He called back, "Just a minute and I'll come and look at it." Barnhouse, from the high seat of the grader could see Elsye and the children about 100 yards away in the woods in a group, looking at something. He could not tell what it was.

"As Mr. Mitchell stopped his car," Barnhouse wrote later that day in his official statement, "there was a terrible explosion. Twigs flew through the air, pine needles began to fall, dead branches and dust and dead logs went up."

There was a moment of stunned inaction. Then all four men ran down the hill. Archie Mitchell was the first to arrive. Another smaller explosion occurred as he came on the scene. It was gruesome. The mangled bodies of Elsye and the children were scattered about a gaping hole three feet across and a foot deep. Elsye was still alive. Her clothing was afire. Archie ran to her and beat out the fire with his bare hands, but he could do nothing about her wounds. She died quickly. All of the children except possibly Joan Patzke had been killed instantly.

Aftermath

The four horrified men realized they needed help. The area was littered with debris that could be dangerous, and the bodies had to be removed. Someone had to do something. Barnhouse took the lead. He left Mitchell and Peterson at the scene and took Donathan with him in the pickup truck. He dropped Donathan at the entrance of Dairy Creek Road to act as a guard and went on to the District Ranger's Office in Bly.

The ranger, F. H. Armstrong, was out; so Barnhouse telephoned Hank Casiday, the Lake County sheriff at Lakeview to report the tragedy and to get the authorities moving. Meanwhile Ranger Armstrong came into the office and Barnhouse repeated the story. It was now 11:25 a.m.

Armstrong assembled three other men: Assistant Ranger Jack Smith, Herb Hadley, and a man named Powell. They collected sheets, first aid kits, tools, and rations. Armstrong phoned Henry Sarles at the Forest Supervisor's office at Lakeview and told him of the accident. Then the five men set out for Leonard Creek. Barnhouse was dropped off at the Campbell Ranch to prevent any unauthorized entry into the area. Hadley was posted at the entrance of Dairy Creek Road to guide the ambulance. Armstrong, Smith, and Powell went on to join Mitchell and Peterson at the explosion site. They arrived at 12:05 p.m.

Prior to the arrival of Armstrong's party at the explosion site, Mitchell and Peterson had cut boughs to cover the bodies. Ranger Smith tried to find a pulse in Elsye Mitchell and Joan Patzke, who were the least badly mangled of the dead. The men then carefully covered the bodies with the sheets Armstrong had brought. They waited. There was nothing else they could do.

Meanwhile Sheriff Casiday had contacted Lake County Coroner James Ousley, Assistant Coroner Dr. H. E. Kelty, and District Attorney Tom Farrell. Ousley, Kelty, and an embalmer set out at once in Ousley's pickup for Leonard Creek. Sheriff Casiday and Farrell contacted Army Warrant Officer Sever and left shortly afterwards. While this was going on, Henry Sarles telephoned the Controller in Everett, Washington, and G-2 at Fort Lewis, Washington. The Army promised immediate action and dispatched Lt. Col. C. F. Bisenius, Major B. S. Henry, Mr. Sherman E. Traver of Military Intelligence, and three enlisted men by air to Lakeview.

At 1:15 Coroner Ousley, Dr. Kelty, and the embalmer arrived at the explosion site, followed by Herb Hadley and the ambulance. Dr. Kelty checked the bodies and treated Archie Mitchell's hands, which were stained yellow with picric acid from beating out the fire in his wife's clothing. At 2 p.m. Sheriff Casiday, Tom Farrell, and Warrant Officer Sever arrived. A little later Navy Lieutenant Jess Faha and seaman T. Dempsey arrived as an advance party from the Naval Air Station at Lakeview. The bodies farthest from the explosion crater had been moved to Ousley's pickup. The others were left where they lay because Lt. Faha thought it was too risky to move them. Faha then departed for Bly to meet the Military Intelligence man and the Army party from Fort Lewis.

By 4 p.m., Moss Richardson, a local cattleman, and Klamath County Deputy Sheriff Willis Pankey were on the scene. At 5 p.m. Herb Hadley went back to Campbell Ranch to relieve Barnhouse. By 5:30 p.m. Lt. Col. Bisenius, Major Henry, Mr. Traver, and Navy Lieutenant H. P. Scott, the bomb disposal officer at Lakeview Naval Air Station, had arrived together with State Patrolman George Giese, Lt. Faha, several sailors from Lakeview, and the three soldiers from Fort Lewis.

Lieutenant Scott and the ordnance people checked the remains of the balloon and found several explosives still capable of doing damage.

These were deactivated and the military personnel then began to collect the debris from the explosion. The Navy men rolled up the balloon, and the remaining bodies were turned over to Coroner Ousley and Dr. Kelty. By this time it was 6 p.m. and most of the evidence had been collected and the area cleared. The party of investigators, witnesses, and officials then left the scene except for Ranger Jack Smith who remained until 9 p.m. to check the area once more.

In Bly, meanwhile, the swarm of lawmen and uniformed personnel did not go unnoticed. They roused a feeling that all was not well. The feeling grew as the day went on and tight-lipped people disappeared into the forest. The townsfolk felt smothered. Rumors began to fly, and by the time the quietly grim Army, Navy, and Forest Service men returned, people were gathered in small groups in the street guessing about what was going on.

Ranger Armstrong, Col. Bisenius, Sheriff Casiday, District Attorney Farrell, and Herb Hadley had the distasteful task of informing the parents of the dead children. The five men first went to the Gifford house. No one was at home. The Engen house was next. No one was there, either. At the Patzke house, Mrs. Patzke, an older son Ed, and Ed's wife were present. Col. Bisenius told Mrs. Patzke what had happened and stressed the need for silence about the affair.

The group then visited the Shoemaker house, but the Shoemakers had left for Lakeview. Neighbors said both the Giffords and the Shoemakers had heard rumors of a tragedy involving their children and had gone to Lakeview to check. Sheriff Casiday and Col. Bisenius said they would try to locate them. They left for Lakeview shortly thereafter, taking Archie Mitchell with them. Assistant Ranger Jack Smith arrived in Bly about 10 p.m. in Mitchell's car. Shortly after Bisenius and Casiday left, Armstrong and Hadley asked Wilbur Bock of the Klamath County Sheriff's Office to locate the Engens who were supposed to be in Klamath Falls.

Armstrong then called Merle Lowden, the Assistant Forest Supervisor at Lakeview, who arranged for a conference to be held the next day. The summary of that conference reads as follows:

A conference was held in the Forest Supervisor's office in Lakeview on the morning of May 6 attended by Mr. Traver, Col. Bisenius, Major Henry, Lt. Scott, Supervisor Mays, Assistant Supervisor Lowden, and Mr. Barnhouse and Mr. Donathan. Traver took complete statements from both Barnhouse and Donathan and also various others asked them a number of questions which were made a part of the record. Traver had already secured a statement from Mr. Mitchell and he obtained information from the coroner regarding the condition of the bodies.

A still further search was made of the area on Monday, May 7 and additional evidence was picked up. The bombs and mechanism picked up on May 5 were returned by the military authorities with them to Fort Lewis and the balloon was left at the Lakeview station for later dispatch.

Col. Bisenius was questioned concerning the information that the Forest Service should give out concerning the incident. It was decided that the Forest Service should state that an explosion of undetermined nature had occurred in the vicinity of Bly killing six people but that we were not at liberty to give out any further information on it. The Colonel reported that there had been a number of inquiries by newspapers and that the Office of War Information had cleared the papers to publish a story stating that the people had been killed near Bly from an unknown explosion but they would not be permitted to say that it had been from a Japanese bomb.

In his report of the tragedy, Lt. Scott, the bomb-disposal officer, wrote:

Upon arrival at the scene [I found] a Japanese balloon together with various pieces of its equipment scattered around the nearby area. An explosion, evidently of the bomb carried by this balloon, had occurred and a woman and five children had been killed. It is surmised that one of the party either dropped or kicked the bomb causing it to explode.

It was necessary for me to render safe four incendiary bombs, a demolition charge, a flash bomb, and various blow-out plugs from the balloon undercarriage before the bodies could be removed.

The examination of the fragments from the explosion proved that the bomb was Japanese Army 15 kg. anti-personnel high-explosive. The balloon had evidently been on the ground for some time as several of the parts were rusted, the paper [of the balloon bag was] mildewed and there were from six to eight inches of snow beneath the paper while the surrounding area was entirely free from snow.

On May 6, someone in Bly telephoned Reverend Pollock at The Dalles, Oregon, where he was a guest speaker. "Several of your church people in Bly have been killed," he was told, "but the Army won't let me tell you anything more." The Pollocks returned to Bly.

A mass funeral was held for four of the victims on May 9 in the Klamath Temple in Klamath Falls because the 150-seat C&MA chapel at Bly would not hold the expected crowd. Decades later, people who were there recall the service, which more than 450 attended, as one of the largest funerals ever held in Klamath Falls and as the first mass service in many years. The four small caskets—all closed—rested in a line across the front of the sanctuary but were nearly hidden in the mass of flowers. The American flag stood at one side, the Christian flag on the other. The Reverend Daniel D. Anderson of the Temple conducted the service, assisted by the Reverend T. L. Brooks and the Reverend Floyd Pollock. Archie Mitchell, grief stricken, was visiting his dead wife's parents in Port Angeles and did not attend. Students from the Bly grade and high schools were there, and the Bly Boy Scout Troop, of which all of the boys had been members, served as honorary pallbearers.

Jay Gifford was buried at Siskiyou Memorial Park in Medford. Joan and Dick Patzke and Edward Engen were buried side by side in Linkville Cemetery in Klamath Falls in graves later marked "ALL KILLED BY ENEMY BALLOON BOMB." Sherman Shoemaker's remains were sent to a family plot in Live Oak, California. Archie Mitchell accompanied his wife's body to Port Angeles, where her father, mother, brother, and sister lived. Rites for Elsye were conducted in Port Angeles where she was buried.

Hidden danger

The weapon that had caused the deaths of the six people was already well known to the FBI and the military, but the information was kept secret because of official fears that it would cause panic or worry that would hamper the war effort. Coroner Ousley's six reports dated May 7, 1945, and filed with the County Court of Lake County merely stated, "The cause of death, in my opinion, was from an explosion from an undetermined source."

For weeks preceding the disaster, word-of-mouth warnings had been making the rounds among public officials at every level. School principals, churchmen, peace officers, and politicians had been told that if any strange object was found anywhere to *leave it alone* and call the Army or the FBI. The general public, however, had not been told. Archie Mitchell apparently had some knowledge, but it was not enough.

For three and a half years the war had been waged between Japan and the United States, and in all that time no deaths from direct enemy action had occurred in continental United States. These were the first, and—as yet—the only deaths.

Yet there is no assurance that there may not be more. Although hundreds of balloon parts, bombs, and bomb fragments were recovered prior to the tragedy and more have been recovered since the war, the percentage compared to the total launchings is minuscule.

The high-explosive fragmentation bomb, the incendiary bombs, and the demolition charge that had been delivered to this isolated spot by a hydrogen-filled paper balloon launched from Japan was only one of thousands of deadly cargoes launched. Only a few hundred balloons have been tracked, located, and recovered or destroyed. Of the remaining thousands there is no trace. Logically, there must be other deadly cargoes waiting to have their delayed destiny triggered by a stumbling foot or a careless hand. ☐

Near the spot where the bomb exploded, killing Elsye Mitchell and five children, the Weyerhaeuser Timber Company dedicated a monument in 1950. The surrounding Mitchell Recreation Area is accessible by forest road in the summer season.

X
The Unguided Missiles

DEVELOPMENT of the balloon that was used by Japan as a transpacific weapon took many years. As early as 1933, the Japanese Army experimented with free-floating balloons as a possible means of carrying bombs into enemy territory. An early model tested had a diameter of about 4 meters (13 feet) and flew as far as 62 miles. Studies were promising enough that the military science laboratory decided to investigate the long-distance characteristics of balloons capable of ascending as high as 30,000 feet.

Research continued, but after the successful attacks and invasions following Pearl Harbor, the Japanese High Command lost interest in long-range balloons as potential weapons. They were scoring victory after victory with a sleek, highly maneuverable fighter plane, the Mitsubishi ZERO, later code-named ZEKE. But suddenly in April 1942, the sacred soil of the Japanese home islands was violated by bombs from Jimmie Doolittle's B-25 raiders. The Japanese at once considered retaliatory strikes against the U.S. mainland. In addition to ordering the air attacks by Nobuo Fujita (Chapter VI), they revived the balloon project. In so doing, the Japanese were the first to implement the concept of automated transoceanic warfare. The British are reported to have tried balloon bombing over short distances, but their experiments failed when cross-channel balloons intended for Nazi-occupied France landed in Sweden.

The decision to plan a transoceanic attack by balloons was made in September 1942. Colonel (later Technical Major General) Sueki Kusaba, who had headed the balloon development project previously, was called back to Japan from service in Manchuria. He and a closely knit group of scientists in the Army's Science Research Center at Noborito were directed to study various methods of using free balloons to make one-way, bomb-carrying flights to America. The project was given the code name FUGO.

A share of the credit for the development of the balloons and the mechanisms to accompany them is given to Dr. Toshiro Otsuki. This accomplishment was acknowledged in his obituary following his suicide in 1950 over an unrelated matter. The obituary included the comment that "his invention proved worthless," which is not precisely true.

General Kusaba's group worked diligently to perfect their weapon. Requirements for a workable balloon were so exacting that time and again, after field tests, they had to return to the laboratory for more study and experimentation. The first plan was to launch bomb-carrying balloons from submarines a few miles off the North American coast. It took almost a year to develop a balloon 6 meters in diameter which would stay airborne between 180 and 600 miles. It could remain aloft about thirty hours and reach an altitude of nearly five miles.

By 1943, Japan's naval forces were strenuously engaged in the southwest Pacific, and they did not want to tie up valuable submarines to launch Army balloons in the eastern Pacific. Even though a large number of the 6-meter (20-foot) balloons had been manufactured, work on this model was discontinued. "We were forced to abandon the project," Kusaba wrote after the war, "before we were half finished." These balloons were warehoused for a better day.

General Kusaba's men went back to their drawing boards and designed a balloon that could be launched from the home islands to make a nonstop flight of more than 6,000 miles across the ocean. For years the Japanese had been studying the upper air currents and knew that there were steady, swift westerly winds at an altitude of about 30,000 feet. They did not know, however, if these upper air currents went all the way to the western hemisphere. Even if the air currents were satisfactory, there were other problems involving materials, atmospheric conditions, and altitude control.

To learn what they needed to know for successful balloon operation across the Pacific, the Japanese developed a radio that would transmit data back to Japan about the flight course, altitude,

Major General
Sueki Kusaba

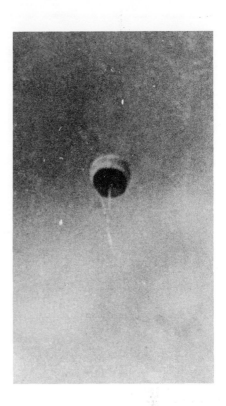

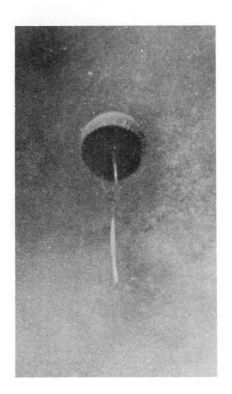

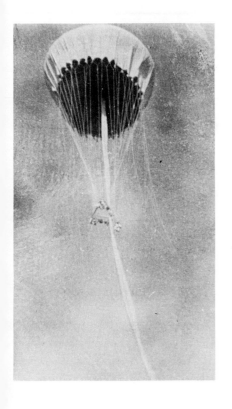

internal bag pressure, and ballast droppings. For this purpose the Japanese Fifth Army Technical Laboratory developed a satisfactory transmitter.

With radio for its load instead of bombs, a test balloon was released. It sent back reports for 80 continuous hours, until it reached 130 degrees west longitude, which is fairly close to the U.S. west coast. Average flight time was computed to be about three days for delivery of a load of bombs from Japan to North America. General Kusaba and others in charge of the balloon project were satisfied. Not only was this delivery system cheaper than sending submarines and GLEN airplanes, it was easier than launching balloons from submarines.

This rare set of photographs shows one of the two early experimental 15-meter balloons being tested in Japan. When General Kusaba sent these pictures to Sergeant Conley in 1961, he included these comments about balloon testing: "In general the cameramen were shut out. The *Kino* [motion picture film] and the pictures which were taken for the record were burned before being developed due to the air raid in Tokyo. We destroyed other documents and pictures at the end of the war. There aren't any left concerning this matter.

"[The balloon in] the pictures I enclose was different from the balloons used for the attack. During the period of research we experimented with this balloon (diameter 15 m) to achieve a higher altitude and a large capacity for carrying weight. The actual balloon used for the air attack had 10 m diameter. It did not have a tail like these pictures. The reason for the tail [was that] we could not make a suitable gas valve for this balloon in time. So we substituted the air pipe for the gas valve. The air pipe kept inside pressure higher than outside of the balloon.

"1. Inflating the balloon on the ground.

"2-3. The moment of launching. To avoid the shock of high speed, it goes up piercing the sand bags and dropping the sand behind.

"4-7. The flight."

101

Navy experimentation

While the Army was developing materials, control mechanisms, armament, and launching techniques for a long-range, bomb-carrying balloon that would fly across the Pacific, the Navy was also conducting experiments. The Navy project was aimed toward scientific study of air conditions and currents over the ocean. A primary purpose was to build a balloon that would carry a radiosonde to high altitude and for a long distance. This small radio transmitter would broadcast by means of precise tone signals information about the upper air. As General Kusaba later wrote, the failure or success of the entire FUGO project rested on the data received from the radiosondes.

Other agencies assisted. The Central Meteorological Observatory and the Navy Meteorological Department worked independently on charting the upper air currents, but they needed more information than their equipment could provide.

The Navy development team experimented with various materials and sizes of balloon envelopes. A 6-meter model was designed to be launched from submarines but was never so used. Two of them were test flown in November 1943. Other models of 6.5- and 8.5-meter diameter were tested in February 1944. The model finally selected for production was 9 meters in diameter and made of silk and rubber. It is designated as Type B.

In early July 1944, the Army and Navy projects were consolidated. Technical Lieutenant Commander Kiyoshi Tanaka, a Naval Ordnance Engineer who had previously worked under Commander H. Yasui of the Ministry of the Navy, continued development of the Navy's balloon and its attachments at the Sagami Naval Arsenal under General Kusaba's direction.

The rubber balloon

The envelope of the Navy's Type B balloon was made of laminated layers of *Habutai* silk impregnated with a thin coating of rubber. It was about 9 meters (29.5 feet) in diameter when inflated. The material was durable and flexible and could be made adequately leakproof.

One of the knotty problems in design was to provide for the great change in the volume of gas in the envelope in the extreme variation in temperature between night and day at high altitudes. Some means had to be used to relieve the pressure

The rubberized silk balloon (above) was developed by the Japanese Navy to obtain meteorological data across the Pacific. It could not carry bombs. Three of these balloons were recovered in or near North America. This one landed near Yerington, Nevada, in August 1944.

The paper balloon (above right) was developed by the Japanese Army to carry incendiary and high-explosive bombs to North America. It was made of tapered panels of four or five layers of tissue paper glued together. Needle and thread were used only on the scalloped band to which the shroud lines were attached. Thousands were launched between November 1944 and April 1945; the landing places of hundreds of them in Canada and the United States have been recorded (see Appendix).

within the bag by day and to conserve the gas in the –50° C temperatures at night.

The Type B balloon was initially designed to operate without a gas relief valve, and the early test models released for data gathering were of this type. The Yerington balloon (*above left*) had no valve, only a sealed tube at the lower end. After only a few experimental flights it was found that while the panels of rubberized silk would withstand high-altitude pressures, the rubber seams holding the balloon together would not. Several balloons split open and were lost at relatively low altitude. Accordingly, to control the high pressure, a special gas relief valve was added.

Three hundred of the Type B balloons were manufactured, but fewer than 40 were ever

launched. A flight log that has recently come to light indicates that between November 1943 and November 1944 the Navy launched 34 balloons. When queried in 1974 about the number of launchings, Mr. Tanaka said that he could account for about 30 of the 9-meter balloons launched, 5 of them of the type without the gas relief valve. Although the Navy balloons were equipped with a payload ejection system, none of these upper-air-testing flights included bombs, only ballast gear and radiosondes.

The remainder of the 300 rubber balloons are reported to have been destroyed by fire at the Fujikura Rubber Company, allegedly as a result of one of the U.S. B-29 raids which began in late November 1944.

The paper balloon

While the Navy group worked to perfect the long-range silk-and-rubber Type B balloon, the Army group had standardized and gone into production on the Type A paper model that was to become the bomb-carrying vehicle.

The paper balloon had several advantages. It was 10 meters (32.8 feet) in diameter, slightly larger than the 9-meter Navy balloon. It was lighter and therefore easier to launch and could carry a heavier payload. It was less expensive to

make and did not require the use of materials that were in increasingly short supply. It weighed only 152 pounds but when inflated had a volume of about 19,000 cubic feet of hydrogen. Its lifting capacity at sea level was about 1,000 pounds and at an elevation of 5 miles about 360 pounds.

The paper envelope was constructed of panels of laminated tissue paper made from the long fibers of the *kozo* bush (*Broussonetia kazinoki*), a member of the mulberry family similar to American sumac, and from the *matsumata* tree (*Edgewortia papyrifera*). The hand-manufactured paper came from companies all over Japan and arrived in various sizes. A great deal of manual labor was required to cement the layers of paper together, to cut the laminated panels to the appropriate shapes and sizes, and to paste the panels together into a gas-tight bag. Each balloon envelope consisted of some 600 separate pieces of paper held together by a hydrocellulose adhesive called *konnyaku-nori*, made from a potato-like vegetable commonly called *arum root*.

The lacquerlike "chemical" used to waterproof the outer surface of the bag puzzled analysts in the United States when samples came into the laboratories. Dard Hunter, paper expert at the Massachusetts Institute of Technology, solved the puzzle. He determined it was the same material used for centuries in Japan to waterproof parasols,

Crew training for launching the B-type rubber balloon at Sagami Naval Arsenal Test Site, February 1944.

tarpaulins, and raincoats—the fermented juice of green persimmons!

Early test balloons were factory made, but with 10,000 balloons scheduled for completion before the favorable winter winds of 1944-45, facilities had to be expanded. Contractors and subcontractors provided various parts. A large percentage of the labor force that worked on this project consisted of nimble-fingered school girls, who had short school hours so they could devote the remainder of the day to the war effort. For testing the finished envelopes for possible leaks, large auditoriums like the Kabuki Theater and the Nichigeki Music Hall in Tokyo and *sumo* wrestling halls were cleared to make room for inflating the 33-foot spheres.

Operating equipment

The bottom of the envelope contained a pressure-operated valve that kept the bag from overinflating and bursting when the gases inside expanded by altitude and by the heat of the sun. Encircling the envelope about one third of the way upward from the bottom was a scalloped belt firmly fixed to the envelope that united the upper and lower hemispheres of the bag. Grommets were set into the free points of the scallops, and through these grommets long (45-50-foot) shroud lines were attached. The free ends of the lines were brought together into a single cable by two large knots. From this cable the payload of instruments, ballast, and weaponry was hung. In some models a heavy rubber "bungee" or shock cord attached the payload to the cable. In other models the shock cord was absent.

The payload was suspended and supported from a four-spoked cast aluminum base ring or "chandelier." The ring contained 36 "T" slots bordered by 72 brass blow-plugs arranged in pairs and set into radial holes drilled around the circumference. Below the spokes were an additional pair of plugs connected to a 64-foot-long slow-burning fuse that led to a packet of flash powder attached to the envelope above the scalloped skirt. Four metal posts extended upwards from the junction of the four spokes and the ring of the chandelier. These posts supported three levels of mechanism: (1) a lower secondary aluminum ring containing the trigger mechanism of the sequential firing system for the blow-plugs in the chandelier, (2) a middle platform supporting 36

The gas relief valve from a paper balloon that was recovered near Legg, Montana, on March 13, 1945. 15689 is the serial number placed on the valve in Japan and used by the U.S. Naval Research Laboratory for identification (incident no. 111).

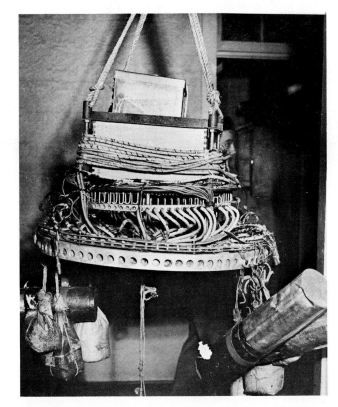

The ballast release mechanism and part of a typical payload: (from top down) battery box, wooden aneroid box, fuses, chandelier ring with holes for blow-plugs, six sandbags, and three incendiary bombs. This gear dropped to the ground after the balloon's envelope burst in a tree near Hayfork, California (incident no. 29).

104

Aneroid barometers closed circuits when balloon dropped to certain altitudes, activating blow-plugs that released ballast or bombs.

Metal hooks on which ballast and bombs were suspended below the blow-plugs.

electrical contact points for the firing system and four aneroid barometers that served as triggers for the firing mechanism, and (3) an upper platform to which was fastened a wet-plate battery, a part of the triggering mechanism, and a self-destruct apparatus consisting of a block of picric acid.

The metal posts ended in four suspension rings which were attached by lines to the lower knot of the shroud cable and to the shock cord if one was present. The mechanism above the second ring was enclosed in a protective cover. Below the chandelier, suspended from each pair of blow-plugs by metal hooks, hung 32 bags of sand ballast and the armament. The paired blow-plugs were connected by wires to the sequential firing mechanism in the upper ring and to the aneroid barometers. A delay mechanism was built into the system that prevented more than one pair of plugs from being fired at a time. In operation, a pair of blow-plugs would be fired each time the balloon descended below a predetermined altitude.

Ideally, the blow-plug ballast system and the escape valve in the bottom of the envelope would maintain the balloon at an average altitude of 30,000 feet. Actually, because of the extreme variation between day and night temperatures and the delay mechanism in the blow-plug firing system, the balloons flew at varying altitudes across thousands of miles of ocean. Indeed, it is possible that this inconstant altitude helped the balloons avoid detection despite the ships, planes, observers, and radar crews searching for them.

Once the sandbag ballast was expended, the jet stream should have (hopefully) carried the balloon over North America. The incendiary bombs would then be dropped one by one by the same mechanism that jettisoned the sandbags. Finally, the high-explosive bomb would be dropped. This action would trigger the self-destruct mechanism. A short fuse to the picric acid block and a long fuse to the magnesium charge on the envelope would be ignited simultaneously. The picric acid block would explode first and blow the rings and platforms to fragments. About an hour later the flash powder would be ignited. The flash powder explosion would rupture the envelope and ignite the hydrogen gas inside. The resulting explosion would destroy the envelope.

If everything worked properly, several forest or grass fires would be set for every balloon launched, and possibly casualties would be inflicted by the high-explosive bomb. It would be very mysterious, because after the self-destruct devices went off, all that might be found would be a few fragments of metal from the rings and rods, some expended blow-plugs, and a wrecked lump of valve apparatus.

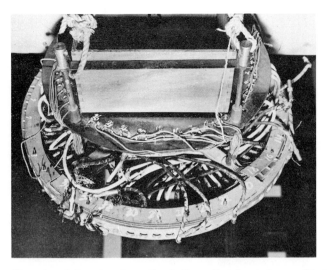

The chandelier ring from the balloon that landed near Bigelow, Kansas, (incident no. 70), showing wires and fuses to blow-out plugs (left). Numbers indicate firing order. Bottom view (right) shows two unfired blow-plugs in center. If the mechanism had worked properly, these plugs would have been the last to fire. Their function was to release the last and largest of the bombs and to ignite the fuses that led to explosives that caused the gear and envelope to self-destruct.

Armament

The armament usually consisted of five bombs and two self-destruct charges:

1. One 15-kilogram (33-lb.) high-explosive antipersonnel bomb with a standard A2(b) instantaneous (point-detonating) fuze. The bursting charge was either TNT or picric acid. The bomb casing was usually made of "shrapnel rings" that gave an effective fragmentation pattern. The danger radius on open ground was about 150 feet with a risk radius of about 300 feet. With one doubtful exception (the Alturas balloon, No. 15, see Chapter XI), this weapon was the only type of antipersonnel bomb recovered. It was the type of bomb that caused the six deaths at Bly. The bomb was carried in the center bottom of the chandelier ring with the release mechanism coupled to the fuse igniters that set off the picric-acid demolition charge and the flash-powder charge to destroy the

A 15-kg high-explosive antipersonnel bomb (right) and a 12-kg incendiary bomb (below).

envelope. On some balloons this bomb was replaced by a 12-kilogram (26-lb.) incendiary bomb, which resembled the antipersonnel bomb in outward appearance. It was fuzed for instant detonation with either an A2(a) or A2(b) fuze. It contained two small explosive charges for ejection of magnesium-thermite pellets and had a danger radius similar to that of the antipersonnel bomb.

2. Four smaller thermite incendiaries weighing 5 kilograms (11-lbs.) each fuzed for instant detonation. All bombs of this type apparently contained a bursting-ignition charge of two small cotton bags of flash powder to ignite the thermite and rupture the casing. Those most frequently recovered were 4 inches in diameter and about 19 inches long. They were crudely constructed from sheet metal and looked like elongated black pork-and-beans cans.

3. One 2-pound picric acid block carried in the automatic ballast-dropping apparatus for the purpose of self-destruction after the payload of bombs had been dropped. If it was hooked up in a certain way, it could function as a booby trap. In handling the many intact recoveries, however, no injury to bomb disposal men from the picric acid charge was reported. If the picric acid block exploded on the ground, fragments from the chandelier assembly could be expected to shower a radius of up to 150 feet.

4. A small packet of magnesium flash powder intended to destroy the balloon. The charge was attached to the side of the envelope above the scalloped belt.

Launching

To launch the balloons, a Special Balloon Regiment of three battalions was formed under the command of a Colonel Inoue. It was this unit's responsibility to prepare launching sites, arrange for gas-producing and inflating facilities, train personnel, establish direction-finding stations, and launch balloons. The regiment had a total strength of about 2,800 officers and men.

When selecting launching sites, officers recognized that the north island, Hokkaido, was closer geographically to North America than the other islands, but balloons launched from there might stray into the Soviet Union and cause an international incident. The Japanese were not at war with the Russians at the time and had no desire to provoke them. More important considerations were to

A two-pound block of picric acid in a metal container was designed to explode and destroy the ballast gear after the last bomb was dropped.

have the launch sites close to rail lines and hydrogen-generating plants and accessible to the balloon manufacturing and assembly facilities. Three locations were therefore chosen on the east coast of Honshu east and northeast of Tokyo. Six launch stations were prepared at Nakoso in Fukushima Prefecture, nine at Otsu in Ibaraki Prefecture, and six at Ichinomiya in Chiba Prefecture. The Otsu site had its own gas-generating plant. The others depended on hydrogen transported in tanks from plants on the Kanto Plain north of Tokyo.

One can begin to realize the extent of the backup measures required for the project by reviewing the hydrogen requirements alone. According to General Kusaba, 30 cylinders of gas were required for each balloon, and each of these cylinders weighed about 60 kilograms (132 pounds). Transportation of nearly two tons of iron from factory to launch site was necessary for each balloon filled.

In comparison with other weapons of war, the Fugo balloon was remarkably inexpensive. It has been estimated that the balloons alone cost about 4,000 yen to manufacture (about $920 at the prewar rate of exchange). Including cost of buildings and facilities the figure has been estimated at 10,000 yen each. The total cost was something like $2,000,000 at the prewar rate of exchange.

Production and launching estimates vary. The secret nature of the operation at the time, destruction caused by B-29 bombings, and last-minute destruction of records by the Japanese make precise information impossible to find. General Kusaba, while assisting Conley in collecting balloon information, once wrote him, "It is with great regret that I have to tell you that there are no

107

records or documents. The pictures which were taken for the record were burned before being developed due to an air raid in Tokyo. We destroyed other documents and pictures at the end of the war."

General Kusaba's best estimate was that about 9,000 balloons were built and about 6,000 launched.

In an article in the Japanese magazine *Shizen* in March 1951 (p. 77), Teiji Takada, one of the scientists who worked on the FUGO project, included this table of "approximate number of launches each month":

Year	Month	Number
1944	November	700
	December	1,200
1945	January	2,000
	February	2,500
	March	2,500
	April	400
Total		9,300

In a letter in August 1973, Vice Admiral Hiroichi Samejima wrote:

According to the testimonies made by the persons for the investigation of the War History Division, manufacturing of 10,000 A-type [paper] balloons and 300 B-type [rubberized silk] was ordered in May 1944 and about 9,000 balloons (mostly A-type) were launched during the period between November 1944 and April 1945.

According to the records kept in the War History Division, planned quantity of launchings between November 1944 and March 1945 was 15,000 balloons. Therefore it is considered that manufacturing quantity might exceed 10,300 balloons.

In early November 1944, with a large stock of completed balloons and their payloads assembled, the Special Balloon Regiment was ready to launch the first bomb-carrying transpacific missiles. From the Japanese point of view this was a good time psychologically. German V-2 rocket attacks on England were causing alarm in the United States about possible transatlantic weaponry. Japanese *kamikaze* attacks in the Pacific were showing the extent to which a fanatical people might go to destroy their enemies. Also, some sort

of success by the Japanese military was needed to boost civilian and military morale.

More important to the timing of the attacks, however, was the increasing intensity of the winds out of Siberia in the winter months. From November through March, the weather studies showed, the jet stream would be strong enough to carry balloons across the ocean in three or four days. Ironically, this was also the safest time of the year for the forests and croplands of North America. Incendiaries would do the least damage at this season, and the chance of starting major fires in the wet, frozen, snow-covered fields and forests was virtually zero.

At the same time, winter conditions made launching difficult. High-velocity surface winds made filling the envelopes with hydrogen and controlling them until the moment of release both difficult and dangerous. A light *offshore* breeze was needed to prevent the balloons from being blown back inland and dropping their bombs on the home islands. Clear skies were important because moisture collecting on the balloons could turn to ice, adding weight that could prevent the balloon from reaching operating altitude. It was estimated that in the five-month period from November through March only 50 days would be favorable for launching, but the promoters of the project felt that the winter season gave the best chance for success.

Launching 10,000 balloons in 50 days meant that the 21 stations at the three sites must average a total of 200 launches a day, or about ten per station. Preparing each balloon and launching it required the work of 30 men for 30 minutes to an hour. Under ideal conditions, each station could launch ten balloons in five to ten hours. The task was possible, but it would be difficult.

On November 3, 1944—the birthday of Emperor Meiji, the farsighted leader who had done more than anyone else to bring Japan out of feudalism and into the twentieth century—the first bomb-laden missile in the Japanese balloon offensive lifted off its launching pad and started its flight eastward toward America. □

XI
Silence--
The Best Defense

ON THE EASTERN SIDE of the Pacific Ocean, the first warning of the Japanese balloon attack came, coincidentally, on the day after the first bomb-carrying balloon was launched. On November 4, 1944, a U.S. Navy patrol craft recovered a deflated rubberized silk balloon from the sea 66 miles southwest of San Pedro, California. Bright golden-yellow shroud lines of woven silk were attached to a skirt around the white envelope, and a small radio transmitter was dangling from the shroud lines. It was one of the early experimental models that had been launched to gather data and carried no bombs.

As were most of the subsequent balloons and parts recovered, this material was sent to the Technical Air Intelligence Center, Naval Air Station, Anacostia, D.C., and turned over to the Naval Research Laboratory for analysis. The envelope was later shipped to New Jersey and inflated with helium at the Lakehurst Naval Air Station and examined for markings and construction details. To the investigators it appeared to be a well-made data-gathering model that had been sent aloft in or near Japan to obtain weather information.

Another rubberized silk balloon with smashed instruments attached had landed near Yerington, Nevada, in August 1944. Sam Ellison, the cowboy who found it, and Charles Ragsdale, the ranch owner, pulled it down from the cottonwood trees where it was snagged and tied it to a fence (see photo page 102). Ragsdale notified military authorities, but no one came to investigate. Days later the ranchers deflated the envelope and stored it in a barn. Still later they cut it up to make haystack covers. Hence, it was not available for scientific study.

The second balloon shipped to the Naval Research Laboratory came down in the sea five miles from Kailua in the Hawaiian Islands. On November 14, 1944, Coast Guardsmen saw the balloon descend and sent a boat to pick it up. It had a good deal more gear attached to it than the San Pedro balloon, including an assembly of switches, fuses, and barometric devices. The envelope was made of laminated paper. After analyzing the balloon, the Naval Research Laboratory concluded:

The presence of automatic ballast release equipment increases the possibility that the balloons are coming from a considerable distance, perhaps from Japan itself.

The purpose of the self-destructive feature is apparently to avoid recovery of the equipment by the Allies or to avoid detection of the operation. This slightly favors the theory that radiosonde or plane detection equipment, rather than incendiaries, are involved. It is still in the realm of possibility that the ballast units might contain insect pests, disease germs, or the like.

In the coming months, as increasing numbers of balloons floated over North America, the threat of biological warfare was constantly in mind. The FBI, very active in the search for balloons, was on the lookout for evidence of pestilence brought by the balloons. Some search teams carried long-handled tongs and special clothing to wear when approaching grounded payloads. These precautions proved needless because no evidence was ever found that the balloons carried living matter or insidious chemicals.

In addition to whatever actual damage the balloons might do on the American mainland, the Japanese expected them to cause sufficient panic to disrupt the Allied war effort and possibly force a withdrawal of troops and other resources from the southwest Pacific to protect the homeland.

Another expectation was to convince the Japanese people that the U.S. mainland had been successfully attacked by a new and ingenious weapon. Even though little or no actual information about the effectiveness of the program reached Japan, the propaganda machine went to work. Conley has outlined some of the efforts:

> The first reference to the balloons in Japanese propaganda appeared on 17 February 1945 in a Domei broadcast beamed to the United States in English. The Japanese claimed that 500 casualties had been inflicted . . . and numerous fires had been started. The broadcast also announced that the government authorities in the United States had found it necessary to issue general warnings against attacks . . . and thus had agitated the people. It was emphasized that these occurrences had shattered the American feeling of security against attacks by the Japanese. . . .

☆ ☆ ☆ ☆ ☆ ☆ ☆

> Subsequent Japanese broadcasts beamed to Europe, Southeast Asia, and China repeated this same theme and, in one instance, added that several million airborne troops would be landed in the United States in the near future. . . .

☆ ☆ ☆ ☆ ☆ ☆ ☆

> A broadcast from Singapore in June 1945 claimed that balloons were causing havoc in the U.S., even though thus far they had only been released on an experimental scale.

☆ ☆ ☆ ☆ ☆ ☆ ☆

> . . . When the experimental period was over, "large-scale attacks with death-defying Japanese airmen manning the balloons would be launched."

Effective silence

American and Canadian newspaper and radio editors must be given credit for the most effective defense against the balloon attacks—*silence*. In the first two months there were a few newspaper stories published, but beginning early in 1945, newspaper and radio cooperation (some called it censorship) was effective.

By the end of 1944, eight balloon-bomb incidents had been recorded: In addition to No. 1 off San Pedro and No. 2 in the Hawaiian Islands, there were two in Wyoming, one in Montana, two in Alaska, and one in Oregon (see lists in Appendix). News of some of them appeared in the press, but for the 300 incidents recorded in the next six months, the editors respected the government's request for secrecy.

On November 17, 1944, Walter Cox, editor of the *Mason Valley News* in Yerington, Nevada, published a comment about the strange balloon that had landed on the Ragsdale ranch. Since it had carried only smashed instruments and was not recognized as being Japanese, no insidious significance was attached to it. Cox assumed it had blown over from California.

The balloons that came down at sea off San Pedro and in the Hawaiian Islands were recovered by the Navy and Coast Guard. They received no publicity.

The Thermopolis balloon

In what must have been the first news story of the balloon/bomb attack, the *Northern Wyoming Daily News* at Worland, on December 8, 1944, described the puzzling events of two days before:

Phantom Plane Is Being Sought Near Thermopolis

THERMOPOLIS—(Special)—Stories of four explosions, flares in the night sky, and the figure of a man parachuting to earth kept Sheriff Kem Moyer and his men busy yesterday. . . .

The weekly *Independent Record* at Thermopolis gave more details the following Thursday and ended on an indignant note:

Thermopolis Has Airplane Mystery; Bomb Dropped Nearby

No Plane Heard but Parachute With Flares Seen Near Highway

Thermopolis had a plane mystery last Wednesday night—which still remains a mystery.

Sheriff Kem Moyer was notified that three men and a woman at the Ben Goe coal mine, west of Thermopolis, saw a parachute in the air, with lighted flares and after hearing a whistling noise, heard an explosion and saw smoke in a draw near the mine at about 6:15 p.m. The sheriff investigated that night and the following day continued the search as it was thought there was a man with the parachute. The searchers found fragments of a heavy bomb which had exploded about a mile and a half from the mine, near the Meeteetse-Thermopolis highway, the sheriff reports.

Captain Tim, investigator for the Casper air base was sent here when the case was reported, and flew over the area, but could find no trace of the parachute. He took fragments of the bomb for examination, and Sheriff Moyer reports he was notified that the Casper air base has no bombs of that type, but it was identified as a bomb. Fragments have been sent to national headquarters to determine where the bomb may have come from.

Louis Artman, who herds sheep for Tom Sanford, is reported to have seen the parachute land in the area northwest of Thermopolis, and that the flares burned for about 10 minutes after landing. . . .
Sheriff Moyer states that the search has been abandoned on the supposition that the parachute seen was a landing flare.

No plane was reported as seen or heard on the night the bomb was dropped, but it is said that a plane with that type of bomb could have been flying too high to be seen or heard. No planes were reported missing.

A bomb so carelessly dropped from a great height could have done extensive damage, and might even have hit the town as it was only 15 miles out where the bomb fragments were found.

A fragment of the envelope and the bomb fragments were forwarded to the Naval Research Laboratory. The bomb was identified as a Japanese 15-kilogram high-explosive, but this information was not made public.

The Kalispell balloon

With incident No. 4 news began to flow. On December 11, 1944, two woodcutters, O. B. Hill and his son Owen, who had been working in a mountainous forest 17 miles southwest of Kalispell, Montana, reported to the sheriff's office the discovery of an object which they thought was a parachute. This is how James H. Morrow of Bozeman, Montana, a former FBI agent, remembers his connection with the incident:

I was on deck at the Butte office of the FBI when the sheriff of Flathead County called describing a peculiar thing that had been found in the woods. I phoned George Rhoades, resident agent at Missoula, and asked him to drop everything and go see what the sheriff had. Within two hours Rhoades phoned in and described a large paper envelope with ropes on it that obviously was not a weather balloon. The Director of the FBI was notified. Contacts were made with the Army, Navy, and Air Corps. Scientific, balloon, and explosives experts were flown in to Butte. The sheriff and Rhoades had arranged to have the thing brought to Butte. We laid it out on a garage floor. George Rhoades wrote the first official report of the Japanese balloons. The few in Kalispell who knew about it were asked to keep it secret.

The Kalispeel balloon being examined by Capt. W. Boyce Stanard, U.S. Army Intelligence; Major J. E. Bolgiano, U.S. Army Air Force; and W. B. Banister, FBI.

In Libby, Montana, however, the editor of the weekly *Western News* saw no need for suspressing such unusual news. His December 14, 1944, issue scooped the nation with this story:

Jap Balloon Found In Timber

Joe Kujawa, mail carrier to the district south of Libby, brought a story back to town Wednesday to the effect that a Japanese balloon had been found by pulpwood cutters. . . . The balloon was said to be large enough to have carried from six to eight men, and had Jap flags at both ends of it. There was no basket on the balloon but in its place was a bomb which had failed to explode when the balloon came to earth. . . .

The Libby editor ran a followup story the next week giving more details about the balloon, quoting FBI and Associated Press sources. "The bag itself," the story mentions, "is of high grade processed paper. There appeared on the balloon Japanese characters indicating completion of construction at the factory on October 31, 1944."

Fragments of balloons were recovered at Manderson, Wyoming, on December 19; at Marshall, Alaska, on December 23; and at Holy Cross, Alaska, on December 24, but they received little or no publicity.

In its New Year's Day edition in 1945, *Newsweek* magazine reported the Kalispell incident, stating that "On December 18, a Federal Bureau of Investigation announcement gave the news to the rest of the country." The writer was puzzled:

Had the balloon carried any passengers? If so, where were they? Where were the parachutes or the gondola? Had the big bag come from an enemy sub operating off the west coast, or had it been flown all the way from the Jap homeland?

Time magazine's January 1 issue also reported the incident, calling the balloon "quaint" and asking why a balloon with "a 70-foot fuse connected to a small incendiary bomb on the inflammable paper bag" had been sent. "Residents of Kalispell," the article concludes, "were engaged in fascinating discussion about what odd people the Japanese are."

Near Estacada, Oregon, soldiers from Fort Lewis, Washington, search for parts of balloon that caught in a tree on New Year's Day 1945.

The Estacada balloon

On January 2, 1945, the Portland *Oregonian* ran a picture of soldiers who had been rushed from Fort Lewis, Washington, the day before, searching through underbrush near Estacada, Oregon, apparently looking for something alive and elusive. They actually were looking for parts or other evidence of a balloon (No. 8) that had floated over downtown Portland within the past few days.

As Larry Miettunen was driving along a road about seven miles southeast of Estacada, he saw something that looked like an upside-down parachute hanging in a tall Douglas-fir. He went to town and got a 6-foot crosscut saw and with the help of Dave Horner, proprietor of a market in Estacada, sawed through the 3-foot butt of the tree and brought it down. State police took charge of the torn bag made of "heavy oil paper, timing mechanism, wet flash powder, burned fuses, and about 1/4 of a metal wheel." The balloon and parts were taken to the Estacada high school and spread out on the tennis court for study. "There was a lot of quarter-inch rope that we wanted," Miettunen says, "but the Army wouldn't let us have any."

Two weeks later (January 15) *Newsweek* gave the balloons some more space. Early returns from government investigations, the article said, suggested that the balloons usually could not travel farther than 400 miles and concluded that they must have been launched from submarines.

The experts were puzzled. After analyzing the Kalispell balloon, the Naval Research Laboratory issued a secret report on January 8, 1945. It described in great detail the balloon envelope, the shrouds, relief valve, fuses, ignition or flash charge, and a "rubber-rope assembly probably intended to act as a shock absorber." Two containers of melted snow forwarded with the balloon were also described. Insofar as these water samples were concerned, the investigators found "no evidence of any chemical materials . . . other than what would result from contact with the balloon envelope."

"While the balloon is undoubtedly of Japanese manufacture," the report continued, "the evidence thus far available does not permit any definite conclusions as to how and why it arrived at Kalispell." The investigators speculated that it might have been launched from a submarine, may have carried personnel, or could have escaped from weather-reporting or plane-interference duty in Japan and drifted across the Pacific in air currents reported to flow "at a speed of 30 to 60 miles per hour." Little did they realize then—in January 1945—that the jet stream attains speeds many times as fast as that.

It was very difficult at first for the investigators to conceive of a massive, purposeful attack launched from the Japanese home islands. The enemy knew about the jet stream, but these high-velocity, high-altitude winds were almost unknown to the Allies. The next two balloons examined, the ones from Hawaii and Oregon, did little to shed light on the source or purpose of the balloons. The Naval Research Laboratory reported on January 15:

The additional information secured through an examination of this [Estacada] balloon is insufficient to warrant changing any of the conclusions made in regard to the Kalispell balloon. The only evidence of any value is that the two balloons are identical in construction and this would indicate that they are not just experimental models.

The report on the Sebastopol, California, balloon (No. 11), which was completed three days later (January 18), shows more concern:

It is now presumable that the Japanese have succeeded in designing a balloon which can be produced in large numbers at low cost and which is capable of reaching the United States and Canada from the western Pacific carrying incendiaries or other devices. . . .

It must be assumed that a considerable number are coming over. This argues against their being launched from submarines. . . . It seems fairly certain that the balloons are coming from Japan. . . . It is to be expected that the number will increase and when the dry season arrives considerable damage will result unless effective countermeasures are developed.

Countermeasures

This authoritative warning was enough to stir officials who had access to it into action. The problem of what to do about the balloons was attacked at many levels. Generals and admirals of the Western Defense Command and the Western Sea Frontier considered it a challenge. Interservice meetings were held to determine which agency or branch of the service should have "authority" over the balloons. At a regional meeting at Fort Lewis, Army, Navy, and FBI representatives tried to determine the purpose for the balloons. They discussed who would chase the balloons and who would do what with them when they and their occupants—if any—were captured. At a meeting at Fort Douglas, Utah, admirals, generals, foresters, FBI representatives, and Army counterintelligence men studied parts of retrieved balloons and listened to technical papers presented by visiting scientists.

Balloons and any recovered parts, it was agreed, would be shipped either to the Naval Research Laboratory or to the California Institute of Technology at Pasadena to be examined and cataloged. Scientists throughout the nation were given research and analysis assignments, many of which required burning midnight oil and careful homework. Inventory forms and instructions on how to use them were designed to be used as checklists for recovery teams. The reports based on these studies ultimately spelled out what the Japanese were doing and how and where they were doing it—even to determining where they got the sand for the ballast bags. These reports are voluminous and comprehensive and reasonably accurate when compared with data obtained from Japan after the war.

P-38 Lightning

F6F Hellcat

Several balloons were taken to the Lakehurst Naval Air Station in New Jersey for testing. One inflated with helium got away and began lifting toward its 30,000-foot ceiling. The Navy SNJ airplane sent out to chase it had a ceiling of 21,500 feet. All the pilot could do was watch the balloon sail out over the Atlantic.

Commanding General H. H. "Hap" Arnold of the Army Air Force well understood the danger of incendiary bombs to Pacific Northwest forests. In the early 1920's he had been one of six aviators in the first organized aerial forest fire patrol in that region. One of the photographs from that time shows the six airmen alongside their DeHaviland 4 aeroplanes at Humptulips Field near the Olympic National Forest. When the Japanese balloons menaced the forests he had once helped protect, General Arnold acted swiftly to make fighter planes available to attack the high-floating bomb carriers.

In the AAF and Navy inventory of planes, the P-38 Lightning and the F6F Hellcat fighter planes were adequate to pursue balloons insofar as altitude requirements were concerned, but advance warning of approaching balloons baffled the best radar units of that time because the balloons did not contain enough metal to reflect the radar signals.

One study included a plan that called for installation of 200 SCR-584 radar units and a minimum of 200 90- or 120-mm guns along 1,000 miles of coastline—at a cost estimated from $31 to $88 million for the installation plus an additional ammunition cost of $2.5 million per 1,000 balloons detected. The planners acknowledged that such installations "might fail to detect as many as fifty percent of the balloons passing overhead."

The Fourth Air Force initiated a plan called Sunset Project and ordered equipment for six radar sites along the Washington coast, but by the time the equipment arrived the balloon offensive had been discontinued.

Another defense scheme called for stationing 200 picket ships offshore for every 1,000 miles of coastline. The estimated cost of this operation was astronomical—far greater than the millions calculated for onshore defenses. As a result of these cost estimates, no further consideration was given to this type of defense. The consensus of the planners was, "Unless the payload [becomes] something very much more dangerous, it is clear that the measure of success to the enemy . . . will be the amount of men and equipment which we divert to defensive measures against it."

Countermeasures organized and partially implemented included two other projects. Under the Firefly Project, a joint plan developed by the Ninth Service Command, Fourth Air Force, and Western Defense Command, a number of planes and about 2,700 troops were stationed at critical points to be used in firefighting missions if needed. The Lightning Project was a precautionary plan organized through the U.S. Department of Agriculture to deal with any evidence of biological warfare.

The menace spreads

Canada received its first recorded balloon (No. 9) near Stony Rapids, Saskatchewan, as a New Year's Day surprise in 1945. On January 2, Oregon's second incident (No. 10) occurred in Medford. An incendiary bomb—apparently released as it was designed to be—came hurtling out of the overcast sky and exploded near a house on South Peach Street, puzzling both townspeople and authorities.

California got its first balloon on January 4, when parts of No. 11 were recovered from a snowfield near Sebastopol, 55 miles north of San Francisco. Samples of the surrounding snow were packed in dry ice—to be analyzed for possible biological warfare agents—and were sent along with the recovered parts to the Naval Research Laboratory.

On January 5, at sea southwest of Kodiak, Alaska, a merchant vessel's armed guard shot No. 12 out of the air as it dropped within range. Nothing was recovered.

Although the balloons tended to concentrate in Alaska, western Canada, and the Pacific Northwest, others landed over a much wider area as the winds aloft kept them moving. Of the 102 findings reported in Canada between December 1944 and August 1945, British Columbia counted 57, Alberta 20, Manitoba 6, the Northwest Territories 4, Saskatchewan 9, and the Yukon Territory 6. Three balloons were reported to have landed in northern Mexico.

In the continental United States the count was Arizona 2, California 23, Colorado 3, Idaho 12, Iowa 3, Kansas 1, Michigan 2, Montana 35, Nebraska 5, Nevada 7, North Dakota 2, Oregon 45, South Dakota 9, Texas 3, Utah 5, Washington 28, and Wyoming 11. (See lists in Appendixes A and B.)

One incident that was never credited to Idaho involved a wild chase between Pocatello and Blackfoot. Sheriff William A. "Dell" Clough followed a balloon in his patrol car for nearly thirty miles, while it floated at treetop level with its ropes trailing. Finally it disappeared over a hill in the direction of Wyoming.

Search and recovery in Alaska

George Corey, who was an Army counterintelligence officer assigned to chasing balloons around Alaska, was involved in many of the 36 recorded findings in that area. He says:

We picked up about 18. We probably had five times that many reports—many were duplications because the native guard stations would radio in what they saw passing overhead.

My orders were to take a small chartered plane piloted by Bill Fike and with FBI man Bill Delius attempt to locate the balloons which were on the reports. Many came in over the lower Yukon and Kuskokwin rivers. Our plane had ski landing gear and sometimes we would put down and then hire a dog team to get to the site. Delius would

disarm the bombs if necessary, then we would fold and pack the balloon and any parts we found into the airplane, go back to Anchorage, and ship what we recovered to Washington, D.C., for study.

Some units recovered had never dropped any of the sand bags or bombs. The Marshall, Alaska, balloon [No. 6] was recovered intact on December 23, 1944. It is the one on which the battery was never connected.

I recall no fires, probably because in the winter time practically all of Alaska is frozen.

The Alturas balloon

It is difficult nowadays to feel the anxiety and tension of the situation in 1944-45. Sitting at home decades later reading about what happened then does not convey the feelings that a member of a bomb disposal team might experience at the scene of a balloon recovery, knowing that any second he might be blown to bits. But was the thought of being blasted foremost in the minds of the men who disarmed the balloons? Possibly, but it was not apparent among those men with whom I talked. The filtering effect of time might have something to do with their detached, almost clinical attitude, but I have the feeling that most of the balloon chasers considered danger a part of the job.

Supervisor Mel Barron and Fire Dispatcher Roland Sherman at the Alturas headquarters of the Modoc National Forest in northeastern California, are examples of these men. Both told me they were too busy doing their jobs to worry about bombs exploding. "Sure," said Barron, "we were told to watch out for bombs, and maybe we would have been a little more worried if we had heard of any ever hurting anybody." When they chased the Alturas balloon on January 10, 1945, the killer explosion at Bly was still months away.

The Alturas balloon (No. 15) is famous mostly because it was the basis of a long report by the Western Defense Command. It was one of the earliest balloons recovered virtually intact. Its other claim to fame has to do with an item of allegedly attached ordnance. Who sighted No. 15 first is unknown, but a P-38 was dispatched to chase it over Crater Lake. At last within range, over Lakeview, Oregon, bullets from the pursuing plane's guns ripped into the gas bag, but it did not catch on fire. As the balloon descended over the Tule Lake region of California, the P-38 continued to lace it with machine gun fire. It finally caught in a tree about a mile northeast of Happy Camp Lookout in the Modoc National Forest. The mili-

The Alturas balloon being inflated and tested at Moffett Field, California.

tary called for forest-ranger assistance in locating the downed balloon. Mel Barron responded and later recounted his experience:

Navy pilot Lieutenant Jenkins from the Klamath Falls Naval Air Station picked me up at Alturas in a Piper Cub. We flew to the reported site but had trouble finding the balloon. While we were in the air EOD [Explosive Ordnance Detachment] men were going in by truck.

Since the little airplane had no radio, I took a standard Forest Service "S" radio along. This little set was very good in line-of-sight transmission but required an antenna. I hung the antenna wire out the window of the airplane with a small weight attached to the end.

After cruising around a bit, we got in touch with the ground party, headed by Roland Sherman, who also had an "S" radio. We were to work as a team.

When the pilot located the balloon snagged in a tree, he did a power dive over the spot to show the ground people where it was. I yelled into the microphone, "Here we are!" Sherman called back, "Gotcha!"

Just then, the antenna got caught in the tree and almost pulled the set off my lap and out the window. I managed to hold it back, but the wire was jerked out of the radio. End of transmission!

Lt. Jenkins took me back to Alturas and I went back to the forest site in my car, arriving in time to see the EOD men packing up everything and stuffing it into the back of a weapons carrier [truck]. Sherman said the balloon was a paper model, rather than the silk model we had heard about. It had landed at about 5,000 feet elevation in a rough, logged-over area. The military people took pictures and told us it was all very confidential.

We were told plenty clear that the Forest Service job was just to get the military to the spot—and then stand back. Everybody was wet and cold. There was much snow at that elevation. It was the 10th of January.

The Alturas balloon was shipped to Moffett Field, Sunnyvale, California. The bullet holes were

patched and the bag was inflated with gas. Whether what happened next was an official test or an extra-curricular one is not clear. The balloon was taken out of the dirigible hangar just as a puff of wind came along. The few men hanging onto the control ropes had a hard time restraining their helium-filled captive, but eventually kept it from blowing away.

This balloon has been the subject of controversy concerning its attached bombload. Normally, investigators found a maximum of five bombs—four incendiaries and one high-explosive—and two self-destruct units per balloon, as described in Chapter X. Inspectors checking this particular balloon when it arrived at Moffett Field found a bomb of peculiar shape *hanging from the shroud lines*. A Navy cameraman took a picture of this bomb at the time, and recently I obtained a copy of it. I took the photo to the Explosive Ordnance Detachment at Vancouver Barracks, Washington. The Ordnance people immediately identified the projectile as a Japanese 81-mm mortar shell. I asked if it could have been used in the balloon bombing in 1945. They answered that it was technically possible, but after searching the literature on known uses of this ammunition said that it was not likely to have been used on a balloon.

To solve the mystery of the 81-mm shell, I added a stock question—"Did the Japanese balloons ever carry 81-mm mortar shells?"—in letters to and interviews with former bomb-disposal and FBI men and military history buffs. No one I con-

116

The Japanese 81-mm mortar shell that was found tangled in the shroud lines of the Alturas balloon.

The Hayfork balloon exploded when caught in a tree. The ballast gear and incendiary bombs dropped to the ground without exploding.

tacted had knowledge of any such deviation from the usual pattern. My comments about the discrepancy were sometimes shrugged off, "So the Japs ran out of the right kind of ammunition and substituted."

The idea that two types of high-explosive bombs were used did not appeal to me. I was aware of the respect for specifications which is typical of the Japanese, and this sort of thing was out of character. Then I found an article on the balloon bombing in the April 1965 issue of *Airpower* (pp. 51-55) in which Clark G. Reynolds had used pictures from the National Archives as illustration. One showed an 81-mm mortar shell with a 12-inch ruler alongside. This seemed fairly good evidence that the 81's *were* used—until I realized that the photo in *Airpower* was another print of the same one I had taken to Vancouver Barracks. No new evidence here.

John F. Green, formerly a major in Army Intelligence, finally gave what I believe is the explanation of this mystery. He wrote from Palos Verdes Peninsula, California, that the 81-mm mortar shell in the photograph looked like one he had found tangled in the rigging of the Alturas balloon *after* it arrived at Moffett Field. He went on to say:

We are reasonably certain the shell was not placed in the rigging by the Japanese . . . but was entangled in the rigging when . . . thrown on top of a collection of such shells . . . confiscated from soldiers returning from overseas. When the balloon was repaired and inflated, the shell was found hanging from one of the ropes.

The Hayfork balloon

In regard to balloon No. 29 (February 1, 1945), Ray Beals, Hayfork District Ranger in the Trinity National Forest in northern California, wrote in his diary:

Got phone call at approx. 6:20 p.m. that a balloon was floating over the [Hayfork] valley. Ran to the office for field glasses, spotted balloon over lower Salt Creek and Tule, fairly high but losing altitude, drifting slightly west of north. Appeared to have an object hanging below. Balloon settled fast and disappeared behind trees in lower [west] end of valley.

Sent Al Muncy and Frank Hoelling to go to it as guards. Mrs. Allen Laffranchini phoned—said she could see it hung up on the ridge.

Walter Glass and I drove over to get exact location, then I returned to station and phoned Lt. Col. Quigley at Presidio [of San Francisco]. Glass and I went back out to look at it and found Frank and Al there. They had just got the few other people well away from it when it blew up.

It was after dark now so I posted a guard then went back to station where message was waiting that FBI in San Francisco wanted all possible details.

Feb. 2, 1945:

6:15 a.m. Lt. Col. Quigley and party arrived. Got them some coffee and then took them to the balloon where their experts dismantled the various objects. Had four incendiary bombs, a demolition bomb, battery, and some other items. Fragments of the balloon showed it was made of paper. Army officials seemed very pleased at the condition of the equipment—said it was the best they had got yet. Didn't want the incident published but did tell us there had been others. They left about 11 a.m.

Feb. 3, 1945:

Three Army intelligence officers called late last evening to get details of balloon incident. . . . Weather cleared so

117

Sheriff Warren W. Hyde of Box Elder County, Utah, and the balloon he finally captured after an hour-long struggle near Tremonton.

went to scene of balloon landing with Hoelling and Muncy and searched thoroughly for another bomb the Army thought should be there.

Nothing further was found. The balloon had landed in the top of a 60-foot fir tree. Exactly what caused the magnesium flash powder and gas-filled balloon to explode has never been determined. No one was hurt. The fir tree had its top blown off, and other trees in the area were blackened. There was no fire.

The Tremonton balloon

Western sheriffs as well as Forest Service people had encounters with the paper bags from Japan. One of them, Warren W. Hyde, sheriff of Box Elder County, Utah, had a wild and unforgettable ride back and forth across a canyon on the shroud lines of an armed balloon (No. 68). It began with a telephone call from Floyd Stohl, who reported a balloon on his ranch. Hyde, who was one of those informed, called the FBI and was asked to "do everything possible" to salvage the balloon. Hyde drove to the Stohl Ranch to watch over the balloon until the authorities arrived. His

car became stuck in the mud about two miles from the landing site. Sheriff Hyde ran from his car to the hilltop where the balloon—its gas expanding in the morning sunlight—had become airborne. It led Hyde a merry chase on foot over Blue Creek Divide and into a narrow canyon. The payload bounced off a sagebrush, but since it did not explode, Hyde decided that it probably would not blow up if he caught it. He therefore continued his pursuit and caught the balloon. But the balloon was not to be easily subdued. Caught by the wind, it lurched into the air dragging the sheriff with it, and for the next 55 minutes an epic battle between the stubborn man and the obstinate balloon went on in the box canyon.

The balloon soared across the canyon and struck the top of the rim. Hyde tried to anchor it to some brush. No luck—the wind caught the bag again and swept the balloon back across the canyon. Another attempt to tie it down failed, and once more Hyde was hoisted into the air and carried across the ravine. Finally the balloon came down near the only chokecherry bush in the draw, and Hyde looped the rope around one of the protruding roots—the rope held; the balloon was secured. The FBI arrived, followed by the military, and by midafternoon there was a long line of parked cars on the road to Floyd Stohl's ranch. The balloon was deflated, the bomb detonated, and a tired, bruised, and battered Sheriff Hyde returned to Brigham City. He was later honored at a ceremony in Salt Lake City attended by the governor and Army, Navy, and civil defense officials.

The Bigelow balloon

The Japanese bombs were intended to burn down forests and destroy lives in northwestern America, but one of them led to romance in faraway Kansas. Edwin North, a bachelor who lived on a farm near Bigelow, about thirty miles north of Manhattan, Kansas, discovered a huge strange-looking balloon (No. 70) on the cold, snowy morning of February 23, 1945. It was wobbling in the sky, snagged in a tree. First he took a picture of it. Then he called on his neighbors, Otis Armstrong and Michael Hays, for help. Together they deflated the balloon. "I took the basket apart," Mr. North said, "then hitched a team because the roads were all snowbound and hauled the thing to Bigelow."

When news of the Japanese balloon offensive was released to the public in August 1945, this snapshot taken by Ed North near Bigelow, Kansas, in February was distributed by the Associated Press.

(KX1)BIGELOW,KAS.,AUG.17--JAP BALLOON SNAGS KANSAS TREE--THIS JAP BOMB-CARRYING BALLOON CAUGHT IN A TREE ON THE ROLAND E. NORTH FARM NEAR HERE, FEB. 23, 1945. THE BALLOON WAS THE ONLY ONE REPORTED TO HAVE LANDED IN KANSAS. NO BOMBS WERE FOUND; NO DAMAGE INFLICTED. THIS PHOTOGRAPH WAS TAKEN BY NORTH WITH A KODAK BEFORE THE BALLOON WAS DEFLATED. (⸺⸺⸺⸺⸺⸺⸺⸺)(RB060940USA)1945

Lena K. Potter, who was postmistress at Bigelow at the time, recalls,

Ed brought the apparatus to me at the Post Office and asked my opinion. I said we'd best call the sheriff who should take custody of the mysterious thing and have it investigated. Ed called Sheriff Charles A. Anderson and the thing remained at the Post Office 'till the sheriff came. The thing that stays clear in my memory all these years is some colored paper adhering someplace on the box-like center of the ring. It was like fire cracker wrappings and I got the impression of Japanese behind this apparatus.

When the government officials appeared, North says,

We looked for bombs and other parts all over my place but in 18 inches of snow it was tough going. We didn't find any.

About 30 residents of the area knew about my find, but when the Army and FBI made the rounds everyone agreed to keep still about it. An Army photographer took lots of pictures. A year later another part of the mechanism was found during a coyote roundup. It was displayed in a Marysville [Kansas] store for a while but when the government found out they picked it up.

I was lucky I didn't get blown up, because when I found the thing, I jerked the basket out of the tree and it landed right beside me. I supposed it was some sort of weather balloon.

Without realizing that the balloon had explosive charges attached to it, Ed North and his neighbors pulled it down from the tree where he had found it, tied it to a fence post, and deflated it.

119

Mr. and Mrs. Roland Edwin North and their two-months-old daughter, Linda Kay, at Christmas, 1946. (right) Linda Kay North Smith in 1973.

North was disappointed when the Army removed the deflated balloon. He had planned to use sections of the waterproof mulberry paper as haystack covers. He did receive some consolation, however. The commander of the Seventh Service Command in Topeka wrote a week later thanking him for his help and his "ability to talk but little."

Six months later, in August, when news of the balloons was made public, the snapshot North had made with his 116 Kodak Hawkeye folding camera was picked up from the Army files by the Associated Press for national release. North later received $10 for use of the photo.

"When the news was released," Postmistress Potter says, "Mr. North received much mail."

The Army's district intelligence officer sent prints of North's pictures and a letter commending him for his cooperation and for maintaining his "information in strict confidence until censorship was lifted."

Another letter was from a widow in Arkansas wanting to learn more about the balloon. The initial letter started a correspondence, and letters flew between Ravenden, Arkansas, and Bigelow, Kansas. Ed North went to Arkansas to visit her. Later she started for Kansas "to inspect the North farm," but he met her en route and they were married. Their daughter, Linda Kay, who was born the next year and later became Mrs. Phillip L. Smith of Spokane, provided some of the information on this incident.

120

The Goldendale balloon

A girl reporter had a long-remembered adventure with balloon No. 77, which came to rest in trees between Goldendale and Satus Summit, Washington. About midnight, February 27, 1945, Sheriff Russell Woodward received a call about the strange object and asked Z. O. Brooks, the county attorney, to go out with him and have a look. State Patrolmen Dwight Nye and Gordon Hyland joined them.

Attorney Brooks' daughter Jerrine, a reporter for the weekly Goldendale *Sentinel*, got wind of the expedition, grabbed her camera and flashbulbs, and tagged along. A quarter century later she still vividly remembered the close call they all had that night:

When we got to the mountain, here was a balloon as wide as a city street tangled in the trees. At the bottom of the balloon was a small box like a car battery with little things hanging from it. We curiously examined this apparatus, dragged it around, took a couple of pictures of it, and wondered what in the world it was.

The "government" was contacted and we were told to have one of the men stay the night as guard and to take no pictures and avoid the press! It was to be kept extremely hush-hush. There was to be no publicity, we were told, so the Japanese would not know their balloon had arrived.

Most everyone went home that night to return early in the morning, when the demolition experts had arrived.

The gas relief valve on the Goldendale balloon and the "small box like a car battery with little things hanging from it" as surreptitiously photographed by *Sentinel* reporter Jerrine Brooks.

The handful of townspeople who knew about the incident watched as the Army men got out of an armored car and donned strange "space suits." They took long poles and manipulated the parts from the carriage at presumably safe distance.

All five of us who had been there the night before looked at each other in horror. We glanced around the circle and telegraphed the message, "I won't tell if you won't tell how we had been bouncing this thing around." How foolish we had been—how ignorant—*and how lucky!*

Dad developed the contraband film himself. We all kept our word and nothing ever appeared in the paper. A REAL SCOOP down the drain! As a souvenir of the night's escapade I did manage to snitch a little piece of the balloon.

"Our" balloon did not self-destruct. This is believed to be because the wet-cell battery had frozen and rendered the circuits inoperative.

On June 15, 1972, Jerrine Brooks May (wife of the publisher of the Goldendale *Sentinel*), who was back on the newspaper after a 25-year absence, published her two "illegal" pictures. She explained that although the State Patrolmen were directed to pick up any pictures, a courtesy was allowed on the promise that they would not be used in the paper until after the war. She ended her article: "I'm 25 years late with the darn scoop. The war IS over, isn't it?"

The Hanford balloon

Less than two weeks after the Goldendale incident, beyond Satus Pass northeast of Goldendale, another balloon caused a three-day interruption in the war effort. The operation which was involved was so supersecret at the time that the cause of the interruption became as secret as the project. So few people were told of the reason for the shutdown of the Hanford plutonium plant that ascertaining details of the incident has been difficult. This is the story as pieced together from various sources:

It will be recalled that the development of chain reaction technology began with the self-sustaining reaction in the Argonne National Laboratory under the stands of the University of Chicago football stadium in December 1942. In May 1943, the crash program to produce atomic bombs to aid the war effort was turned over to the U.S. Army Corps of Engineers under the code name Manhattan Engineer District, also known as the Manhattan Project. A large plant was built—with great speed and secrecy—to manufacture plutonium for nuclear reactors and for explosive charges for atom bombs. This plant, called the Hanford Engineering Works, was located on a huge res-

On the same day that a Japanese balloon caused a power outage at the top-secret Hanford Engineering Works, another balloon (above) was shot down near the Yakima Road barricade (below) near Cold Creek, Washington.

ervation along the Columbia River upstream from Pasco and Kennewick, Washington. From materials produced there, the first atomic bomb was constructed at Los Alamos, New Mexico, and exploded near Alamogordo on July 16, 1945.

On March 10, 1945, four months before the first atomic explosion, one of the Japanese balloons (No. 94) came floating low across the Yakima Valley thirty or so miles west of the Hanford works. At 3:23 p.m., about three miles southwest of the Alfalfa townsite and about six miles southeast of Toppenish, the balloon struck the main transmission line bringing power from Bonneville Dam to Hanford. The resulting short circuit triggered safety controls and in a fraction of a second shut down the whole Hanford plant. The balloon apparently touched the power lines momentarily, but long enough to activate circuit breakers. Power was restored almost immediately as an intertie circuit switched in, but in that split second the damage was done.

One of the plant workers recorded in his diary, "The 100-B and 100-D reactors were delayed 10 minutes and the 100-F reactor was delayed 68 minutes." In her history, *Manhattan Project*, Stephane Groueff says that the interruption "necessitated three days of work to get the piles back to full capacity. . . . Only the top Du Pont people [who operated the Hanford Works for the government at the time] were informed confidentially about the cause of the trouble."

Several months previously the patrol personnel guarding the Hanford Works had been alerted to watch for Japanese balloons, and a number had been sighted passing over or near the project. As indicated by the Incident Lists in the Appendix, parts from several balloons were recovered in south-central Washington in mid-March—on March 10 at Ephrata, Satus Pass, Toppenish, and Moxee City and on March 11 at Cold Creek. The former townsite of Cold Creek was on the border of the Hanford reservation, near the western entrance into it. On March 10, the same day that No. 94 caused the power outage, two Hanford patrolmen assisted by two military policemen shot down No. 100 a quarter of a mile outside the Yakima Road barricade. They were later told that "this balloon was the most intact of any that had been recovered to that date." So far as can be ascertained from records now, none of the balloons actually landed within the reservation.

Word-of-mouth warning

Not until May 31, 1945, did the Western Defense Command at the Presidio of San Francisco release "Japanese Balloon Information Bulletin No. 1." It included these special instructions:

The information in this bulletin is to be conveyed to the general public by word-of-mouth and under no circumstances is to be given publicity in the press or on the radio. . . .
This bulletin will not be posted on any bulletin boards or transmitted to individuals other than those authorized to receive it from the agency concerned. . . .
You are being informed about these balloons because they are dangerous. Six persons have been killed. . . .

You are now in on the secret. Do not write about it in any letters and do not be unduly alarmed. Let us all shoulder this very minor war load in a way such that our fighting soldiers at the front will be proud of us.

The Army and Mr. O'Toole

Not all participants in balloon discoveries accepted the secrecy mandate gracefully. Mr. A. C. O'Toole of Medford, Oregon, had an angry confrontation with Army officers from Camp White in July 1945. While he and his family were on a camping trip at Hyatt Lake, balloon No. 274 was found. O'Toole cautioned others not to disturb it. It was obviously not the weather balloon for which the Army had advertised a $25 reward. O'Toole had heard by word of month of the fate of the Mitchell party and he wanted none of that. He took photographs of the balloon, intending to use them to show others what to avoid.

"You are off limits here," he told Army officials who later came to his home to confiscate the undeveloped film. "I have a perfect right to that film as this is a free country and the star in the window represents a son fighting to keep it free. There are a lot of kids in school whose dads are doing the same. I will do my little bit by having the pictures posted on the school bulletin boards so that the kids will know the difference between it and the one you are offering a reward for."

The Army officials listened but finally took the film, promising to have it developed and to put out a bulletin to the schools. They returned all the prints except those of the balloon, which they were to return "after the war."

Before school opened in the fall, the need for secrecy ended. The balloon offensive had stopped and the war was drawing to a close. In mid-August information on the balloons was released to press and radio, and editors were permitted to publish anything they wanted to about them. But news of the unguided missiles was overshadowed by the more dramatic atomic bombs and surrender of the Japanese military forces. As for Mr. A. C. O'Toole, he was still angry in 1975—the Army still had not returned his balloon pictures!

How effective?

Was the balloon bomb operation successful? Did the project pay off? How many fires were started? How many people were killed? According to Japanese radio propaganda, the balloon bombs were fantastically effective. Reality, how-

This balloon crossed the state of Washington and came down near Farmington on the Idaho border. This photo was one of the first released to newspapers in August 1945.

ever, was not so bright. Operationally, the idea was a fiasco from a destruction viewpoint. The balloons and bombs were treated with poker-faced silence by the usually gabby Americans. An estimated two-million-dollar investment had generated virtually no visible return in panic or propaganda. No fires attributable to balloon-bomb explosions were ever verified. The "thousands" killed (according to the propagandists) were actually five members of a Sunday School class and a minister's wife, and even this bit of encouraging information was denied to the High Command. The Japanese could hardly be blamed for closing down the project.

The long-range balloons, however, were much more effective than the Japanese realized. They were a headache for the Canadian and American military and security people and created more paperwork and disrupted more routine than any other Japanese attack against the North American mainland. Not entirely in jest was the observation

that the furor created by the balloons and attempts to set up defensive plans against them used more paper than was required to build the things! The money, material, and effort expended in defense and investigation caused more time and monetary damage to the Allied war effort than the two million dollars the Japanese spent to build, equip, and launch the balloons.

As an economic measure, the balloon bombs gave the Japanese a good return on their investment. Unfortunately for them, it was not good enough. The losses were absorbed by the immense military machine that the United States and Canada had created, and the war went on with undiminished fury.

The major failure of the Japanese scheme was the sheer immensity of the North American forest regions, the excellence of the defenses against forest fires established by the U.S. and Canadian governments decades before the war, and the fact that these attacks were launched during the season when damage would be minimal. Had the attacks been carried into the summer, the story might have had a different ending.

Several writers have speculated that the bombing threat to the security of North America may have been used as a partial justification for the atomic bombing of Hiroshima and Nagasaki. This is extremely doubtful, and a request to the Chief Archivist of the Truman Library brought the following reply in 1972:

> We were unable to find any evidence in our collections that the paper balloons had an effect on those decisions. If we should come across any information regarding a relationship between Japan's use of the paper balloons and our use of the atomic bomb, we will let you know.

Discovery of the jet stream

The swift-flowing river of air that brought the unguided missiles from the other side of the globe to the American continent in three or four days came as a surprise to pilots of the Army Air Force when the attack on the Japanese home islands began. As previously mentioned, the best information available in the Naval Research Laboratory as late as January 8, 1945, was that at 20,000 feet winds reached "a speed of 30 to 60 miles per hour, perhaps even faster. At 25,000 feet there is reputed to be a 60 mile per hour air current that crosses Japan, veers southward to Hawaii, then swings to the north crossing Northern California and on over Montana, where it again veers southward."

On November 1, 1944, when Captain Ralph D. Steakley took his B-29 reconnaissance plane, the *Tokyo Rose*, on the first U.S. flight over the Japanese capital since the Doolittle raiders in 1942, the crew had not been warned to expect heavy winds at high altitudes. He says:

We took off from Saipan and flew "on the deck" nearly all the way. We climbed to about 30,000 feet for our target run.

I found myself over Tokyo with a ground speed of about 70 miles an hour. This was quite a shock, particularly since we were under attack from antiaircraft guns and were a sitting duck for them. Obviously, the head wind was about 175 miles an hour. To my knowledge, this was the first experience by B-29's with the jet stream.

After our return to Saipan, we gave a debriefing which included this information. The weather officer seemed to have some knowledge about high winds but had not anticipated the velocity. He took our information and applied it to subsequent reconnaissance and bombing missions.

Steakley made two more flights over Tokyo in early November to provide photographs from which bombing targets could be selected. Again the B-29 crew experienced extremely high winds, and on one flight (he does not remember whether it was on the 5th or the 7th of November) he saw a strange sight in the sky:

At about 30,000 feet we saw a large balloon about 100-200 miles southeast of Tokyo. It was actually above us and was very large. It could very well have been one of those the Japanese had launched with incendiaries.

When the B-29 Superfortress attack was launched, beginning on November 24, 1944, the bombers, although partially prepared for it, encountered an unexpected difficulty. As a report written in 1945 describes the situation:

Greatest hindrance to bombing accuracy was the high winds over the target. At 30,000 feet, high wind velocities up to 230 m.p.h. were met, causing ground speeds as high as 550 m.p.h. when bombing downwind. These velocities were far beyond the maximum provided for in the AAF bombing tables.

The AAF had to alter tactics to compensate for the high winds and eventually sent most of their planes in at low level.

After the war, Theodore R. Gillenwaters, a member of the special staff of meteorologists with the 5th Air Force in the Philippines, went to Japan to review the comprehensive meteorological studies and calculations on which the balloon-bombing project was based. He developed considerable respect for the Japanese civilian meteorologists and their ability to decode Russian weather reports. In regard to the jet stream, he said, "We recognized that the Japanese had greater knowledge of the upper air mass than we did [and] they knew how to take advantage of their knowledge."

When General Curtis LeMay, commander of the 20th Bomber Command, launched the first nonstop flight of three B-29's from Hokkaido to the United States in September 1945, his pilots were directed by AAF meteorologists who had been briefed by Japanese experts.

The jet stream, which Robert Buck describes as a "hose-like band of high-speed winds at high levels [that] wanders in serpentine fashion" at 200 to 300 knots, is now much better known and easier to locate than it was in 1945. Commercial and military aircraft now take it for granted, avoiding it on westward flights and riding it eastward around the globe. The air stream used briefly as a river of death has become a corridor for peaceful transportation. □

Capt. Ralph D. Steakley (right) and crew of the Boeing B-29 Superfortress which encountered the jet stream on their reconnaissance flights over Tokyo in early November 1944.

XII
Epilogues

EPILOGUE A. Archie Mitchell's Ordeal

The U.S. Congress approved a bill that President Truman signed on June 7, 1949, providing $20,000 for survivors of the Mitchell tragedy—$5,000 to Reverend Mitchell and $3,000 for each child to the bereaved parents. The Department of the Army argued that this matter should be settled by treaty with Japan or under a general statute applying to all claimants for combat damages. The Senate, however, held "that in this unique case where loss of life occurred to innocent citizens . . . who were unaware of any danger from enemy activity, the persons who suffered [bereavement] should be compensated in a reasonable amount." Although no negligence was attributed to the Armed Forces, the Senate held that the Armed Forces were "aware of the danger from these Japanese bombs and took no steps, for what may have been valid reasons, [to warn] the civilian population." (United Press dispatch, May 9, 1949.)

The Reverend Archie Mitchell about 1962, when he was taken prisoner in Viet Nam.

In later life, the Reverend Archie Mitchell suffered again—as a civilian—at the hands of military enemies of the United States. Two years after the balloon-bomb incident at Bly, Oregon, he married Betty Patzke, an older sister of the boy and girl who were killed with Elsye Mitchell. Their parents, Mr. and Mrs. Frank Patzke, had ten children and had lived in Minnesota before moving to Oregon. They had been strong supporters of the work Archie and Elsye Mitchell had started in the Sunday School and church in Bly. Soon after Archie and Betty Patzke were married, the newlyweds enlisted in the foreign missionary field of the Christian and Missionary Alliance Church. They were sent to Indochina to work in a leprosarium at Banméthuot in the central highlands. Four children were born to them.

On June 1, 1962, United Press International released this dispatch:

Today word came from South Viet Nam that three Americans had been kidnapped by Communist guerillas. One of them is Reverend Archie E. Mitchell, a former pastor at Bly in southeast Oregon. He has been in Viet Nam since 1947. . . .

When prisoners of war, both military and civilian, were released by the North Vietnamese and the Viet Cong in 1973, no mention was made of Archie Mitchell and his two companions. The headquarters of the C&MA church in New York had received no news of them. If they were still living and were still held against their will at that time, they were confined longer than any of those prisoners who were released.

In 1973 Betty Mitchell returned to the United States on furlough as she had done in earlier years, but she always goes back to Vietnam, having faith that her husband will "walk out of that jungle just like he walked in."

(For details of the kidnaping see *The Alliance Witness*, June 27, 1962; October 14, 1964; March 13, 1968; February 5, 1969; and May 24, 1972.)

In 1950 the Weyerhaeuser Timber Company dedicated a monument and picnic area at the site where the bomb exploded to the memory of those who lost their lives there. It is called the Mitchell Recreation Area. (See "Tree Farm Parks" by Albert Arnst in *American Forests*, April 1951, pp. 20-21.) □

A signpost on the Klamath Falls-Lakeview highway a mile east of Bly (above) guides visitors to the Mitchell Recreation Area, dedicated in 1950 (left) near the spot where Mrs. Archie Mitchell and five children were killed by a Japanese bomb.

EPILOGUE B. Fujita's Return

In the spring of 1962 the Junior Chamber of Commerce of Brookings and Harbor, Oregon, embarked upon a courageous course of action designed in part to promote international understanding and in part to publicize Brookings' Azalea Festival. The Jaycees invited Nobuo Fujita, the pilot of the only Japanese plane to bomb the U.S. mainland, to be their guest at the Festival. The act took moral courage and a staunch belief in the Jaycee creed: "The brotherhood of man transcends the sovereignty of nations."

Veterans protest

There was instant, vocal, and unbridled opposition despite a message from President Kennedy, transmitted through the State Department and the U.S. Information Agency, and encouraging remarks from Mark Hatfield, the governor of Oregon, and other supporters. Records of the Brookings-Harbor Jaycees have some interesting comments on the project and the opposition to it. The opposition was mainly led by a local flower grower and a commander of a veteran organization. Despite the opposition of people who could not bring themselves to approve, the Jaycees went ahead with their plan, no doubt feeling much as the man in San Fernando, California, who wrote: "Surely after twenty years, bitterness should be over and acts of bravery, no matter by whom, commended."

Forced to defend their position, Jaycee members stated, "The thoughts recently expressed lack the American way of thinking that we teach in our churches and our schools. This is an endeavor to offer the hand of Brookings in friendship and brotherly love, which is so often preached and so often forgotten."

The affair received international publicity, some good, some bad, with the consensus that the Jaycees of Brookings-Harbor were brave but foolhardy. From Japan, Mr. Fujita wrote, "If you can give us this valuable opportunity, we firmly believe that this invitation will have as much value, as much important meaning, as that of a top-level leader's meeting."

In a letter to Mayor C. Fell Campbell, Governor Hatfield wrote: "The invitation is in keeping with the spirit of cooperation, hands across the sea. If we who fought the Japanese are able to forgive, I trust that those few who have protested this invitation will reconsider."

The U.S. Department of State wrote: "There can be no overestimating the extent to which direct people-to-people projects of this kind have been a positive force for greater international understanding."

Editorially, newspapers were generally favorable. The Eugene *Register-Guard* opined: "If President Kennedy can be polite to the enemy sailor who sank his boat, maybe the people of Brookings can be gracious, too."

Portland's *Oregon Journal* commented: "If there are those who still think Nobuo Fujita, ex-pilot, still harbors a desire to burn down the Oregon woods, they might think over the advisability of inviting him to see the beauty of Brookings in the spring and consider the error of his ways."

Salem's *Oregon Statesman* said, "Fujita . . . was serving his country. . . . So far as is known he never killed nor injured anyone. We have been quite busy as a nation doing just what the Brookings Junior Chamber of Commerce wants to do—convince the Japanese that we are not the kind of people [the Japanese] had been led to believe."

A Tokyo newspaper quoted by radio KURY published a letter from one K. Suehiro of Fujisawa who described the Jaycee invitation as "A beautiful gesture of war and peace. The war and its tragedies are still vivid not only in the minds of Americans, but in the minds of all Japanese. We do not resent the pilots who pushed the fateful button to wipe out Hiroshima and Nagasaki. I sincerely hope the nice people of the town in Oregon will fully enjoy the coming festival and pave the way to mutual understanding and friendship."

Eddy Waldrop, mayor of Bandon in 1962, a former commander of U.S. Army troops stationed along the southern Oregon coast declared, "I have no animosity toward him. Fujita was just doing his job as we were doing ours."

The opposition also had its say.

The U.S. Information Agency in a classic of irony wrote: "[We] might suggest that you contact the various veterans organizations who might be interested in assisting this project." To this, the commander of the Brookings VFW Post No. 966, replied, "I talked with the veterans and they are definitely against it. We were against it since we first heard of it. If [Fujita] wants to come over on his own money, that's all well and good. But if it's our money . . . we should spend it on our own heroes."

The Crescent City, Calif., American Legion Post No. 175 sent an official letter of protest to the Brookings Jaycees over the signature of their commander. A resident of Snohomish, Wash., observed that if Brookings welcomed Fujita, the Jews might as well make Adolf Eichmann a national hero.

Portland's *Oregon Journal* carried a piece by columnist Doug Baker who repeated a suggestion someone made to him, "Why not invite the survivors of the Bataan death march at the same time?"

The New York correspondent for the *London Daily Express* telephoned Brookings Jaycee project chairman Douglas Peterson and festival chairman Tex Bates, and asked if police protection for Fujita would be required.

And so the comments went. . . .

Naturally the pros and cons of the invitation did not escape the Fujita family in Tsuchiura, and naturally Nobuo Fujita did not want to bring his family into a hostile community. Neither did the Japanese consulate want a Japanese family in the middle of an unpleasant incident. A delegation from the consulate visited Brookings to see if there was appreciable hostility or trouble brewing. The delegation visited city officials and the Jaycees and expressed concern over possible violence. The Jaycees were emphatic that there would be none and that demonstrations were most unlikely. The opposition, they said, was more over money than anything else.

The Jaycees also reiterated that the Fujitas would be guests and not placed on public display any more than any other honored guest. Jaycee President Dr. William McChesney said, "If we felt Fujita or his family would be in an uncomfortable position, we would not ask them to visit us."

The Brookings Ministerial Association issued a statement of agreement with the project. A few at a time, most of the people in Brookings who opposed the project changed their tune if not their minds. At a PTA meeting, the votes in favor of Fujita's visit outnumbered the opposition two to one. Money arrived from across the nation as well as from local people, clubs, and businessmen. As the collection deadline drew near, a question arose: Will there be enough money in the pot to meet the anticipated expenses? A travel agency put together a package but the cost exceeded the donations. The Jaycees had already supported their project with $300 from their own treasury, but when it was apparent the contributions would be insufficient, they borrowed an additional $700.

All during the money-raising campaign and the pro-and-con street-corner and tavern arguments, correspondence was being exchanged between the Fujitas in Japan and the Brookings-Harbor Jaycees. Fujita wrote:

Frankly speaking, we were surprised to hear from the United Press International and Associated Press, that some people opposed the invitation. All of us were, to some extent, embarrassed and worried very much if we made lots of trouble to all you friendly people of Brookings. Because we never want to make any trouble to you even though we are wishing very much to meet every one of you. But now we understand that you are still going to carry out this plan and we realize at this moment that a greater meaning and responsibility has come out to us, to meet such people, who don't know the fact that we Japanese people can make friends with you American people.

Fujita wrote further of his feeling that if people of both countries could meet and talk about their problems "with faith and frankness," it would be better than "if only political or diplomatic leaders have lots of meetings."

In Japan, the Foreign Office informed the Fujitas not to worry about their reception in Brookings. Two days before their arrival in the United States, the Reverend Del Roth, publicity chairman for the Jaycees, issued a news bulletin:

The Brookings-Harbor Jaycees are counting on the generous nature of the citizens of the community to make the stay of the Fujitas a happy and memorable occasion.

The Fujitas arrive

At 6:30 a.m. May 24, 1962, Pan American Airways flight 892 touched down at Portland International Airport. The Fujitas had arrived. Daughter Yoriko, 21 and recently married, had announced earlier that she would not make the trip because of pregnancy. When Mr. and Mrs. Fujita, and their son Yasuyoshi, 26, alighted, a representative of the mayor of Portland presented a bouquet of roses to the former pilot's wife, Ayako. Brookings Mayor Campbell gave her husband the key to his city. Also among the greeters were Jaycee President McChesney, a small group of newsmen, and several Japanese.

With a broad smile, Nobuo Fujita responded through his interpreter son, expressing his thanks to everyone who had made his visit possible. He said, "It is a wonderful day in my life."

The group went to the KGW-TV studio in Portland for a telecast and about noon left for a

The Fujitas, with Brookings Mayor C. Fell Campbell, at the Portland International Airport on arrival in 1962. Mrs. Fujita holds a bouquet of roses presented by Mayor Terry Schrunk of Portland.

Ayako, Nobuo, and Yasuyoshi Fujita in the home of one of their hosts in Brookings.

leisurely, 300-mile drive along the Oregon coast. There was a moment of concern when the automobile was stopped at a roadblock near Port Orford, 50 miles north of Brookings. All were relieved when the blockers unveiled a large sign, "Welcome Fujita."

At a reception in the McChesney home in Brookings, Yasuyoshi translated: "My father was impressed by the size of the jet liner. He says it is a little larger than the plane in which he made his first trip to this country." The reception was friendly, warm, and, as prophesied, without unpleasant incident.

The Fujitas were houseguests of the McChesneys their first night in Brookings and then went to the Henry Kerr home for the rest of the week. They graciously received many courtesies. They were not rushed. They visited homes and inspected the physical development of the city. Mr. Fujita commented that "Oregon highways are much better than those in Japan."

He photographed and expressed astonishment at such things as automatic car washes, trainloads of new automobiles, and farm machinery. The Jaycees took the party to the Harris Beach State Park and Azalea State Park to see the blossoms in profusion on a beautiful spring day, pointing out that Brookings is the only city in Oregon with two state parks within the city limits. Yasuyoshi commented that during the flight from Japan his father's face was pressed to the jet's window almost constantly as they approached the mainland: "From dawn he was looking outside, searching the coastline that he had approached three times before as part of an attack force."

The recollections of those past trips must have rushed through Nobuo's mind, particularly the trip on which he piloted his airplane from the submarine and dropped bombs into an American forest. Now, after twenty years, he was approaching the same mainland, again at dawn, but this time as an invited guest.

Gratitude for the invitation and the significance of the visit had been expressed by Yasuyoshi in a letter he wrote to William Landis in Brookings before they left Japan:

We are thinking this invitation is not only for us but to all our Japanese people. People read of this program through newspapers and are requesting us to take messages of friendship to all of you. My father knows too much about the misery of war.

In the front seat are Mr. and Mrs. Fujita, with son Yasuyoshi facing camera, as they start up the scenic Rogue River on their 1962 visit to southern Oregon.

On Saturday morning of the Azalea Festival, the Fujitas gathered with many townspeople and visitors for breakfast of pork sausage and hotcakes at the Presbyterian Church. From the place where he was standing on a street curb during the morning parade, the elder Fujita darted out into the line of march to shake hands with a startled, six-year-old Mark Meade, who was driving by in a homemade midget racing car. Amateur and professional cameramen, including Yasuyoshi, grabbed up their cameras to record the event.

At the coronation of the Azalea Festival Queen, Elaine Nonemaker, the Fujitas were introduced to the more than 2,000 people assembled. Ayako Fujita, whose given name means "very soft and tender girl," wore the traditional silk kimono and obi sash with leather zoris and white tabis on her feet. Nobuo wore a white carnation in the buttonhole of his western-style suit. In response to the applause of the crowd, the Fujitas stood up and bowed three times—once to each side and once to the front.

After the parade, the Japanese visitors mixed with the crowd. Nobuo was especially interested in the bagpipes played by the Eugene Highlanders. At the suggestion of Hector Smith, leader of the group, Nobuo tried his lungs on one of the bagpipes. He blew hard, but his effort was rewarded only by a sad squeal. The crowd laughed when Smith clapped Fujita on the back and declared, "You'll make a Scotsman yet!"

In the afternoon, while witnessing a water fight between two groups of firemen, Yasuyoshi observed, "We could never have such a time in Japan because of the national water shortage." When he took pictures and got caught in the blast of water, his father clapped his hands in glee.

The Fujitas joined the crowd on the sidewalk to watch the Azalea Festival Parade.

"You'll make a Scotsman yet." Hector Smith told the former pilot when he produced a squawk on Smith's bagpipe.

Nobuo was often surrounded by former military men who wanted to talk of soldiering. Through his son-interpreter he described his life on the *I-25* and the frustrated feelings of a flyer accustomed to the sky as his ceiling, confined. Often his only duty, he said, was as the conning tower watch and periscope officer. On some missions, his aircraft was never taken from its hangar. After one long trip, he recalled that he had difficulty walking because of swelling in his legs from beriberi. Submariners were usually given liberty at the end of a mission and Fujita's destination, like many of his American counterparts, was home and the embrace of his "very soft and tender girl."

Some of the foresters who had worked the small fire caused by his bomb chatted with the former flyer. Fred Flynn jested, "Wasn't much of a fire. You're one of the world's worst fire setters." When Yasuyoshi translated, the elder Fujita clapped his hands and laughed in agreement.

In its account of the event, the *Japan Times* on May 28 reported,

Everywhere Nobuo and Ayako and their son appeared there were smiles, applause, and the inevitable autograph line. When he had a chance to relax, Yasuyoshi said, "In Japan people have never seen such a wonderful parade."

In the afternoon Bill Landis, the Jaycee vice president, took Nobuo, Yasuyoshi, and a *Time/Life* cameraman for a flight in a Piper Tri-Pacer.

At the Brookings Azalea Festival in 1962, Nobuo Fujita met Howard Gardner, the forest lookout who sighted his plane and reported it in 1942.

Once aloft, Bill offered to turn over the controls, and Fujita readily accepted. Bill noted that the former pilot had lost none of his skill and that he handled the plane like a professional. Fujita flew smoothly over Mt. Emily and then over Wheeler Ridge, where he had released one of his bombs twenty years before. He said he remembered Mt. Emily from that foggy morning in September 1942.

He later told questioners that he received no decoration, promotion, or bonus for his unique flight. He had become aware of the necessity for peace following the war and had set up a wholesale distribution business to benefit the families of his friends who had been killed.

The Fujitas agreed that most Japanese want friendship with the United States. "We are very ashamed," they said, "of the hate when President Eisenhower wanted to come to Japan. Ninety-nine per cent of the people wanted to welcome President Eisenhower. Just one per cent of the crazy young people made demonstrations and we are very angry with them."

When Jaycee wives and other women of Brookings learned that the Fujitas' daughter Yoriko did not make the trip to America because she was expecting her first child, they organized a typically American event. They decided to have a "grandmother" shower. Mrs. McChesney decorated a cake with booties in pink frosting. Others gathered gifts for the Fujitas to take back to Japan—a myrtlewood bowl, hand-knit baby clothes, a cuddly musical panda, and other toys.

Assisted in translation by Mrs. Yukiko Duncan, a Japanese war bride living in Brookings, Ayako Fujita talked of the kimono of handmade silk she was wearing and showed how the long obi sash is wound about the waist. She also demonstrated *origami*, the ancient art of paper folding. She made a complicated good-luck bird and taught several of the Jaycettes how to make simpler paper birds for decorations.

The climax of Nobuo Fujita's visit was the banquet in his honor. Space was limited and the dining room was packed. After the meal, President McChesney thanked all who had assisted in making the event possible and pointed out that "the warm reception you have given our guests has made Brookings a finer place in which to live than it was one week ago."

Then with Yasuyoshi translating, Nobuo addressed the group:

I never imagined I would be back in Japan alive after my flight over America, and I never dreamed that I could ever visit the United States again. But at this moment I am here again with my family on this visit arranged by your broadminded citizens.

This is the finest possible way of closing this story. It is in the finest Samurai tradition to pledge peace and friendship by presenting a sword to a former enemy.

With this remark he produced the centuries-old Samurai-type sword he had carried with him on his bombing missions. He handed it to his son. The room was hushed as a solemn-faced Yasuyoshi gravely passed the sword on in the name of his father to Mayor Campbell. As the priceless symbol changed hands, the audience gasped. With his father speaking in Japanese, Yasuyoshi translated into English the history of the blade and explained how to handle it. The mayor began to say, "Friends, I don't know how to thank you enough," but was interrupted by the scrape of chairs being pushed back from the tables and a standing, lengthy applause.

A decade later, the ornate Fujita sword, photographs, and other mementos of the visit were on display in the Brookings City Hall. At that time, father and son were operating their own business, Fujita Metal Company, Ltd., specializing in building materials. Yasuyoshi was managing director, planning to succeed his father as head of the company. From the ashes, devastation, and economic disaster left by World War II, they were doing their part in rebuilding the country and rejuvenating the economy in the land of the rising sun. □

Yasuyoshi Fujita has just presented his father's sword to the people of Brookings. Nobuo smiles approval as the weapon he carried at his side on his wartime flights over southern Oregon is accepted by Mayor Campbell.

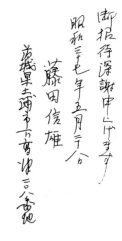

The former pilot signed hundreds of autographs: "I deeply appreciate your kind invitation. May 28, 1962. Nobuo Fujita, 208 Shimo-Takatsu, Tsuchiura-Ibaraki."

"This sword," says Mr. Fujita, "is judged by experts to be of the Kamakura period. The name of the *Katana-kaji* or blacksmith is not known, although he was one of the best of the period. The handle, lapping, and scabbard were redesigned and remade later in the Showa period for Japanese Navy service men. The engraving is not only decorative but also is the distinctive pattern of the blacksmith who made the sword. According to an expert, this is the pattern of a blacksmith in Bungo Takada, near my birthplace in Kyushu. I always carried this sword during my service in the Navy and, of course, had it beside my seat when I flew my missions."

Appendixes

Incident Lists

The numbering system used in the incident lists follows the pattern established by Conley (1965) and Mikesh (1973). For publication here modifications have been made:

1. Additional incidents have been included in their chronological sequence by adding "a," "b," etc., to numbers already assigned. For example, the balloon reported to have landed near Yerington, Nevada, in November 1944 is not included by Conley or Mikesh. It has been given the number "1a."

2. Place names have been corrected or clarified where supplemental information has come to light.

3. Additional data have been included in the Remarks column based on reports of the Naval Research Laboratory and other sources.

Definitions

INCIDENT: A finding of physical evidence identifiable as part or parts of a Japanese balloon or its cargo.

ENVELOPE: The spherical gas bag. A few of the early experimental or test envelopes made of woven silk covered with rubber are included in the list and are so designated. Others were made of laminated tissue paper four or five layers thick. Reported dimensions vary slightly but the paper envelopes fully inflated were about 100 feet in circumference, 33 feet (10 meters) in diameter. In color they were usually either light tan or bluish white.

ENVELOPE DESTRUCTOR: A paper sack containing 250 grams (8.7 ounces) of magnesium flash powder cemented to the envelope. The long-burning fuse to detonate the envelope destructor was lighted at the time that the 15-kg antipersonnel bomb was released. Its purpose was to ignite the hydrogen in the envelope, causing an explosion that would destroy the envelope. Sometimes the only evidence of a balloon found was a scorched fragment of paper. Complete envelopes that were recovered were ones that escaped destruction because of a malfunction in the system.

ENVELOPE DESTRUCTOR FUSE: A paper cord fuse that burned at the rate of about one foot in a minute and six seconds. It was designed so that about an hour would elapse between the time the last bomb was dropped and ignition of the envelope destructor.

GAS RELIEF VALVE: A metal disk valve 19½ inches in diameter with a 17-inch opening. It was cemented into the opening at the bottom of the envelope for the purpose of releasing hydrogen when the gas expanded at high temperatures.

SHROUDS: On the paper envelopes, ¼-inch hemp ropes that connected the envelope to the shock absorber or the ballast gear and armament. Normally there were 19 shrouds.

SHOCK ABSORBER: A bundle of 250 3/64-inch rubber bands inserted between the envelope and ballast gear to reduce effect of sudden movements of the envelope. It was not found on all balloons recovered.

BALLAST GEAR: An automatic altitude control mechanism that included a 2.2 volt one-cell wet battery and a surrounding solution to prevent the battery from freezing; a box of aneroid barometers; fuses and arming wires; and an aluminum wheel 32½ inches in diameter that had 72 tapered holes bored horizontally to receive the tapered blow-plugs. The aluminum wheel is also known as the chandelier ring and ballast ring.

BLOW-PLUGS: Small metal cylinders (also known as blow-out plugs) that fitted tightly into the tapered horizontal holes in the aluminum wheel. The plugs contained a charge of black powder which was fired electrically to release the ballast or bombs hanging below them.

DEMOLITION CHARGE: A 2-pound block of picric acid in a metal container next to the battery case. Its purpose was to destroy the ballast gear after the last bomb was dropped.

SANDBAGS: Ballast in paper sacks weighing from 3 to 7 pounds each that hung on hooks below the blow-plugs.

TYPE A BOMB: A 12-kilogram, fin-type incendiary bomb.

TYPE B BOMB: A 5-kilogram, candle-type, incendiary bomb.

TYPE C BOMB: A 15-kilogram high-explosive, fin-type, anti-personnel bomb.

Abbreviations used in Remarks column:
N,S,E,W: Compass directions
USN: United States Navy
USCG: United States Coast Guard
USA: United States Army
USAAF: United States Army Air Force
PWT: Pacific War Time
MWT: Mountain War Time
NRL: Navy Research Laboratory

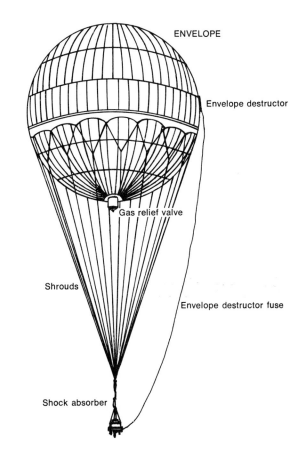

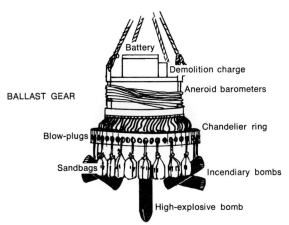

The Type A Paper Balloon

Japanese Balloon/Bomb Landings

Recorded Incidents from November 1944 through August 1945 by State and Province

Incident number	Location

Territory of Alaska

6	Marshall (Fortuna Ledge)
7	Holy Cross
12	Kodiak Island
13a	Unalaska Is., Aleutians
23	Holy Cross
23a	Rat Is., Aleutians
24	Buldir Is., Aleutians
25	Kashunuk River
34a	Attu Is., Aleutians
57	Ekwok
74a	Attu Is., Aleutians
78	Bethel
86a	St. Lawrence Island
87a	Platinum/Goodnews Bay
107a	Nunapitchuk/Bethel
110	Gambell
120	Phillips
130	Mumtrak (Goodnews)
138	Kinak Bay
160	Dillingham
172	Bethel
211	Attu Is., Aleutians
213	Attu Is., Aleutians
214	Little Sitkin Is., Aleutians
216	Midas Creek
217	Adak Is., Aleutians
218	Bethel
219	Amchitka Is.,. Aleutians
220a	Bering Sea
222	Platinum
226	Tikchik Lake
237	Akiak
260	Egegik
264	Anchorage
286	Nunivak Island
293	Unalaska Is., Aleutians

Alberta

32	Provost
59	Manyberries
101	Edson
108	Baril Lake
128	Hay Lake
150	Fort Chipewyan
153	Olds
154	Wimborne
155	Foremost
157	Delburne
173	Athabasca
174	Delburne
178a	Medicine Hat
182	Strathmore
188a	Medicine Hat
241	Stettler
246	Milo
253	High River
262	Whitecourt
297	Wood Buffalo National Park

Arizona

26	Nogales
272	Ajo

British Columbia

21a	Boundary Bay
51	Takla Landing
66	Chase
82b	Mayne, Galiano Island
83	Nanaimo
84a	Duncan
85	Big Creek
86	Stuart Lake
91	Galiano Island
95	Nicola
97a	Galiano Island
102	Kunghit Island
104	Coal Harbor
107b	Rupert Arm Inlet
109	Port Hardy
124	Gambier Island
131	Williams Lake
132	Chase
133	Baker Creek
136	Fort Babine
139	Alexis Creek
146	Cedarvale
151	Williams Lake
152	Denman Island
165	Ashcroft
170	Barrier Lake
176	Britain River
176a	Jervis Inlet
179	Hanson Island
184	Whitewater/Fort Ware
195a	Barrier Lake
207	Merritt
223	Boundary Bay
223a	Moresby Island
224	Morice Lake
227	Vedder Mountain
229	Chilliwack
232	Queen Charlotte Island
234	Kitchener
237a	Dome Creek
237b	Vanderhoof/Stuart Lake
244	Chilliwack
251	Vanderhoof
254	Chilanko River
265	Mahood Lake
267	Yahk
271	Dease Lake
272a	Nanoose Bay
275	Alberni
280	Salmo
282	Lillooet
287	Adams Lake Plateau
289	Sicamous
290	Chase
292	Kettle River Valley
295	McBride
296	Hillcrest

California

1	San Pedro
11	Sebastopol
13	Napa
15	Alturas
16	Adin
19	Ventura
20	Moorpark
21	Moorpark
27	Julian
28	Red Bluff
29	Hayfork
34	Camp Beale
42a	Cohasset
43	Calistoga/Elmira
55a	Oxnard
99	Meridian
103	West Cloverdale
127	Grimes
129	Big Bend/Redding
140	Guerneville
166	Volcano
199	Hoopla Indian Res.
252	Soldier Mountain

Colorado

121	Delta
148	Timnath
259	Collbran

Territory of Hawaii

2	Kailua (Kona)

Idaho

34b	Blackfoot
34c	Twin Falls
45	American Falls
69	Rigby
75	Boise
117	American Falls
164	Rogerson
209	Plano
234a	Lucile
268	Gilmore
269	Hailey
294	Idaho Falls

Iowa

30	Laurens
82	Holstein
126	Pocahontas

Kansas

70	Bigelow

Manitoba

89	Nelson House
106	Oxford House
145	Marie Lake
193	Waterhen Lake
204a	Lawford Lake
208	Southern Indian Lake

Mexico

147	Sonoyta, Sonora
183	Laguna Salada, Baja California
229a	Coahuila

Michigan

71	Grand Rapids
180	Farmington

Montana

4	Kalispell
18	Lame Deer
36	Lodge Grass
37	Hardin
38	Riverdale
41	Cascade
44	Eden
46	Hardin
49	Flathead Lake
50	Deer Lodge
60	Hays
74	Boyd
75a	Laurel
88	Bernice
98	Hammond
107	Whitehall
111	Legg
112	Divide
116	Bench!and
122	Harlowton
123a	Broadus/Hammond
135	Coram/Nyack
137	Sula
141	Glen
144	Laurel
162	Glen
191	Bozeman
197	Dillon
205	Turner
231	Phillipsburg
235a	Loring/Dodson
255	Pryor
273	Boulder
277	Monida
291	Babb

Nebraska

31	Schuyler
39	Burwell
67	Ellsworth
149	Chadron
177	Osceola

Nevada

1a	Yerington
163	Reno
188	Pyramid Lake/Nixon
204	Massacre Lake
230	Elko
279	Jiggs
285	Indian Springs

North Dakota

56	Ashley
190	Grafton

Northwest Territories

22	Fort Simpson
47	Marie River
200	Hay River
243a	Snowdrift

Oregon

8	Estacada
10	Medford
14	Medford
31a	Ontario/Vale
61	North Bend
72	Burns
73	Deer Island
76	Eugene
79	Deer Island

90 Wolf Creek
96 Vale
114 Echo
118 Malheur Lake
123 Ontario
125 Yamhill
134 Coquille/Riverton
142 The Dalles
156 The Dalles
159 Murphy
168 Rome
175a Parkersburg
186 Adrian
187 Nyssa/Mitchell Butte
202 Harper
206 Provolt
210 Bald Mountain
212 Rome
215a Grants Pass
220 Tyee
233 Lake of the Woods
236 Beatty
239 Huntington
240 Bly
242 Enterprise
245 Enterprise
248 Harper
250 Summer Lake
256 Jordan Valley
257 Mahogany Mountain
258 Mahogany Mountain

274 Hyatt Lake
276 Hyatt Lake
281 Mt. McLoughlin
284 Mt. McLoughlin
288 Bald Mountain

Saskatchewan
9 Stony Rapids
17 Minton
35 Moose Jaw
63 Porcupine Plain
161 Camsell Portage
192 Consul
196 Ituna
201a Yorkton
243 Kelvington

South Dakota
40 Nowlin/Rapid City
87 Buffalo
169 Ree Heights/Wolsey
181 Kadoka
194 Red Elm
195 Marcus
215 Wolsey
236a Buffalo
249 Madison

Texas
171 Desdemona
175 Desdemona
178 Woodson

Utah
68 Tremonton
143 Garrison
189 Duchesne
221 Snowville
235 Paragonah

Washington
42 Spokane
48 Prosser
52 Asotin
53 Ephrata
54 Spokane
55 Sumas
58 Ephrata
77 Goldendale
80 Lakebay
81 Vaughn (Gig Harbor)
82a Tacoma
84 Puyallup
92 Ephrata
93 Satus Pass
94 Toppenish
97 Moxee City
100 Cold Creek
113 Farmington
115 Paine Field (Everett)
119 Chimacum
198 Tampico
201 Colville
203 Walla Walla
225 Wapato

238 Moxee City
239a Mount Rainier
247 Asotin
266 Tampico

Wyoming
3 Thermopolis
5 Manderson
24a Worland
33 Newcastle
36a Casper
62 Kirby
64 Powell
65 Glendo
158 Gillette
167 Basin/Sheridan
205a Casper

Yukon Territory
185 Canol Road
228 Watson Lake
261 Skukum Creek
263 Mayo
270 Old Crow River
278 Aishihik

Miscellaneous
105 At sea: 30°18'N-132°52'W
107c At sea
222a North Pacific Ocean: 41°46'N-171°47'W
283 North Pacific Ocean

APPENDIX B

Japanese Balloon/Bomb Landings

Recorded Incidents from November 1944 through August 1945 listed chronologically

Incident number and location	Date	Remarks
	1944	
1. San Pedro, California	Nov. 4	Balloon retrieved from sea 66 miles SW of San Pedro by USN vessel. White envelope was made of four layers of silk cloth impregnated with rubber. Shrouds had 27-strand woven silk core covered with bright golden yellow silk sheath. Small radio transmitter was attached.
1a. Yerington, Nevada	Nov. 9	Rubber balloon found by ranchers in August but not immediately recorded. Western Defense Command Intelligence Study No. 2 lists it as having been recovered on Nov. 9. Conley gives May 1, 1945, as the date reported (see photo p. 102 and notes p. 171).
2. Kailua (Kona) Hawaii	Nov. 14	Fragments of a paper balloon envelope, shrouds, fuses, and ballast gear recovered by USCG five miles at sea.
3. Thermopolis, Wyoming	Dec. 6	Observers saw bright red flame in sky and heard an explosion at 1800 MWT 15 miles SW of Thermopolis and reported seeing what appeared to be a parachute descending. Fragments of type C bomb recovered Dec. 7. (See pp. 110-111.)
4. Kalispell, Montana	Dec. 11	Paper envelope 100 feet in circumference, gas relief valve, 19 shrouds, fuse, shock absorber, and envelope destructor recovered between Libby and Kalispell; estimated to have landed between Nov. 11 and 25. (See pp. 111-112.)
5. Manderson, Wyoming	Dec. 19	A 3-by-4-foot fragment of paper balloon envelope recovered.
6. Marshall (Fortuna Ledge), Alaska	Dec. 23	Three large sections of envelope, gas relief valve, remains of ballast gear, shrouds, two 32-foot fired fuses, and two sandbags recovered.
7. Holy Cross, Alaska	Dec. 24	Several large sections of envelope, gas relief valve, shrouds, a 60-foot fuse, shock absorber, part of ballast gear, and one sandbag recovered.
8. Estacada, Oregon	Dec. 31	Balloon found hanging in a tree. Envelope, gas relief valve, shrouds, envelope destructor, two fuses, shock absorber, and pieces of ballast gear recovered. (See pp. 112-113.)

		1945	
9.	Stony Rapids, Saskatchewan	Jan. 1	Several fragments of envelope found.
10.	Medford, Oregon	Jan. 4	Whistling sound and explosion heard. Fragments of type B bomb found in a field near Peach Street, a mile SW of Medford. (See also No. 14)
11.	Sebastopol, California	Jan. 4	Skirt from envelope, 19 shrouds, remains of envelope destructor, gas relief valve, 60 feet of fuse, shock absorber, damaged ballast gear, parts of four type B bombs, and two 32-foot fired fuses recovered. (See also No. 13)
12.	Kodiak Island, Alaska	Jan. 5	The armed guard of a merchant vessel at 52°5′N-160°W shot down a white balloon SW of Kodiak. Nothing recovered.
13.	Napa, California	Jan. 5	Fragments of balloon found about 30 miles SE of Sebastopol. May have been part of No. 11.
13a.	Unalaska Is., Aleutians, Alaska	Jan. 5	Burned fragment of envelope reported.
14.	Medford, Oregon	Jan. 7	Fragments of type B bomb recovered. Possibly from No. 10.
15.	Alturas, California	Jan. 10	Balloon was forced to a lower altitude and shot down by USN plane; landed in forest 30 miles W of Alturas; recovered intact with envelope destructor, 19 shrouds, gas relief valve, and ballast gear. (See pp. 115-117.)
16.	Adin, California	Jan. 10	Balloon reported at this location probably same as No. 15.
17.	Minton, Saskatchewan	Jan. 12	Balloon observed descending at 1630 MWT about six miles north of U.S.-Canadian border and releasing type C bomb, which did not explode on impact. Parts of ballast gear and four sandbags broke loose and were recovered after balloon rose and disappeared.
18.	Lame Deer, Montana	Jan. 13	Balloon landed at 1600 MWT; envelope, 19 shrouds, and gas relief valve recovered.
19.	Ventura, California	Jan. 15	Explosion heard at 1800 MWT at Saticoy, eight miles E of Ventura. Fragments of type C bomb recovered. Possibly dropped from No. 20.
20.	Moorpark, California	Jan. 17	Balloon reported 15 miles E of the Saticoy explosion (No. 19).
21.	Moorpark, California	Jan. 17	Balloon recovered with envelope, envelope destructor, gas relief valve, five unexploded blow-plugs, and parts of an exploded type C bomb. Probably same balloon as Nos. 19-20.
21a.	Boundary Bay, British Columbia	Jan. 17	Fragment of balloon reported.
22.	Fort Simpson, Northwest Territories	Jan. 19	Envelope, envelope destructor, gas relief valve, ballast gear, and demolition charge recovered.
23.	Holy Cross, Alaska	Jan. 21	Large fragments of envelope, gas relief valve, 19 shrouds, four blow-plugs, parts of ballast gear, and one sandbag recovered eight miles SW of Holy Cross. Possibly a duplicate report of No. 7.
23a.	Rat Is., Aleutians, Alaska	Jan. 24	Fragment of burned envelope reported.
24.	Buldir Is., Aleutians, Alaska	Jan. 25	Balloon sighted at 28,000-foot altitude and shot down by fighter plane 40 miles SW of Shemya Island in the Aleutians. Nothing recovered.
24a.	Worland, Wyoming	Jan. 28	Envelope and shrouds reported found. Possibly from No. 3.
25.	Kashunuk River, Alaska	Jan. 30	Fragment of envelope found.
26.	Nogales, Arizona	Jan. 31	Small fragment of envelope found.
27.	Julian, California	Jan. 31	Envelope, gas relief valve, ballast gear, shrouds, envelope destructor, and demolition charge recovered.
28.	Red Bluff, California	Feb. 1	About one-quarter of an envelope (all from the lower half) and the gas relief valve recovered.
29.	Hayfork, California	Feb. 1	Balloon observed descending at about 1825 PWT 3½ miles NW of Hayfork Ranger Station, where it caught in a treetop. The envelope exploded but the gas relief valve, shrouds, ballast gear, four type B bombs, and seven sandbags crashed to the ground. (See pp. 117-118.)
30.	Laurens, Iowa	Feb. 2	Fragments of envelope with charred edges, envelope destructor and fuse, 19 shrouds, and gas relief valve recovered. The envelope destructor was found unexploded in a paper cylinder. Destruction of the balloon by its demolition charge possibly produced the fragmentation and charring.

31.	Schuyler, Nebraska	Feb. 2	Triangular envelope fragment about six feet long recovered. It had charred edges similar to fragments found the same day at Laurens, Iowa, (No. 30) and may have been from the same balloon, although these locations are 140 miles apart.
31a.	Ontario/Vale, Oregon	Feb. 2	A fragment of 4-ply envelope paper, 19 shrouds, and pieces of the ballast gear reported.
32.	Provost, Alberta	Feb. 7	Envelope, gas relief valve, and ballast gear recovered.
33.	Newcastle, Wyoming	Feb. 8	Balloon landed at 1800 MWT 25 miles W of Newcastle; envelope, 19 shrouds, gas relief valve, and ballast ring recovered.
34.	Camp Beale, California	Feb. 8	Envelope recovered with gas relief valve, battery gear without battery and barometers but with 16 pairs of unexploded blow-plugs and one single blow-plug in the ballast ring.
34a.	Attu Is., Aleutians, Alaska	Feb. 8	Fragment of burned envelope reported found on Point Alexia.
34b.	Blackfoot, Idaho	Feb. 8	Fragment of envelope reported.
34c.	Twin Falls, Idaho	Feb. 8	Fragment of envelope reported.
35.	Moose Jaw, Saskatchewan	Feb. 9	Envelope, shrouds, and ballast gear recovered.
36.	Lodge Grass, Montana	Feb. 9	Top one-third of envelope recovered.
36a.	Casper, Wyoming	Feb. 9	Fragment of envelope reported.
37.	Hardin, Montana	Feb. 12	Fragments of an envelope, 19 shrouds, gas relief valve, and remains of a type A exploded bomb recovered.
38.	Riverdale, Montana	Feb. 12	Fragments of three type B bombs found following explosion.
39.	Burwell, Nebraska	Feb. 12	Large fragment of envelope recovered with 19 shrouds, gas relief valve, ballast gear, six pairs of unexploded blow-plugs, five arming wires, and two type B bombs. Paper cylinder normally used to hold envelope destructor was empty.
40.	Nowlin/Rapid City, South Dakota	Feb. 12	Alerted by explosion, search team found one sandbag and remains of two exploded type B bombs.
41.	Cascade, Montana	Feb. 12	Recovery team retrieved bomb fragments that smelled of ammonia. Bomb type not specified.
42.	Spokane, Washington	Feb. 12	Two unexploded bombs, one type A, one type B, found with paint unmarred seven miles N of Spokane. (See No. 54)
42a.	Cohasset, California	Feb. 12	Remains of one exploded type A bomb found in Butte County, N of Chico.
43.	Calistoga/Elmira, California	Feb. 23	(out of sequence) Balloon shot down by P-38 fighter plane; envelope fragment found near Elmira, 39 miles SE of Calistoga.
44.	Eden, Montana	Feb. 13	Fragment of 5-ply envelope paper and 19 shrouds found.
45.	American Falls, Idaho	Feb. 13	Fragment of envelope and shrouds recovered.
46.	Hardin, Montana	Feb. 13	Gas relief valve and shrouds recovered.
47.	Marie River, Northwest Territories	Feb. 13	Envelope fragment found.
48.	Prosser, Washington	Feb. 15	Envelope, gas relief valve, and ballast gear with two unfired blow-plugs and five arming wires recovered. NRL comment: "No reason for the failure of the balloon to destroy itself was apparent."
49.	Flathead Lake, Montana	Feb. 17	Fifty-square-foot fragment of 5-ply paper recovered. It was apparently from upper portion of envelope; seams were covered with blue tape.
50.	Deer Lodge, Montana	Feb. 18	Two fragments of envelope paper recovered.
51.	Takla Landing, British Columbia	Feb. 19	Envelope partially inflated, gas relief valve, shrouds, shock absorber, 11 pairs of blow-plugs, demolition charge, and one sandbag recovered.
52.	Asotin, Washington	Feb. 20	Two-thirds of an envelope and pieces of shrouds recovered.
53.	Ephrata, Washington	Feb. 21	Balloon touched ground and lost three sandbags, then ascended and disappeared. (See No. 58)
54.	Spokane, Washington	Feb. 21	One type C (antipersonnel) bomb and one type A or B (incendiary) bomb reported. Possibly a duplicate report of No. 42. Type A was sometimes mistaken for type C as both are fin-type bombs.

55.	Sumas, Washington	Feb. 21	Balloon shot down near U.S.-Canadian border; recovered by Canadians.
55a.	Oxnard, California	Feb. 21	Envelope reported found.
56.	Ashley, North Dakota	Feb. 22	Envelope, 19 shrouds, and gas relief valve recovered.
57.	Ekwok, Alaska	Feb. 22	Balloon hit ground, dropping battery. Fragments and gas relief valve recovered on March 13.
58.	Ephrata, Washington	Feb. 22	Three sandbags recovered. May be duplicate report of No. 53.
59.	Manyberries, Alberta	Feb. 22	Envelope, gas relief valve, ballast gear, demolition charge, and ring containing five unexploded blow-plugs recovered.
60.	Hays, Montana	Feb. 22	Envelope, 19 shrouds, gas relief valve, ballast gear, and three sandbags recovered.
61.	North Bend, Oregon	Feb. 22	Balloon shot down by fighter plane at 12,000 feet altitude. Envelope, envelope destructor, and 19 shrouds recovered.
62.	Kirby, Wyoming	Feb. 22	Balloon was observed grounding. Envelope, gas relief valve, shrouds, ballast gear, and demolition charge were recovered. Battery was in discharged condition; antifreeze solution had drained out through crack in outer box.
63.	Porcupine Plain, Saskatchewan	Feb. 22	Envelope, shrouds, gas relief valve, and ballast gear recovered.
64.	Powell, Wyoming	Feb. 22	Balloon observed exploding in air. Fragment of 4-ply paper 12 x 20 feet, shrouds, gas relief valve, ballast gear, and one type A and two type B bombs recovered. Remains of a 25-pound bomb of undetermined type were also recovered.
65.	Glendo, Wyoming	Feb. 22	Balloon observed as it grounded. Recovered with 19 shrouds, gas relief valve, ballast gear, two sandbags (one weighing 6 pounds), one type B bomb, and many unfired blow-plugs. Envelope destructor missing, possibly never installed. Four fuses had failed to ignite; defective battery may have caused malfunction.
66.	Chase, British Columbia	Feb. 22	Fragment of envelope paper recovered.
67.	Ellsworth, Nebraska	Feb. 22	Gas relief valve and several pieces of shroud lines recovered.
68.	Tremonton, Utah	Feb. 22	Envelope, envelope destructor, 19 shrouds, gas relief valve, and ballast gear including demolition charge recovered. Malfunction of self-destruct mechanisms may have been due to short fuses and poor connections. This balloon carried a man! (See p. 118.)
69.	Rigby, Idaho	Feb. 23	Balloon found with gas relief valve, ballast gear, demolition charge, and one arming wire.
70.	Bigelow, Kansas	Feb. 23	Farmer discovered balloon snagged in a tree. Envelope, envelope destructor, 19 shrouds, gas relief valve, and ballast gear recovered. (See pp. 106, 118-120.)
71.	Grand Rapids, Michigan	Feb. 23	Envelope, gas relief valve, ballast gear with battery, and one sandbag recovered.
72.	Burns, Oregon	Feb. 23	Envelope, gas relief valve, ballast gear with battery, and one sandbag recovered.
73.	Deer Island, Oregon	Feb. 23	After an explosion in the air, a fragment of envelope was found on this island in the Columbia River 25 miles NW of Portland. (See No. 79.)
74.	Boyd, Montana	Feb. 23	Envelope with 19 shrouds, ballast gear with battery, demolition charge, and one ballast bag recovered.
74a.	Attu Is., Aleutians, Alaska	Feb. 24	Balloon shot down at 51°49′N-172°6′E. Nothing recovered.
75.	Boise, Idaho	Feb. 25	Envelope, envelope destructor charge, shrouds, ballast gear with battery, demolition charge, and one sandbag recovered.
75a.	Laurel, Montana	Feb. 25	Envelope with shrouds reported.
76.	Eugene, Oregon	Feb. 26	Fragment of an envelope and gas relief valve found.
77.	Goldendale, Washington	Feb. 27	Envelope, shrouds, gas relief valve, ballast gear with battery, and demolition charge recovered. (See pp. 120-121.)
78.	Bethel, Alaska	Feb. 27	Balloon shot down. Burned envelope found 70 miles from Bethel.
79.	Deer Island, Oregon	Feb. 27	Fragment of envelope reported. Possibly duplication of No. 73.
80.	Lakebay, Washington	Feb. 28	Damaged envelope and ballast gear found.
81.	Vaughn (Gig Harbor), Washington	Feb. 28	Pieces of balloon and parts reported found.
82.	Holstein, Iowa	Feb. 28	Fragments of type B bomb found.

82a.	Tacoma, Washington	Feb. 28	Fragment of envelope found.
82b.	Mayne, Galiano Island, B.C.	Mar. 1	Small fragment of envelope found 30 miles N of Victoria.
83.	Nanaimo, British Columbia	Mar. 3	Envelope, gas relief valve, ballast gear, and one incendiary bomb recovered on east coast of Vancouver Island.
84.	Puyallup, Washington	Mar. 3	Fragment of paper envelope found.
84a.	Duncan, British Columbia	Mar. 3	Envelope reported found.
85.	Big Creek, British Columbia	Mar. 4	Envelope, shrouds, ballast gear, and one type A bomb recovered.
86.	Stuart Lake, British Columbia	Mar. 5	Fragments of balloon recovered near Fort St. James.
86a.	St. Lawrence Island, Alaska	Mar. 5	Fragment of balloon envelope found.
87.	Buffalo, South Dakota	Mar. 6	Fragments of envelope and shrouds found.
87a.	Platinum/Goodnews Bay, Alaska	Mar. 8	Envelope, aneroid barometers, demolition charge, and three sandbags recovered.
88.	Bernice, Montana	Mar. 10	Envelope, shrouds, and ballast gear recovered.
89.	Nelson House, Manitoba	Mar. 10	Fragments from exploded type A bomb recovered.
90.	Wolf Creek, Oregon	Mar. 10	About half of envelope found in mountains ½ mile SE of village. Reported to have been displayed in store window until FBI learned of it and picked up portion. Remainder was left with finder who stored his large fragment in basement of home for many years.
91.	Galiano Island, British Columbia	Mar. 10	Two balloons sighted. One shot down over Strait of Georgia N of Victoria, other disappeared.
92.	Ephrata, Washington	Mar. 10	Balloon shot down. Envelope, 19 shrouds, gas relief valve, ballast gear, 23 pairs and 3 single blow-plugs, and one sandbag recovered.
93.	Satus Pass, Washington	Mar. 10	Envelope recovered with gas relief valve, ballast gear, 13 pairs of blow-plugs, 3 single blow-plugs, three arming wires, and one sandbag.
94.	Toppenish, Washington	Mar. 10	Burned envelope fragment recovered with gas relief valve, portion of ballast gear, 15 pairs of unexploded blow-plugs, one single blow-plug, four arming wires, one sandbag, and remains of three type B exploded bombs. (See pp. 121-122.)
95.	Nicola, British Columbia	Mar. 10	Envelope recovered with one unexploded type C bomb.
96.	Vale, Oregon	Mar. 10	Remains of envelope and shrouds located; possibly related to explosion reported in January.
97.	Moxee City, Washington	Mar. 10	Envelope, two aneroids, demolition charge, and two type B bombs recovered.
97a.	Galiano Island, British Columbia	Mar. 10	Balloon shot down. See also No. 91.
98.	Hammond, Montana	Mar. 11	One-third of an envelope and 17 shrouds found.
99.	Meridian, California	Mar. 11	Following balloon sighting and explosion in air, paper fragments recovered.
100.	Cold Creek, Washington	Mar. 11	Balloon shot down by military police and civilian security guards just west of Yakima Road Barricade, Hanford Engineering Works. Envelope recovered with shrouds, envelope destructor, gas relief valve, complete ballast gear, seven sandbags, 14 blow-plugs, and much unburned fuse. (See photo p. 121.)
101.	Edson, Alberta	Mar. 11	Balloon landed and recovered.
102.	Kunghit Island, British Columbia	Mar. 11	Balloon shot down on or near southernmost of the Queen Charlotte Islands.
103.	West Cloverdale, California	Mar. 12	Paper fragments reported recovered between West Cloverdale and Guerneville. See No. 140.
104.	Coal Harbor, British Columbia	Mar. 12	Envelope found with gas relief valve and one unexploded type A bomb at W end of Vancouver harbor.

105.	At sea: 30°18'N-132°52'W	Mar. 12	Envelope with gas relief valve and ballast gear retrieved from sea W of Baja California, Mexico.
106.	Oxford House, Manitoba	Mar. 12	Envelope with shrouds and gas relief valve, and ballast gear recovered.
107.	Whitehall, Montana	Mar. 12	Envelope recovered with 19 shrouds, envelope destructor, gas relief valve, ballast gear, demolition charge, one sandbag, and two unexploded type B bombs.
107a.	Nunapitchuk/Bethel, Alaska	Mar. 12	Fragment of envelope and shrouds recovered.
107b.	Rupert Arm Inlet, British Columbia	Mar. 12	Envelope reported found.
107c.	At sea	Mar. 12	Envelope reported found in Pacific Ocean 700 miles SW of San Francisco.
108.	Baril Lake, Alberta	Mar. 13	Balloon found near Lake Athabasca. Condition not stated.
109.	Port Hardy, British Columbia	Mar. 13	Two balloons sighted. One shot down near N end of Vancouver Island; three arming wires found. Second escaped.
110.	Gambell, Alaska	Mar. 13	Paper fragment found on St. Lawrence Island.
111.	Legg, Montana	Mar. 13	Damaged envelope recovered with 17 shrouds, gas relief valve, ballast gear, and 18 pairs unexploded blow-plugs.
112.	Divide, Montana	Mar. 13	Balloon recovered with gas relief valve, ballast gear, 29 blow-plugs, and two arming wires.
113.	Farmington, Washington	Mar. 13	Envelope recovered with 19 shrouds, envelope destructor, and ballast gear. (See photo, p. 123.)
114.	Echo, Oregon	Mar. 13	Envelope recovered with envelope destructor, shrouds, gas relief valve, ballast gear, 22 pairs unexploded blow-plugs, one single blow-plug, demolition charge, three arming wires, 11 sandbags, one type B bomb. (This unit is owned by the Smithsonian Institution and has been displayed in the National Air and Space Museum, Washington, D.C., and in Japan.)
115.	Paine Field Everett, Wash.	Mar. 13	Damaged envelope, ballast gear, and one type B bomb recovered.
116.	Benchland, Montana	Mar. 13	Envelope, 19 shrouds, and ballast gear recovered.
117.	American Falls, Idaho	Mar. 13	Envelope fragments and shrouds located after a report that a balloon was seen exploding in the sky.
118.	Malheur Lake, Oregon	Mar. 13	Envelope, envelope destructor, shrouds, ballast gear, and one type B bomb recovered.
119.	Chimacum, Washington	Mar. 13	Balloon sighted, shot down, and recovered.
120.	Phillips, Alaska	Mar. 13	Fragment of envelope and shrouds found.
121.	Delta, Colorado	Mar. 13	Following an explosion, several balloon fragments and shroud lines recovered.
122.	Harlowton, Montana	Mar. 13	Three arming wires, three sandbags, remains of one exploded type A bomb recovered.
123.	Ontario, Oregon	Mar. 13	Fragment of envelope about two feet square, 19 shrouds, several parts of ballast gear found Feb. 2. (See No. 31a.)
123a.	Broadus/Hammond, Montana	Mar. 13	One-third of an envelope and 17 shrouds recovered.
124.	Gambier Island, British Columbia	Mar. 14	Fragments of balloon found 15 miles NW of Vancouver.
125.	Yamhill, Oregon	Mar. 14	Fragments of balloon and incendiary bomb found following an explosion.
126.	Pocahontas, Iowa	Mar. 14	Fragment of balloon paper and shrouds recovered.
127.	Grimes, California	Mar. 14	Balloon discovered with shroud lines draped across power lines. Ballast ring and bombs dangled about 15 feet above ground on one side. On other side, shrouds led to collapsed balloon laying on highway. Balloon recovered with envelope, gas relief valve, shrouds, ballast gear, six pairs unexploded blow-plugs, five single blow-plugs, three sandbags, and one type A and one type B bomb. See photo page 3.
128.	Hay Lake, Alberta	Mar. 14	Pieces of bakelite insulating disc from ballast gear and one sandbag recovered.
129.	Big Bend/Redding California	Mar. 14	Fragment of envelope, shrouds, and gas relief valve found.
130.	Mumtrak (Goodnews), Alaska	Mar. 15	Envelope with shrouds and gas relief valve recovered.

131.	Williams Lake, British Columbia	Mar. 15	Envelope reported found. See also No. 151.
132.	Chase, British Columbia	Mar. 15	Damaged envelope, gas relief valve, and ballast gear found.
133.	Baker Creek, British Columbia	Mar. 15	Two small fragments of balloon paper reported. Location uncertain—several Baker Creeks in B.C.
134.	Coquille/Riverton, Oregon	Mar. 15	Several fragments of balloon envelope recovered.
135.	Coram/Nyack, Montana	Mar. 16	Fragments of balloon paper found.
136.	Fort Babine, British Columbia	Mar. 17	Fragment of balloon paper found with gas relief valve attached.
137.	Sula, Montana	Mar. 17	Bomb fragments recovered on March 12; type not recorded.
138.	Kinak Bay, Alaska	Mar. 18	Fragments of balloon paper recovered following two explosions.
139.	Alexis Creek, British Columbia	Mar. 18	Large fragment of balloon paper reported to have landed about this date.
140.	Guerneville, California	Mar. 18	Paper fragment found. Possibly from No. 103.
141.	Glen, Montana	Mar. 18	One type B bomb recovered. See also No. 162.
142.	The Dalles, Oregon	Mar. 18	Fragments from one type B bomb recovered. See also No. 156.
143.	Garrison, Utah	Mar. 18	Balloon recovered with 19 shrouds, gas relief valve, ballast gear with battery, 28 pairs of unexploded blow-plugs, and five sandbags.
144.	Laurel, Montana	Mar. 18	Balloon recovered with shrouds and other parts.
145.	Marie Lake, Manitoba	Mar. 19	Balloon reported found W of Barrington Lake.
146.	Cedarvale, British Columbia	Mar. 19	Balloon with gas relief valve recovered.
147.	Sonoyta, Sonora (Mexico)	Mar. 19	Balloon with shrouds and gas relief valve recovered close to Arizona border; believed to have been shot down by U.S. fighter plane.
148.	Timnath, Colorado	Mar. 20	One unexploded type B bomb recovered along with fragments of an exploded type A bomb.
149.	Chadron, Nebraska	Mar. 20	Envelope recovered with 19 shrouds, gas relief valve, and ballast gear attached.
150.	Fort Chipewyan, Alberta	Mar. 20	Envelope, gas relief valve, and ballast gear recovered near W end of Lake Athabasca.
151.	Williams Lake, British Columbia	Mar. 20	Envelope with ballast gear and five ballast bags recovered.
152.	Denman Island, British Columbia	Mar. 20	Envelope recovered E of Vancouver Island with shrouds, ballast gear, and two unexploded type B bombs.
153.	Olds, Alberta	Mar. 20	Fragments from one type B bomb recovered S of Red Deer. See Nos. 154, 157, 174.
154.	Wimborne, Alberta	Mar. 20	Unidentified bomb fragments reported recovered SE of Red Deer. Possibly related to Nos. 153, 157, 174.
155.	Foremost, Alberta	Mar. 20	Balloon and parts of ballast gear recovered E of Lethbridge.
156.	The Dalles, Oregon	Mar. 20	Fragments of type B bomb recovered. Possibly related to No. 142.
157.	Delburne, Alberta	Mar. 20	Envelope with shrouds and one type A bomb found E of Red Deer. Possibly related to Nos. 153, 154, 174.
158.	Gillette, Wyoming	Mar. 21	Fragment of balloon paper found.
159.	Murphy, Oregon	Mar. 21	Fragments of balloon recovered on Powell Creek. See No. 206.
160.	Dillingham, Alaska	Mar. 21	Balloon with gas relief valve and one broken paper ballast bag recovered.
161.	Camsell Portage, Saskatchewan	Mar. 21	Envelope with gas relief valve, ballast gear, and one type B bomb recovered from N side of Lake Athabasca.
162.	Glen, Montana	Mar. 21	Missile seen falling followed by explosion. No fragments found but one unexploded type B bomb recovered. See also No. 141.
163.	Reno, Nevada	Mar. 22	Balloon shot down by P-63 fighter plane. Recovered with 19 shrouds, ballast gear, 12 pairs unexploded blow-plugs, three single blow-plugs, one sandbag, two unexploded type B bombs.

164.	Rogerson, Idaho	Mar. 22	Envelope with gas relief valve, and ballast gear with battery recovered.
165.	Ashcroft, British Columbia	Mar. 22	Balloon reported found in Thompson River valley. No details available.
166.	Volcano, California	Mar. 22	Envelope recovered with shrouds, gas relief valve, ballast gear, six pairs unexploded blow-plugs, eight single blow-plugs, and demolition charge.
167.	Basin/Sheridan, Wyoming	Mar. 22	Fragment of balloon paper recovered.
168.	Rome, Oregon	Mar. 22	Envelope with gas relief valve, shrouds, ballast gear, demolition charge, and three arming wires found in desert near village.
169.	Ree Heights/Wolsey, South Dakota	Mar. 22	Envelope reported found with ballast gear, one single blow-plug, and demolition charge.
170.	Barrier Lake, British Columbia	Mar. 23	Balloon reported recovered. No details announced.
171.	Desdemona, Texas	Mar. 23	Fragment of envelope found with envelope destructor attached, 19 shrouds, gas relief valve, ballast gear with battery, and remains of *two* exploded type A bombs. See also No. 175.
172.	Bethel, Alaska	Mar. 23	Gas relief valve found.
173.	Athabasca, Alberta	Mar. 23	Balloon reported found. No details available.
174.	Delburne, Alberta	Mar. 23	Fragment of balloon paper and shrouds reported. Possibly related to No. 157. See also Nos. 153, 154.
175.	Desdemona, Texas	Mar. 23	Unidentified bomb fragments found, possibly from No. 171.
175a.	Parkersburg, Oregon	Mar. 23	Envelope reported recovered near confluence of Bear Creek and Coquille River about three miles E of Bandon.
176.	Britain River, British Columbia	Mar. 24	Portion of envelope recovered.
176a.	Jervis Inlet, British Columbia	Mar. 24	Fragment of balloon envelope reported found.
177.	Osceola, Nebraska	Mar. 24	Envelope recovered with gas relief valve and shrouds; may have landed March 19.
178.	Woodson, Texas	Mar. 24	Section of envelope with 19 shrouds recovered.
178a.	Medicine Hat, Alberta	Mar. 24	Balloon envelope reported found.
179.	Hanson Island, Briitsh Columbia	Mar. 25	Fragment of balloon paper recovered north of Vancouver Island.
180.	Farmington, Michigan	Mar. 25	Fragments of type B bomb recovered.
181.	Kadoka, South Dakota	Mar. 26	Many small fragments of balloon envelope found.
182.	Strathmore, Alberta	Mar. 28	Balloon identified by aircraft lookout, shot down by Canadian fighter plane W of Calgary. Fragment of envelope and the gas relief valve recovered.
183.	Laguna Salada, Baja California (Mexico)	Mar. 28	Balloon shot down S of Imperial Valley, California, by U.S. fighter plane. Debris crashed in Mexico. Nothing reported recovered.
184.	Whitewater/Fort Ware, British Columbia	Mar. 28	Envelope with gas relief valve recovered along with 12 sandbags and two type B bombs.
185.	Canol Road, Yukon Ter.	Mar. 29	Fragments from an exploded type C bomb recovered. Report does not indicate where along road these fragments were found.
186.	Adrian, Oregon	Mar. 29	Bomb presumed to be type C reported found. See No. 187.
187.	Nyssa/Mitchell Butte, Oregon	Mar. 29	Two sandbags and type C bomb recovered. Perhaps a duplicate report of No. 186. Adrian and Nyssa are only ten miles apart along the Idaho border.
188.	Pyramid Lake/Nixon, Nevada	Mar. 29	Envelope, gas relief valve, shrouds, ballast gear but no battery, eleven pairs unexploded blow-plugs, one single blow-plug, five arming wires, and four ballast bags recovered. Indians chopped down tree to obtain envelope and shrouds.
188a.	Medicine Hat, Alberta	Mar. 29	Envelope from balloon called Medicine Hat No. 2 reported. See also No. 178a.
189.	Duchesne, Utah	Mar. 30	Envelope, gas relief valve, 19 shrouds, ballast gear, and demolition charge found.
190.	Grafton, North Dakota	Mar. 30	Envelope, gas relief valve, shrouds, ballast gear, demolition charge, and sandbags recovered.

191.	Bozeman, Montana	Mar. 30	Envelope, ballast gear, and four broken paper ballast bags recovered.
192.	Consul, Saskatchewan	Mar. 30	Envelope found with one unexploded type A bomb.
193.	Waterhen Lake, Manitoba	Mar. 30	Envelope with gas relief valve found.
194.	Red Elm, South Dakota	Mar. 30	Envelope with gas relief valve, shrouds, and ballast gear recovered.
195.	Marcus, South Dakota	Mar. 31	Fragments recovered from one type A bomb.
195a.	Barrier Lake, British Columbia	Mar. 31	Envelope and shrouds recovered.
196.	Ituna, Saskatchewan	Mar. 31	Envelope with gas relief valve recovered W of Yorkton.
197.	Dillon, Montana	Apr. 1	Fragments of envelope, gas relief valve, and shrouds found.
198.	Tampico, Washington	Apr. 1	Balloon fragments, parts of ballast gear, and one type B bomb found.
199.	Hoopa Indian Reservation, California	Apr. 1	Heavily damaged balloon, gas relief valve, shrouds, ballast gear, and demolition charge recovered.
200.	Hay River, Northwest Ter.	Apr. 1	Fragment of envelope, ballast gear, seven sandbags, two unexploded type B bombs found near Great Slave Lake.
201.	Colville, Washington	Apr. 1	Envelope, envelope destructor, and unknown number of shrouds recovered.
201a.	Yorkton, Saskatchewan	Apr. 1	Envelope reported found.
202.	Harper, Oregon	Apr. 3	Fragments of envelope, gas relief valve, shrouds, and ballast ring found.
203.	Walla Walla, Washington	Apr. 3	Envelope recovered with gas relief valve, ballast gear, four single blow-plugs, demolition charge, and one arming wire.
204.	Massacre Lake, Nevada	Apr. 5	Envelope, gas relief valve, shrouds, ballast gear, and other parts recovered.
204a.	Lawford Lake, Manitoba	Apr. 5	Fragment of paper envelope found.
205.	Turner, Montana	Apr. 6	Balloon reported recovered. No additional details.
205a.	Casper, Wyoming	Apr. 6	Balloon envelope reported found.
206.	Provolt, Oregon	Apr. 7	Fragments of balloon recovered. Possibly related to No. 159.
207.	Merritt, British Columbia	Apr. 8	Envelope, gas relief valve, shrouds, ballast gear, picric acid demolition block, and one type C bomb recovered.
208.	Southern Indian Lake, Manitoba	Apr. 10	Envelope and other parts reported.
209.	Plano, Idaho	Apr. 10	Sandbag and attaching hook found about 6 miles NW of Rexburg. Possibly from No. 69.
210.	Bald Mountain, Oregon	Apr. 10	Envelope recovered along with ballast gear, two sandbags, one type A and four type B unexploded bombs. (Location not clear; could be in Polk or Curry county.)
211.	Attu Is., Aleutians, Alaska	Apr. 12	Balloon intercepted by F6F Navy fighter plane, shot down W of Massacre Bay. Nothing recovered.
212.	Rome, Oregon	Apr. 12	"Complete" balloon and parts found.
213.	Attu Is., Aleutians, Alaska	Apr. 13	Nine balloons shot down over Massacre Bay by Navy 6F6 fighter planes at 30,000-37,000-foot altitudes; none recovered. Many more tracked by 11th Air Force but not intercepted. Signal Corps radar sets used included SCR-588, -516, -270-D, -270-AA, and -270-DA. According to War Dept. Mil. Intell. Div. General Report No. 5, 1 June 1945, "Tracking was difficult because of high altitude . . . and number of balloons."
214.	Little Sitkin Is., Aleutians, Alaska	Apr. 13	Balloon shot down at sea—not recovered.
215.	Wolsey, South Dakota	Apr. 13	Large fragment of balloon found, perhaps from No. 169.
215a.	Grants Pass, Oregon	Apr. 14	Fragment of envelope paper found.
216.	Midas Creek, Alaska	Apr. 15	An Indian boy found remnants of a balloon about Apr. 10 on a tributary of the Noatak River at 67°50'N-156°30'W and, taking his first plane ride, guided Sgt. Albert Leverson from Ladd Field to it. A fragment of envelope, shrouds, ballast gear, a blow-plug, the demolition charge, and four arming wires were recovered.

217.	Adak Is., Aleutians, Alaska	Apr. 15	Balloon shot down at sea at 52°46′N-178°30′W. Nothing salvaged.
218.	Bethel, Alaska	Apr. 15	Two boxes of type usually containing aneroids found.
219.	Amchitka Is., Aleutians, Alaska	Apr. 15	Envelope, gas relief valve, shrouds, and ballast gear recovered.
220.	Tyee, Oregon	Apr. 15	Fragments of balloon recovered.
220a.	Bering Sea, Alaska	Apr. 15	Discovery of envelope in sea at 55°46′N-172°24′W, north of the Aleutian Islands reported.
221.	Snowville, Utah	Apr. 16	Large fragment of balloon paper recovered.
222.	Platinum, Alaska	Apr. 16	Balloon reported shot down.
222a.	North Pacific Ocean	Apr. 16	Fragment of envelope and part of ballast gear found at 41°46′N-171°47′W.
223.	Boundary Bay, British Columbia	Apr. 17	Balloon found near U.S. border with gas relief valve and two bombs, one type C and one incendiary type not identified.
223a.	Moresby Island, British Columbia	Apr. 23	Balloon envelope reported found.
224.	Morice Lake, British Columbia	Apr. 17	Balloon recovered complete with envelope, gas relief valve, shrouds, ballast gear, 22 sandbags, and two unexploded type B bombs.
225.	Wapato, Washington	Apr. 19	Fragments of balloon paper found.
226.	Tikchik Lake, Alaska	Apr. 20	Envelope, with damaged gas relief valve, ballast gear, demolition charge, and other parts recovered.
227.	Vedder Mountain, British Columbia	Apr. 20	Balloon reported grounded near U.S. border. Recovered by Canadian search team.
228.	Watson Lake, Yukon Ter.	Apr. 20	Parts of a balloon reported found.
229.	Chilliwack, British Columbia	Apr. 20	Envelope and unstated number of shrouds found.
229a.	Coahuila, Mexico	Apr. 20	Balloon envelope reported found.
230.	Elko, Nevada	Apr. 21	Fragment of envelope with gas relief valve found.
231.	Phillipsburg, Montana	Apr. 21	Envelope with gas relief valve recovered.
232.	Queen Charlotte Is., British Columbia	Apr. 23	Rubberized silk balloon with gas relief valve No. 15, salvaged from ocean W of Queen Charlotte Islands at 53°3′N-135°52′W.
233.	Lake of the Woods, Oregon	Apr. 23	Fragment of envelope found with shrouds, shock absorber, ballast gear, and demolition block. See Nos. 281, 284.
234.	Kitchener, British Columbia	Apr. 24	Envelope with shrouds found E of Creston.
234a.	Lucile, Idaho	Apr. 24	Fragment of envelope reported found.
235.	Paragonah, Utah	Apr. 25	Fragment of balloon paper found.
235a.	Loring/Dodson, Montana	Apr. 25	Envelope fragment and shrouds recovered.
236.	Beatty, Oregon	Apr. 26	Fragment of balloon paper found.
236a.	Buffalo, South Dakota	Apr. 26	Fragment of balloon envelope reported found.
237.	Akiak, Alaska	Apr. 28	Envelope with gas relief valve, three single blow-plugs, five arming wires, and two sandbags found about 25 miles N of Bethel.
237a.	Dome Creek, British Columbia	Apr. 29	One type B incendiary bomb reported found.
237b.	Vanderhoof/Stuart Lake, British Columbia	Apr. 29	Fragment of balloon envelope reported found. See No. 251.
238.	Moxee City, Washington	Apr. 30	Balloon parts recovered, possibly from No. 97.
239.	Huntington, Oregon	May 2	Paper fragments recovered.
239a.	Mount Rainier, Washington	May 3	Burned fragment of envelope reported found.

240.	Bly, Oregon	May 5	Envelope, envelope destructor, gas relief valve, eight sandbags, and four type B bombs recovered after type C bomb had exploded killing a woman and five children. (See Ch. IX)
241.	Stettler, Alberta	May 5	Envelope fragments found.
242.	Enterprise, Oregon	May 12	Unidentified incendiary bomb found. See No. 245.
243.	Kelvington, Saskatchewan	May 15	Gas relief valve and assorted ballast gear recovered.
243a.	Snowdrift, Northwest Ter.	May 15	Envelope with shroud lines recovered.
244.	Chilliwack, British Columbia	May 20	Envelope recovered with gas relief valve, shrouds, ballast gear, two sandbags, one type A bomb, and two type B bombs.
245.	Enterprise, Oregon	May 21	Balloon fragments found. Possibly related to No. 242.
246.	Milo, Alberta	May 23	Fragments of balloon paper found.
247.	Asotin, Washington	May 25	Fragments of balloon parts found in mountains W of Snake River.
248.	Harper, Oregon	May 25	Fragments of balloon parts recovered.
249.	Madison, South Dakota	May 26	One unexploded type B bomb recovered.
250.	Summer Lake, Oregon	May 26	Small fragments of envelope, shrouds, and ballast ring found.
251.	Vanderhoof, British Columbia	May 26	Fragments of paper balloon found W of Prince George. Possibly duplicate of No. 237b report.
252.	Soldier Mountain, California	May 26	Fragments of envelope found.
253.	High River, Alberta	May 28	Damaged envelope and ballast gear recovered S of Calgary.
254.	Chilanko River, British Columbia	May 29	Fragments of envelope, two type B bombs, and other parts recovered.
255.	Pryor, Montana	June 1	Fragment of balloon envelope recovered.
256.	Jordan Valley, Oregon	June 7	Small fragments of envelope found. (Location indefinite. Two Jordan Valleys in Oregon several hundred miles apart.)
257.	Mahogany Mountain, Oregon	June 8	Fragments of envelope and parts of ballast ring found. A paper tag had this notation in Japanese: "No. 168 balloon, 31 January 1945. 7 hours 50 minutes, No. 10 squad." Probably refers to assembly of the balloon. (Military History Div., War Dept. General Report No. 7, "Japanese Free Balloons and Related Incidents," 1 Aug 1945). See No. 258.
258.	Mahogany Mountain, Oregon	June 9	Additional fragments found. See No. 257.
259.	Collbran, Colorado	June 12	Small fragment of envelope recovered.
260.	Egegik, Alaska	June 14	Balloon reported grounded—other details lacking.
261.	Skukum Creek, Yukon	June 15	Fragment of balloon envelope found at 60°11′N-135°23′W.
262.	Whitecourt, Alberta	June 15	Two fragments of balloon found NW of Edmonton.
263.	Mayo, Yukon Ter.	June 16	Fragments of balloon envelope recovered.
264.	Anchorage, Alaska	June 18	Envelope recovered with gas relief valve, ballast gear, three sandbags, two type B bombs, and one type C bomb.
265.	Mahood Lake, British Columbia	June 18	Fragments of envelope recovered.
266.	Tampico, Washington	June 21	Balloon, complete with parts, recovered.
267.	Yahk, British Columbia	June 23	Paper fragments recovered.
268.	Gilmore, Idaho	June 24	Balloon with shrouds recovered in Lemhi Mountains.
269.	Hailey, Idaho	June 24	Balloon with shrouds and ballast gear found.
270.	Old Crow River, Yukon Ter.	June 24	Fragments of envelope found.
271.	Dease Lake, British Columbia	June 27	Envelope, additional parts found with one type B bomb and fragments from two exploded type B bombs.
272.	Ajo, Arizona	July 2	Damaged envelope, gas relief valve, and shrouds recovered.

272a.	Nanoose Bay, British Columbia	July 2	Envelope, gas relief valve, ballast gear, eight sandbags, and one type A bomb recovered.
273.	Boulder, Montana	July 4	Approximately 25 percent of an envelope found.
274.	Hyatt Lake, Oregon	July 5	Damaged balloon with gas relief valve and shrouds found in trees near lake about 25 miles E of Ashland. Official report lists one type B unexploded bomb recovered. An eyewitness claims "three or four round cylinders plus one bomb that had dropped off near the [lake] shore that two boys had found but stayed away from because the Bly incident had been a warning." Plausible that bomb mentioned in Nos. 10, 14 had ejected from this balloon, then balloon not discovered for six months because of winter snows in Hyatt Lake area. (See p. 122.)
275.	Alberni, British Columbia	July 5	Vancouver Island recovery team found envelope with gas relief valve, ballast gear, one type C bomb, and one unexploded incendiary bomb.
276.	Lake Hyatt, Oregon	July 5	Duplicate entry of No. 274.
277.	Monida, Montana	July 6	Envelope with shroud lines recovered.
278.	Aishihik, Yukon Ter.	July 11	Envelope found with gas relief valve, shrouds, and ballast gear.
279.	Jiggs, Nevada	July 12	Envelope with shrouds, ballast gear parts including aneroids recovered.
280.	Salmo, British Columbia	July 16	Fragments of envelope and shrouds recovered.
281.	Mt. McLoughlin, Oregon	July 18	Incendiary bomb, condition and type not stated, found on mountain formerly known as Mt. Pitt NE of Medford. Possibly related to No. 233.
282.	Lillooet, British Columbia	July 19	Envelope with shroud lines reported found.
283.	North Pacific Ocean	July 19	Balloon shot down by U.S. Navy aircraft 420 miles ESE of Tokyo. Sank before recovery. Not likely a bomb-carrying balloon as launchings of these ceased nearly three months earlier. (Chapter X)
284.	Mt. McLoughlin, Oregon	July 20	One type B bomb (unexploded) found. See Nos. 233, 281.
285.	Indian Springs, Nevada	July 20	Envelope, gas relief valve, and shrouds recovered about 40 miles NW of Las Vegas.
286.	Nunivak Island, Alaska	July 20	Small fragment of envelope recovered.
287.	Adams Lake Plateau, British Columbia	July 24	Balloon reported found about 50 miles NE of Kamloops.
288.	Bald Mountain, Oregon	July 24	Balloon had landed several months earlier but was not seen until snows melted (elevation 7,445 ft.). Sighted by Jean P. Groth, Bald Mountain lookout on Fremont National Forest; recovered following day by military and Forest Service team. In addition to nearly intact balloon with shrouds and ballast gear were five bombs, recorded only as "incendiary—unexploded."
289.	Sicamous, British Columbia	July 25	Small fragment of balloon paper found.
290.	Chase, British Columbia	July 25	Envelope, shrouds, and ballast gear recovered.
291.	Babb, Montana	July 27	Damaged balloon recovered. No other details.
292.	Kettle River Valley, British Columbia	Aug. 1	Small fragment of paper found about 40 miles E of Penticton.
293.	Unalaska Is., Aleutians, Alaska	Aug. 2	Ballast gear recovered on Cathedral Point.
294.	Idaho Falls, Idaho	Aug. 9	Envelope, gas relief valve, and unstated number of shrouds recovered.
295.	McBride, British Columbia	Aug. 13	Envelope, shrouds, ballast gear, and two unexploded type B bombs recovered.
296.	Hillcrest, British Columbia	Aug. 13	Several small fragments of balloon paper found.
297.	Wood Buffalo National Park, Alberta	no date	Remains of ballast gear recovered by a trapper in the park who carried them to the Royal Canadian Mounted Police at Fort Vermilion by dog team.

Numbered incidents: 297. Sub-numbered incidents: 45. Total incidents: 342.

APPENDIX C

Postwar Balloon/Bomb Incidents

In early October 1945, on Coleman Rim east of Bly, Oregon, three hunters (Joe Rinard, J. S. McDonald, and J. W. Teague) from Medford found a large piece (about 80%) of a partially exploded 5-kg candle-type incendiary fused to a rock. The site is 17.5 miles east and .6 miles north of Bly in Township 36-S, Range 17-E, Section 34 Willamette Meridian, below the east ledge of Coleman Rim. Rinard dug the bomb and attached ballast ring mounting hook out of the rock with his pocket knife and reported his recovery to Army authorities at Camp White near Medford.

The U.S. Forest Service Bulletin for October 1945 reports the finding of remains of a balloon or bomb near Klamath Falls, Oregon, on October 17.

In the fall of 1946, near Merlin, Oregon, a damaged ballast ring was found in the top of a tree felled by loggers. The ground near the tree was scorched in three places. In the center of each six-foot-wide burned area was a spent blow-plug. The recovered ring contained three unfired blow-plugs.

On April 26, 1947, Captain G. I. Cunningham and Frank Armstrong, while digging clams on a beach near Eureka, California, found three thermite bombs, which they identified as the type dropped from Japanese balloons.

In the summer of 1948, Archie Ostrander and another hiker found the remains of a balloon, deteriorated rope, and pieces of metal near highway 199 in the Six Rivers National Forest in Del Norte County, California. The site is about 800 yards north of the confluence of Myrtle Creek and the Middle Fork of the Smith River, in Township 16-N, Range 1-E, Section 3, Humboldt Meridian —about 5.5 miles southwest of Gasquet Ranger Station.

On March 4, 1949, near Montesano, Washington, Grays Harbor Sheriff Mike Kilgore recovered a 14 x 20 inch fragment of an envelope, a ballast ring with wiring and fuse links, about 15 blow-plugs, 3 aneroids, remains of a 5-kg candle-type incendiary, and a picric acid self-destruct charge. He turned them over to Navy Explosive Ordnance men from Seattle.

In August 1954, Ralph G. Merton and another hiker in the Modoc National Forest sighted large balloon fragments and ropes near Emerson Peak. Because the terrain was rugged and they were carrying loaded backpacks, they made no attempt to retrieve any of the pieces.

In 1954 near the Scheenjek River in Alaska, bush pilot Don Hulshizer spotted a balloon on the ground. Because of the rough terrain, the Air Force helicopter sent to recover it could not land but dropped Intelligence Officer Lt. Harold L. Hale to investigate. Hale hid the paper envelope under a tree to avoid it being reported again; then he loaded the rest of the gear into the hovering helicopter. Analysis of the bombs at an ordnance center indicated that the explosives were still potent.

In the summer of 1956 two fishermen in southern Oregon found a double ballast ring with bakelite insulation plate and a picric acid self-destruct block in the forest about 3.5 miles south of Pelican Butte Lookout in Winema National Forest. The demolition charge was picked up by an explosive ordnance team from Kingsley AFB, Klamath Falls. The ballast rings are now on display at Klamath County Museum in Klamath Falls.

In January 1966, on Neah-Kah-Nie Mountain near Nehalem, Oregon, Frank Corder and another man found an undamaged ballast ring with bakelite insert disc, several blow-plugs and arming wires and a picric acid self-destruct block. The Tillamook County Sheriff's Department turned the items over to the 53rd Army Ordnance Detachment demolitions experts from Vancouver Barracks, Washington.

In early 1968, at Clatskanie, Oregon, members of the 53rd Army Ordnance Detachment from Vancouver Barracks, Washington, retrieved assorted parts from a Japanese balloon. □

Remnants of Japanese balloons found in the Pacific Northwest since World War II. (left) A partially burned out incendiary found on Coleman Rim in southern Oregon. (opposite page) Unexploded blow-plugs in the chandelier ring found near Merlin, Oregon (top left). Fragment of envelope, chandelier ring, aneroid barometer, and picric acid block found near Montesano, Washington (top right). Chandelier ring and gear found on Pelican Butte, now on display in the Klamath County Museum, Klamath Falls, Oregon (below right). Chandelier ring, insert disc, and picric acid block found near Neah-Kah-Nie, Oregon (below left).

149

Some of the former officers and crew members of the Japanese submarines *I-25* and *I-26* who contributed information for this book. Nobuo Fujita with his grandson Toshiki in 1970. Meiji Tagami in 1973. Minoru Hasegawa in 1973.

Fujita *(I-25)*

Tagami *(I-25)*

Hasegawa *(I-26)*

Shoji Aizawa

Sadao Iijima

Kou Maki

Togoro Okamoto

Sensuke Tao

Crew members of *I-25*, above and left.
Crew members of *I-26*, right.

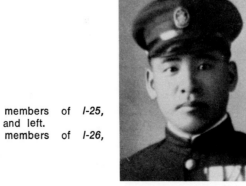

Saburo Hayashi

Takaji Komaba

150

Sources, Acknowledgments, and Notes

General Acknowledgments

Several individuals in addition to those mentioned in the Preface deserve special recognition for their assistance. During the early months of this project, my friend and colleague, Richard J. Portal, head of the reference department of the Jackson County Library System in Medford, Ore., guided me over, around, and under stumbling blocks that had defied others. Another friend and neighbor, Robert G. Emmens (Col. USAF Ret.), one of Doolittle's Tokyo Raiders, provided published materials and background information and introduced me to Ted W. Lawson, another of the Raiders. David L. Barker, also of Medford, with much-appreciated persistence searched the literature on the GLEN aircraft and provided information. J. Larry Kemp, Concord, Calif., loaned his extensive files and photo collection on Japanese submarine attacks along the Pacific Coast. Tom Harlan, U.S. Forest Service Region 6, supplied maps of all of the national forests of the region, which were a great help, especially in studies of balloon and bomb landing sites.

Authors of several of the references listed in this section gave encouragement and additional information. These include Carroll V. Glines, James A. Gibbs, Marshall Hanft, Emanuel R. Lewis, Kou Maki, Robert C. Mikesh, George Nicholson, Clark G. Reynolds, Grahame F. Shrader, Joanne Stathos, and Amos L. Wood.

In Japan quite a number of former servicemen, librarians, archivists, and newspapermen have provided indispensable assistance. Those with a special knowledge of the subject matter of this book who gave unstintingly of their time and effort to provide accurate information include:

Nobuo Fujita, pilot of the reconnaissance plane on the *I-25* submarine

Meiji Tagami, wartime commander of *I-25*

Tatsuo Tsukudo, first (or executive) officer on *I-25*

Minoru Hasegawa, formerly Minoru Yokoda, wartime commander of *I-26*

Kiyoshi Tanaka, who was the officer in charge of the Japanese Navy's long-range balloon development team.

I am indebted to the "Action Line" desk of the *Mainichi Daily News,* Tokyo, for putting me in touch with Mr. Fujita.

Rear Admiral James S. Russell (USN Ret.), Tacoma, Wash., has given valued advice and assistance, especially in corresponding with Vice Admiral Hiroichi Samejima, Fleet Air Force, Japan Maritime Self-Defense Force. It was through them that I obtained the address of Mr. Hasegawa and started an extensive correspondence with the former submarine commander.

I am fortunate in having Mrs. Keiko Nakamura Thurston of Central Point, Ore., not only as a translator and interpreter but also as a perceptive adviser. As a graduate in physics from the Tokyo College of Science with a fluent command of English, Mrs. Thurston has added professional insight in her translation of technical papers. She has made a vital contribution to this book. □

General References

Bergamini, David. *Japan's Imperial Conspiracy*. Morrow, 1971.

Conn, Stetson, Rose C. Engelman, and Byron Fairchild. *Guarding the United States and Its Outposts, U.S. Army in World War II: The Western Hemisphere.* Chief of Military History, Department of the Army, Washington, D. C., 1964.

Craven, Wesley Frank and James Lea Cate. *The Army Air Forces in World War II*. Vol I. University of Chicago Press, 1948.

Emmens, Robert G. *Guests of the Kremlin*. Macmillan, 1949.

Fujita, Nobuo. "Only Man to Attack American Mainland," in *Tora! Tora! Tora!*, Pacific War Documentary, Vol. I, pp. 147-168 (in Japanese). Tokyo: Konnichi no Wadai Co., 1967, 3rd printing, 1970. Also in *Today's Topix*, No. 4, Special Issue [ca. 1954], pp. 10-13, 26-35.

Fujita, Nobuo and Joseph D. Harrington. "I Bombed the U.S.A." United States Naval Institute *Proceedings*, June 1961, pp. 64-69.

Glines, Carroll V. *Doolittle's Tokyo Raiders*. Van Nostrand, 1964.

Gibbs, James A. *Pacific Graveyard*. Binfords, 1955; *Shipwrecks of the Pacific Coast*. Binfords, 1962; *Shipwrecks of Juan de Fuca*. Binfords, 1968; *Disaster Log of Ships*. Superior, 1971.

Hanft, Marshall. "The Cape Forts, Guardians of the Columbia." *Oregon Historical Quarterly*, Dec. 1964; reprinted by Oregon Historical Society, 1973.

Hashimoto, Mochitsura. *Sunk! The Story of the Japanese Submarine Fleet 1941-1945;* tr. by E. H. M. Colegrave. Holt, 1954.

Holmes, William J. *Undersea Victory*. Doubleday, 1966.

Ito, Masanori. *The End of the Imperial Japanese Navy*. Norton, 1962.

Lawson, Ted W. *Thirty Seconds Over Tokyo*. Random House, 1943.

Maki, Kou. *The Mission of I-25: Secret Document on American Mainland Attack* (in Japanese). Tokyo: Ushio Publishing Co., 1956. Based on Maki's diary when he was known as Kou Okamura, a chief petty officer in the *I-25*. Also published in revised form with pencil sketches by the author in *Today's Topics* (in Japanese), Vol. 102, June 1962.

Merrill, James M. *Target Tokyo*, Rand McNally, 1964.

Morison, Samuel Eliot. *History of the United States Naval Operations in World War II*. Little, Brown and Co. Vol. III, "The Rising Sun in the Pacific, 1931-April 1942," 1958; Vol. IV, "Coral Sea, Midway and Submarine Actions, May 1942-August 1942," 1950; Vol. VII, "Aleutians, Gilberts and Marshals, June 1942-April 1944," 1951.

Roscoe, Theodore. *United States Destroyer Operations in World War II*. U.S. Naval Institute, 1953.

Rush, Philip S. *A History of the Californias*. Privately printed, 1958.

Shrader, Grahame F. *The Phantom War of the Pacific Northwest*. Privately printed, 1969.

Watts, Anthony J. and Brian G. Gordon. *The Imperial Japanese Navy*. Doubleday, 1971.

152

PREFACE

A number of historians have come to the conclusion that the Japanese attacks on North America were motivated by the Doolittle raid of April 1942. Conn, Engleman, and Fairchild (1964), for example, say that the final west coast submarine operation of August/October 1942 "was undertaken expressly as a reprisal for the American bombardment of Tokyo," (p. 93) and quote a Tokyo press story after the war as stating, "The balloon bomb was Japan's V-1 weapon in efforts to get revenge for the Doolittle raid." (p. 113) See also: Craven and Cate (1948), Vol. I., pp. 298-299; Glines (1964), p. 395 (listed in General References).

SOURCES FOR INCIDENTS MENTIONED IN THE PREFACE:

The accidental shelling of the Southern Pacific passenger train on May 12, 1944, was reported in the San Luis Obispo *Telegram-Tribune* the next day and on May 15. See also Del Schrader, "Lifting the Lid on Old War Secrets," Los Angeles *Herald-Examiner*, May 13, 1973, p. A9. As a result of the explosion, Vertie Bea Loggins, a kitchen worker from Los Angeles, lost her arm. HR 4491, 79th Congress, 1st Session, Oct. 24, 1945, provided her with a Congressional award of $5,000. According to relatives, she died from an unrelated cause in 1958. The others hurt were Alice Jones and Emil Strong of Los Angeles. The report filed by the claims officer, Lt. Lyle G. Weller, was dated 27 Sep 1944 and filed with the Service Command Unit No. 1908, Camp Cooke, California.

Vertie Bea Loggins

The sketch of bamboo periscopes is reproduced with the author's permission from *Today's Topics*, Vol. 102, June 1962, p. 52.

The news story about a submarine hull found at Cape Kiwanda with James Buchanan's by-line appeared in the *Oregon Journal*, Aug. 3, 1972.

For loss of *M. S. Clevedon*, see Gibbs (1971), p. 62; *Merchant Vessels of the United States*, Vol. 1944, p. 753.

Tahoe incident: San Francisco *Chronicle*, Jan. 27, 1942. Mr. Hasegawa says that soon after the alleged incident he met his friend Genichi Shibata, commander of *I-23*, in Kwajalein. Shibata "did not say anything to me and I did not hear anyone else tell of bumping into a garbage boat, nor did I see any scar or damage to *I-23* to indicate such an occurrence. *I-23* was sunk with all hands on its next mission." (Letter, 1974.) For sinking of *I-23*, see Roscoe (1953), p. 112; Ito (1962), p. 245; Watts and Gordon (1971), p. 334.

Shrader (1969) relates a number of other incidents suspected of being caused by enemy action but which turned out to be the result of other causes. □

INTRODUCTION

Of the many books and articles about the Doolittle raid among the best are Lawson (1943), Emmens (1949), Glines (1964), and Merrill (1964).

One of the B-25 Mitchell bombers that lifted off the deck of the *Hornet* on the morning of April 18, 1942, and started its 620-mile flight toward Japan was piloted by Lt. Edgar E. McElroy. Lt. Richard A. Knobloch was co-pilot, Lt. Clayton J. Campbell, navigator, Sgt. Adam R. Williams, engineer-gunner, and Sgt. Robert C. Bourgeois, bombardier. Admiral Halsey had hoped to be much closer to Japan before launching Lt. Col. Doolittle's flight of 16 Army planes on their bombing mission, but a Japanese patrol craft had been sighted and Halsey assumed—correctly, as it turned out—that it had radioed a warning of the approaching American force. He therefore changed the attack plan and ordered an immediate launch. This early launch meant more flying time and a daylight rather than a night attack on Japanese cities.

The McElroy-Knobloch B-25 (No. 40-2247) was the thirteenth ("Lucky 13th") to take off from the carrier and was assigned to strike the naval yard at Yokosuka, on a peninsula 30 miles south of Tokyo. As the plane came in over Tokyo Bay and flew over the naval station at low altitude, Lt. Knobloch picked up his pocket camera and snapped pictures out of the right cockpit window, taking what turned out to be the only photographs of the raid that finally got back to the United States (Glines, chapter 19).

Ahead of them in an inner harbor lay a ship and four submarines in adjacent drydocks. Bombardier Bourgeois dropped his four 500-pound bombs, one of which hit the 10,000-ton submarine tender *Taigei*, which was being converted into an aircraft carrier and which was later renamed *Ryuho*.

Two officers of the I-25 submarine witnessed the attack. First Officer Tatsuo Tsukudo wrote me his recollections (in English) in 1974: "When the Doolittle's plane bombed the 'Taigei' in Yokosuka, I was on board the I-25 which was dry docking next to Taigei's with three other boats of the same squadron. We were [notified of]

the approach of the U. S. carrier task group on Saturday (18 Apr.) morning and expected the air raid at night or next day dawn. But near the Saturday noon, condition yellow (*Keikai Keiho*) [seek immediate cover] was ordered.

"I made all the shipyard worker go outboard and the crew stay inside the hull in order to avoid unnecessary casualty. My boat was stripped of its 14-cm deck gun. So I only left Mr. Fujita and several enlisted men on the bridge as lookout. I believed Fujita would make best recognition for enemy aircraft.

"Sometime between 1230 and 1300 [hours], a Mitchel plane bombed the 'Taigei' in Dry Dock No. 4 [which] was about 100 meter from my boat in Dry Dock No. 5. The shock was like a medium grade earthquake. The damage was kept secret in that time except for a short news, 'hull and personnel suffered minor damage.'"

Warrant Officer Fujita had received special aircraft recognition training because he was the pilot of the submarine's reconnaissance aircraft. He remembers that day well. He told me by telephone in August 1974 that earlier that day in 1942 he had taken a harbor boat over to the submarine mother ship *Brazil* to obtain aircraft repair parts. He had returned to the I-25 and looked up to the bridge just as a lookout shouted, "The enemy plane!"

Mr. Fujita also describes the incident in *Tora! Tora! Tora!* (p. 138): "I heard and felt a tremendous explosion as if we were knocked in the head. It was very swift. There I stood still clutching the aircraft parts. I estimated the altitude of the bomber to be about 300 to 400 meters. I could clearly see the 'star' insignia of the U.S.A. and could easily see the plane had twin engines.

"The chief gunner shouted, 'Start firing!' so [our twin 25-mm machine guns] shot at the plane but the plane banked to a different course to do other bombing and our guns could not reach it.

"We were all tense and expected more planes but all our lookouts could see was a flight of our own planes about 8,000 meters above, but our planes did not seem to know about the plane which had bombed us." (Translations by Keiko Thurston.)

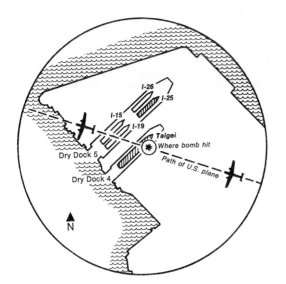 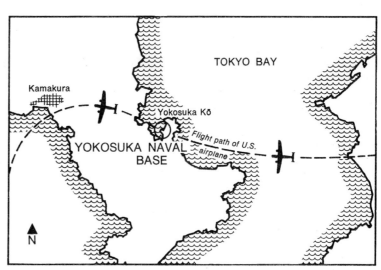

The flight path of B-25 No. 40-2247 over Tokyo Bay and the Yokosuka Naval Base on April 18, 1942, as estimated by Tatsuo Tsukudo, former First Officer of the *I-25* submarine.

At the request of Mr. Tsukudo, the Japanese War History Institute provided some additional information about the damage done: "The bomb hit the starboard outboard, about the height of waterline. The hole was about 8 meter (height) by 15 meter (length) . . . Casualty was five personnels were suffered from medium grade burnt. It is not certain whether they were crew or shipyard workers."

The other submarines docked nearby were *I-15*, *I-19*, and *I-26*. Mr. Hasegawa says he did not witness the bombing because he and most of the *I-26* crew were at Atami, a health resort 35 miles southwest of Yokosuka. He says, "TAIGEI was our prewar mothership on which we sent the men for rest and baths. In April 1942 a U.S. plane bombed TAIGEI, but when I visited the ship two days later I believe the bomb exploded against the inside bottom of the drydock and the blast ripped the hole in the side of TAIGEI. The position of the hole makes it impossible for the bomb to have hit the ship with the bomb falling from the sky. The hole between the bridge and the bow was at least five meters wide."

See also Watts and Gordon (1971), pp. 193, 198; Merrill, p. 97.

After bombing Yokosuka, the U.S. plane headed back out to sea, followed the Japanese coast south, and then swung westward toward China. Late that night, in a heavy rainstorm, when the fuel gauges registered empty, Lt. McElroy ordered the crew to bail out. They landed in rice paddies near Poyang, China. Friendly Chinese eventually led them to safety (Glines, chapter 19).

As a result of the 16-plane raid, "Fifty Japanese were dead, 252 wounded, and ninety factory buildings gutted. A fuel farm and six large gas tanks had been subtracted from Japan's most precious stockpile, her liquid fuel." (Bergamini, p. 911.)

The quotation from Saburo Sakai is from *Samurai!* (Dutton, 1957), p. 148. The cousin he later married was Hatsuvo, "pretty as a movie star—an accomplished pianist . . . She survived the war with me, only to die of poverty and illness two short years later." p. 272. □

CHAPTER I: THE WAR BELOW

General references for this chapter include Morison, III, pp. 87, 221, *passim*; IV, pp. 170, 198; Maki (1956); Watts and Gordon (1971), pp. 297-372.

Daniel C. Carnegie, Ashland, Oregon, a retired steam and diesel engineer on seagoing ships and Puget Sound ferry boats, reviewed and discussed technical data on ship and submarine propulsion plants.

The crew of the *I-25* varied in number from 96 to 108. After the 1941-1942 operations in the eastern Pacific, a number of them were transferred to other duty and survived the war. Others, however, were lost later in the war. Shoji Okuda, Fujita's observer on the submarine's aircraft, is reported to have been killed in October 1944 when he took part in an air attack on the U.S. carrier striking force off Taiwan. Other crew members went down with the *I-25* when it was sunk in the central Pacific in 1943.

Survivors of the *I-25* crew (in addition to Tagami, Tsukudo, and Fujita) who have graciously shared their recollections and diaries, include Shoji Aizawa, Kyozo Suzuki, and Tyojiro Yamamoto, torpedomen; Sadao Iijima and Sensuke Tao (formerly Sensuke Izutu), gunners; Shigeji Minamide and Shinichi Nakagawa, engineers; Moriichi Kikuchi, diesel engineer; Kou Maki (formerly

Kou Okamura), sound detector SONAR; Togoro Okamoto, electric motor engineer; and Shichido Wakabayashi, messenger-lookout-catapult launcher. To all of these gentlemen I extend my thanks and send best wishes for continued good health.

A model of the type B-1 Japanese submarine, similar to the *I-19*, *I-25*, and *I-26* with gun on after deck and hangar, catapult, and reconnaissance plane on forward deck.

THE GLEN AIRCRAFT SOURCES

General View of Japanese Military Aircraft in the Pacific War (in Japanese with English translation). Tokyo: Kanto-Sha, Ltd., n.d., pp. 55-60, 160.

Green, William. *Warplanes of Second World War*, Vol. 6, "Float-Planes." Doubleday, 1962, rev. 1968, pp. 138-140.

Jane's All the World's Aircraft, 1945-46, p. 175c.

Kubota, Akitoshi. *Maru Special Photo Library* (in Japanese). Tokyo, Sept. 1971, pp. 8-13.

Watts and Gordon (1971), pp. 331-335. Discusses specifications and service life of type A-1 and type B-1 submarines which carried GLEN aircraft.

Admiral Samejima says that during the testing of this aircraft, which began in 1937, some modifications were made. The tail design was changed to extend the vertical stabilizer "to prevent excessive side-slip."

A model of the GLEN reconnaissance seaplane of the type used by Nobuo Fujita to drop bombs in Oregon.

154

THE S. S. *Cynthia Olson*

Allen, Gwenfread. *Hawaii's War Years 1941-1944.* University of Hawaii Press, 1950, p. 58.

Bergamini, 1971, p. 844.

Porteus, Stanley. *A Century of Social Thinking in Hawaii.* Pacific Books, 1962, pp. 210-213.

Pratte, Alf, series on sinking of *Cynthia Olson*, Honolulu *Star-Bulletin*, Dec. 3-8, 1966.

Russell, William W. "Eyewitness to Infamy," *V.F.W. Magazine*, Dec. 1973, p. 9.

Webber, Bert. "Some Historians Believe NW Ship Sunk by Japanese Before Pearl Harbor." *Oregon Journal*, Dec. 7, 1972, Sec. 2, p. 1.

Correspondence with Mr. Hasegawa has been graciously translated by the Rev. John M. Tsutada, President of Immanuel Bible College in Yokohama. Correspondence with other surviving crew members of the *I-26* has been translated by Keiko Thurston.

Chief Gunner Saburo Hayashi says that while loading ammunition before leaving Japan it was discovered that the stock of new torpedoes had been exhausted. All *I-26* could get were 10 (capacity 17) obsolete torpedoes which had been warehoused for at least ten years. He says the attack on *Cynthia Olson* took a long time "because the ship would not sink. More than 20 14-cm shells were consumed with about 10 hits. The first firing was from 3,000 meters."

"Immediately after the first shot," Mr. Hayashi continues, "Mr. Osawa, our radioman, reported that the ship was sending SOS. Then we saw the American flag being raised. Two boats were put into the sea, and I believe all the crew got off the ship. After more firing and fearing an air attack in answer to the SOS, *I-26* crash-dived. When no enemy appeared, the submarine resurfaced and found the ship still floating but on fire.

"We switched to torpedo attack, but because the submarine was drifting too close to the flaming ship, we had to back off before we could fire. One torpedo was fired by Chief Torpedoman Takaji Komaba from about 400 meters. This was our first torpedo attack of the Pacific War. We were dismayed because the old torpedo went wild, turned in mid-course, missed the target by a hair's breadth, then went dead in the water.

"Still fearing an air attack, we dived again. When we resurfaced, the ship was in heavy list. The gunners went back to the deck gun for more shooting. About one-third through the 20 shells fired, the electric ammunition elevator broke down, and the men had to hand-carry the heavy shells up through the hatch to the deck. After about 10 shells were carried, the electricians got the hoist working again.

"Although I was Chief Gunner, my duty during the attack was in the control center. While sub-gunners were shooting, I received permission from First Officer Saito to go onto the bridge to take a picture with my Zeiss 6 x 6-cm camera." (Letter, Aug. 1974.)

Mr. Hayashi's photograph of the sinking *Cynthia Olson* is published for the first time in this book.

A letter from Torpedoman Komaba reinforces Mr. Hayashi's memory of the attack. Another crew member, Yukio Oka, Senior Warrant Officer (Diving Officer), through Mr. Hayashi, provided a copy of his article, "Some Tales About *I-26*." It gives additional details and on page 26 a chart giving *I-26's* position at the start of the war as 29°N-140°W, which would be the location of the attack on *Cynthia Olson*.

Lookouts aboard the *I-26* as photographed in 1942 by Saburo Hayashi, a crew member.

According to Hayashi, the photograph of *I-26* used in this book was made by Shizuo Huki off Daikokugin-to during the submarine's shakedown cruise in October 1941.

SUBMARINES IN THE EASTERN PACIFIC

Bergamini, 1971, pp. 825, 840.

Del Norte (Calif.) *Triplicate*, Dec. 26, 1941, reporting an interview with Captain Farrow of the *Emidio*; follow-up article, July 10, 1971.

Gibbs (1955), pp. 178ff; (1968), pp. 118-121, 303; (1971), p. 62.

Glines, Carroll V. "Theirs Was the First," *Air Force Magazine*, Dec. 1966, pp. 88-89. Account of U.S. bomber attacking a submarine at the mouth of the Columbia River on Dec. 24, 1941.

Hashimoto, pp. 62-63, 65.

Hoehling, A. A. *Home Front, U.S.A.* Crowell, 1956, p. 13.

Ito, p. 221.

Lawson, p. 16.

Ships in Gray: THE STORY OF MATSON IN WORLD WAR II. Matson Navigation Co., 1946, p. 42.

Shrader, p. 37.

Stone, Stephen A. "Was Japanese Sub Sunk Off Columbia?" Portland *Oregonian*, June 30, 1963.

"Submarine Operations," General Headquarters, Far East Command, Military History Section, Japanese Research Division, Japanese Monographs: No. 102, pp. 6, 9, 10, 12-16; No. 110, pp. 21-23; No. 111 (Navy), pp. 32-33; No. 184 (Naval War College), pp. 21, 63-64.

Watts and Gordon, 1971, p. 326.

Correspondence was received between 1972 and 1974 from Charles Acebo, Clarence E. Gillingham, Carroll V. Glines (Col. USAF Ret.), Everett W. Holstrom (Brig. Gen. USAF Ret.), Ben J. Norman, and Frank J. Rohan.

Japanese sources indicate that no submarine was sunk off the Oregon or Washington coast at any time. At the

Japanese War History Institute Lt. Col. Kyushro Kawada, assisted by Commander Kengo Tominaga and Atsushi Ebihara, searched records and found "no information" (Oct. 1972). The fact that the I-25 was operating off the northwest coast in December 1941 is verified by several sources. Executive Officer Tatsuo Tsukudo says, "I-25 patrolled off the mouth of the Columbia River during third week [14-20] Dec. 1941. Then, moved to the Bay of Monterey, Calif. So, she was not in vicinity of reported area . . . I do not remember any Japanese submarine being hit by a bomb or lost on or around Christmas near Columbia River." Other members of the crew who have been contacted, Shichiro Wakabayashi, Togoro Okamoto, Sadao Iijima, Kyozo Suzuki, and Shoji Aizawa also have no recollection of such an attack. Meiji Tagami, commander of I-25, wrote (in Japanese) on Feb. 5, 1974, that before his submarine left the area his bilge was pumped. "I suppose the bomber saw our bilge and attacked it heavily."

The only other submarine off the Pacific Northwest coast in December 1941 was I-26. Mr. Hasegawa assures me that it did not come close to the mouth of the Columbia. When he left his operating station at the entrance of the Strait of Juan de Fuca, he sailed for Kwajalein far out at sea.

On December 24, 1941, the I-19 or I-21 fired a torpedo into the freighter Absaroka near San Pedro, Calif., but with decks awash the ship was brought into port. Actress Jane Russell was photographed inside the jagged hole caused by the torpedo, holding a sign close to her bosom: "A slip of a lip may sink a ship." Hoehling (p. 13) says someone had crossed out "may sink" and substituted, "has sunk!"

Sadao Iijima, a chief gunner on I-25, wrote in 1974, "Everybody on the submarine respected and trusted each other in spite of the differences in rank. The friendship was strong, the atmosphere very amiable. No matter how difficult the situation became, everybody shared the burden stoically and was faithful to his duty. At the time of the air raid over Oregon [Ch. VI, VII] and attacks against ships [Ch. I] all of us concentrated on our duties. For these reasons, I believe, we survived and completed our mission. I still treasure the valuable lessons I learned during the two years I was on I-25."

SUBMARINES IN THE NORTH PACIFIC

Hashimoto, p. 44, and Holmes, p. 130, identify the GLEN aircraft destroyed in the Aleutians as having come from I-19. Fujita, who knew all of the reconnaissance pilots personally, says it was from I-17.

Admiral Samejima made a translation of portions of Naval Operations in Northeast Theatre in the Pacific, published by the War History Office of the Japanese Maritime Self-Defense Agency in 1971, and forwarded it to me in 1972 through Admiral Russell. It reads in part, "I-25 conducted reconnaissance off Kodiak Island by its aircraft May 27, 1942, and reported (A) One cruiser and one destroyer entering port. (B) One destroyer and three patrol boats in Woman's Bay and two patrol boats in Kodiak port. (C) No flying boat. Airfield and hangars sighted in vicinity." The translation also mentions that I-9 flew a reconnaissance mission over Kodiak on June 16.

Morison, IV, pp. fn 168-169 lists Aleutian reconnaissance flights from I-9 on May 25/26, from I-19 on May 28/29, and from I-25 on May 26/27.

There may have been as many as 132 aircraft within range of the I-25 when it reconnoitered Kodiak, 42 of them on that island. War Diary, Northwest Sea Frontier, May 30 and June 2, 1942, lists one AT-7, one AT-6, two LB-30, five B-18A, five P-36A, and 28 P-40E.

The Signal Corps Aircraft Warning Service had a radar on Cape Chiniak on Kodiak Island, but even if it were operating at the time of the May 27 and June 16 flights, it is questionable that the wood-and-fabric GLEN aircraft could have been detected. Only the engine and belly of the plane were metal.

ENEMY PLANE OVER SEATTLE?

The erroneous assertion (Morison, IV, pp. 170, 198; Holmes, p. 130; Craven and Cate, p. 285; and Conn, Engelman, and Fairchild, p. 92) that the I-26 flew a reconnaissance plane over Seattle apparently has its source in Interrogation Nav No. 20 (USSBS No. 97) with Commander Masatake Okumiya, who from March 1942 to July 1944 had been a staff officer with the Japanese Second Air Fleet. When interrogated on 10 October 1945 by Captain James S. Russell, USN, the Commander said, "From a position off the Washington State coast, a submarine had launched a reconnaissance seaplane which scouted Seattle harbor and reported no heavy men-of-war, particularly CV's [carriers] there." (United States Strategic Bombing Survey: Interrogations of Japanese Officials, Vol. 1, p. 93.) From several reliable sources it is known that the only Japanese submarine in that vicinity was the I-26, and the commander of that vessel states that such a flight could not have been made because the I-26 carried no aircraft.

When asked for comment in 1974, Masatake Okumiya (Lt. Gen. JASDF Ret.) wrote, "There was no plane which flew over Seattle. As to my answer to Capt. Russell, I think it is a mistake of an interpreter. I have found many mistakes in the reports and documents of the Strategic Bombing Survey, [which] relied on several Japanese who speak English well but have almost no knowledge of military terminology and military operation."

THE S. S. Coast Trader

War Diary, Northwest Sea Frontier, June 9, 1942, pp. 1-2; Shrader (1969), p. 37; Gibbs (1968), pp. 118-121 and Board of Inquiry memorandum, Summary of Statements by Survivors SS Coast Trader 1 July 1942

Mr. Hasagawa says that Takaji Komaba was the torpedoman at his side in the conning tower at the time of the attack. In firing the torpedo Komaba was assisted by Yukio Oka.

THE S. S. Fort Camosun

Unpublished paper, Directorate of History, Canadian Armed Forces Headquarters, Ottawa; letter from Maritime Museum of British Columbia, Victoria, June 1972; Shrader (1969), p. 40.

Sadao Iijima, the gunner who fired on Fort Camosun, wrote in April 1974: "The crew was running on deck at the front of the ship, so I aimed the gun carefully to avoid the men. I hope there were no deaths—please tell me." I was able to tell him there had been no casualties.

THE S. S. Camden

War Diary, Northwest Sea Frontier, June 24, 1942, p. 64; Coos Bay War Diary, NW Sea Frontier, June 22-28, 1942; U.S. Navy memorandum (n.d.) summarizing state-

聲明書

1942年6月に 126 潜水艦 より発進した 偵察機 に
よって、シヤトル 上空の スパイ 飛行 が 行なわれた、との
多くの書き物が ある 事に 対して、此の聲明を 致します。

私は 1941年 11月1日より、1943年 9月18日 まで、
確かに イ26 潜水艦の 艦長で ありました。

然し 1942年6月に 偵察任務を 以て 如何なる 飛行
機をも、シヤトル 上空を 飛行させた ことは ありません。
戦争中 イ26 潜水艦は 飛行機を 搭載した ことがない
からです。

（イ26 の 飛行機格納筒には 自艦用の食糧か 又は 航
空用がソリンを 搭載して、遠く 浮上にて 飛行機 に
燃料を 補給した 事を 申しそえます）

1974年 1月 5日   長谷川　稔
　　　　　　　　　　（旧 横田）

DECLARATION

I issue this declaration concerning the statement found in many documents alleging that a reconnaissance plane from the I-26 submarine conducted a reconnaissance mission over the Seattle sky in June 1942.

It is a fact that I was the captain of the I-26 from November 1, 1941, through September 18, 1943. However, I did not order any reconnaissance missions over Seattle in June 1942. The reason why this is true is that the I-26 did not carry any airplane during the war time.

(I wish to add that the airplane store room of the I-26 was used as storage space for food for the crew and for airplane gasoline to supply fuel for airplanes in distant places in the ocean.)

(Signed) *Minoru Hasegawa*
Date: January 5, 1974   *(former name: Yokoda)*

ments of survivors; letter from Arnold Lyczewski, a survivor, Sept. 22, 1972; information from Arthur E. Rupert, Prosser, Wash.

According to the diary of Shoji Aizawa, two torpedoes were prepared for *Camden* and fired by Kenji Takezawa from 1,000 meters. "The hits," he says, "were confirmed by explosion of the tanker heard on the submarine. Because of the distance, there was no damage to the submarine."

The S. S. *Larry Doheny*

Rush (1958), pp. 217-223; U.S. Navy Memorandum summarizing statements of survivors, Oct. 18, 1942; Maki (1956), p. 166; Hashimoto p. 66; diary of Shoji Aizawa; letter from Sadao Iijima, Mar. 1974; letter from Nobuo Fujita, Mar. 1973.

Aizawa says, "The sound of the [*Larry Doheny*] was detected before dinner and by periscope [the ship] was determined as large tanker. Weather—very dark with heavy cloud. Visibility poor, so gave surface pursuit. [Torpedoman Kenji Takezawa fired two torpedoes. The

first] no hit—continue pursuing. About an hour later another torpedo fired. Success—heard tremendous sound. It hit just under the bridge and caused huge fire."

Iijima also mentions "the huge fire-explosion on the ship."

Maki recalls that *I-25* was low in the water at a distance and obviously not visible to men on the sinking *Larry Doheny*. Because of the success of the attack, Commander Tagami allowed all of the approximately 100 crewmen to come on deck two at a time for a brief view of the scene.

Hashimoto, p. 66, says that immediately after the attacks on the *Camden* and *Larry Doheny* American planes bombed *I-25*, snapping off its radio antenna and causing a small leak. No confirmation of an attack at this time has been found. The attack on *I-25* by a single Lockheed Hudson came nearly a month before (pp. 67, 77, 164-166).

The Soviet Submarine *L-16*

Rear Admiral George M. Lowry (USN Ret.) made public announcement of the fact that the *I-25* sank the *L-16* in an article published in the U.S. Naval Institute *Proceedings* in January 1962, "L-16—Mystery No Longer," pp. 115-116. The previous article in the *Proceedings* by Fujita and Harrington had merely mentioned that the *I-25* on its way back to Japan had fired its last torpedo at two submarines about 600 miles off the Washington coast. So far as is known, neither the Russians nor the Japanese have publicly confirmed how the sinking occurred. Japanese records list it as an American submarine sunk. As described by C. P. Lemieux in another *Proceedings* article, "*L-16* Sinking—'No Mistake, Just Dirty Work,'" June 1963, pp. 118-120, some Russian officials have tried to lay blame for the sinking on the U.S. submarine *S-31*.

The interview with Lt. Commander Komazov is recorded in a letter from Commander, Western Sea Frontier,

Kou Maki's sketch of the *I-25* attack on the *S. S. Fort Camosun*

Former submariners (left to right) Minoru Hasegawa, Nobuo Fujita, and Meiji Tagami, get together in 1973 to discuss their 1942 operations along the North American coast.

to the Commander-in-Chief, U.S. Fleet, "Russian Submarine L-16-loss of," dated 18 Oct. 1942, file (WSF-01-ml) (SC) Serial 1363.

See also Holmes (1966), p. 169; Del Shrader in Los Angeles *Herald-Examiner*, May 13, 1973, p. A9; and Helen Schrader column in Arcadia *Tribune* and Temple City *Times*, Apr. 26, 1973.

Several surviving members of the *I-25* crew have vivid recollections of the incident. Morikazu Kikuchi, a diesel machinist, recalls that the sonar report showed *L-16's* main engine was operating at 150 rpm. At Commander Tagami's request, Kikuchi computed the *L-16's* speed to be between 11 and 12 knots. Basing his firing data on this speed, Tagami scored a direct hit.

According to Aizawa's diary, "The torpedo was fired by Kenji Takezawa at 4:07 a.m. [Tokyo time]. The explosion followed in about 20 seconds with shock and damage to *I-25* because of closeness."

Sadao Iijima remembers his feelings at the time: "For a moment I shudder thinking of the lives lost of the enemy crew and of their poor families. I realized that this very destruction could also happen to us but it was a war—a sad situation. I still pray for the souls of the dead and for the happiness of their families."

Mr. Fujita wrote: "I believe that none of our crew knew that the submarine sunk was Russian. Both Cmdr. Tagami and I discussing this incident now (1973) feel very lucky that this affair did not bring serious diplomatic problems between Japan and the U.S.S.R. at that time."

Oregon Senator Robert Packwood helped add to the meager store of information on the American liaison officer who went down with the *L-16*. He obtained the assistance of James F. Green, Acting Commissioner of the Immigration and Naturalization Service of the Department of Justice, who supplied these details: Mihailoff was naturalized at Seattle, Washington, on July 28, 1917, having

emigrated from Japan in 1908. He was born in St. Petersburg, Russia, in 1890. In 1914 when Milhailoff filed a Declaration of Intention to become a citizen of the United States, he listed his name as Sergius Andrew Victor Micheloff. "Mihailoff," however, was the name granted by the court and is so shown on Certificate No. 790063. He is known to have been married twice and was married at the time of his death.

Repeated attempts to elicit additional information from various Soviet offices have been met with silence. No U.S. office queried has been able to identify the American liaison officer on the other Soviet submarine, the *L-15*.

The photograph of Mihailoff was loaned by the National Personnel Records Center in St. Louis, Missouri, in December 1973.

HISTORY OF THE *I-12*

The Japanese made one additional attempt to send a submarine to the U.S. west coast. The *I-12*, which was completed on April 25, 1944, was dispatched in October 1944 to shake up the Americans, who had not had any interruption in commerce along the coast for two years. Japanese reports show that this submarine disappeared and was never heard from again. It is now presumed to have been the submarine that sank the cargo ship S. S. *John A. Johnson* midway between Hawaii and California on October 30, 1944, and which in turn was discovered and sunk on November 13, 1944 by the U.S. Navy frigate *Rockford* (manned with an all-Coast Guard crew) and the destroyer escort *U.S.S. Ardent* (Deck Log of *Rockford*, PF-48; Holmes, 393, 413).

FINAL DISPOSITION OF *I-25* AND *I-26*

The published lists of the final disposition of the Japanese submarines do not agree in some particulars. Dates given for the sinking of *I-25*, for example, range from July to October/November 1943 and of *I-26* from October 25 to November 17, 1944. According to *Jane's Fighting Ships*, 1947-48, p. 479, *I-25* was sunk by U.S. destroyer *Taylor* on July 11, 1943, and *I-26* by aircraft VC-82 of *U.S.S. Anzio* on November 17, 1944. Watts and Gordon (1971), p. 334, list *I-25* as sunk by *U.S.N. Patterson* on September 3, 1943, and *I-26* as a "marine casualty" east of Leyte in November 1944. Roscoe (1953), p. 229, describes the discovery and sinking of *I-25*. See also *The United States Navy at War 1941-1946*, by E. J. King, Commander-in-Chief of the U.S. Navy (1946), p. 245; Joint Army/Navy Assessment (1947); Ito (1962), p. 245; Holmes (1966), pp. 243, 391. ☐

CHAPTER II: THE WAR ASHORE

SOURCES ON EVACUATION OF JAPANESE-AMERICANS

Conrat, Maisie and Richard. *Executive Order 9066: The Internment of 110,000 Japanese Americans.* California Historical Society, 1972. Photographs of callup and resettlement.

Final Report: Japanese Evacuation from the West Coast 1942. U.S. Army Western Defense Command, Government Printing Office, n.d., pp. ix, 53-54.

Hosokawa, Bill. *Nisei: The Quiet Americans.* Morrow, 1969, pp. 306-307.

Huckleberry, E. R. *The Adventures of Dr. Huckleberry, Tillamook County, Oregon.* Oregon Historical Society, 1970, p. 234.

Kitagawa, Daisuke. *Issei and Nisei: The Internment Years.* Seabury, 1967, pp. 210, 148, 154.

Kitano, Harry H. L. *Japanese Americans: The Evolution of a Subculture.* Prentice-Hall, 1969, p. 28.

McKee, Ruth E. *Wartime Exile: The Exclusion of the Japanese-Americans from the West Coast.* U.S. Government Printing Office, 1946, pp. 51, 104ff, 157. Quotations from General DeWitt from this source.

Mears, Eliot G. *Resident Orientals on the American West Coast.* University of Chicago Press, 1928, p. 471.

Myer, Dillon S. *Uprooted Americans.* University of Arizona Press, 1971, p. 282.

Okimoto, Daniel I. *Americans in Disguise.* Weatherhill, 1971, pp. 21-22.

Okubo, Miné. *Citizen 13660.* Columbia University Press, 1946. Cartoons of situations encountered.

Olson, Joan and Gene. *California Times and Trails.* Windyridge, Grants Pass, Oregon, 1971, pp. 235-236; quoting Earl Warren, p. 236.

Pegler, Westbrook. Los Angeles *Times*, Feb. 16, 1942.

Rush (1958), p. 216.

Sone, Monica. *Nisei Daughter.* Little, Brown, 1953. Describes callup and relocation problems and joys.

"Summary Removal of Japs Demanded." Los Angeles *Times*, Feb. 25, 1942, p. 9.

Violette, Forrest E. *The Canadian Japanese and World War II.* University of Toronto Press, 1948; and *The Japanese Canadians.* Canadian Institute of International Affairs, Vol. VI, No. 2, 1945.

For other references see "Selected Bibliography on the Japanese American Experience," published by the Japanese American Citizens League, San Francisco.

General John Lesesne DeWitt (1880-1962) served in France in World War I and later held commands in the U.S. and the Philippine Islands. He was 61 when the United States entered World War II. His administrative position kept him out of combat operations except for one near-miss in the Aleutians. When the Allies prepared to dislodge the Japanese force that occupied Kiska, Dewitt left Adak on a destroyer and was transferred by small boat in rough weather to the battleship *Pennsylvania*. With other officials including Assistant Secretary of War John J. McCloy and Marine Corps Major General Howland M. Smith, he anticipated battle as Army Major General Charles H. Corlett led 34,426 American and Canadian troops to retake the island. The Japanese, however, a few days before, under cover of a pea-soup fog, had sent two cruisers and six destroyers to Kiska, and in only 55 minutes evacuated 5,183 men—a brilliant and daring achievement undetected by the Allies. When the Allied troops landed, there was no one to fight. (Morison, VII, pp. 58-59, 62. Roscoe (1953), pp. 252-253.)

The initial removal of Japanese-Americans from their homes into assembly centers was an Army operation under the direction of Col. Karl R. Bendetsen. The ultimate management of the relocation centers was a civil operation. Between the Army and the civilian War Relocation Authority, Dillon S. Myer, head of WRA, wrote that there was a long series of frustrations. The points of view of Colonel Bendetsen were so completely opposed to those of the WRA "that relations were nearly always difficult and at times downright impossible." (Myer, 1971, p. 282.) According to Myer, the Caucasian physician who was beaten at the Tule Lake camp hospital on November 1, 1943, was Reece M. Pedicord, M.D. (*Ibid*, pp. 319-320.)

For information on Colonel Bendetsen see *Who's Who in America*, Vol. 25, 1948-49, and Hosokawa, pp. 306-307.

Administrators of the relocation of Japanese-Americans: Colonel Karl R. Bendetsen (left), Assistant Chief of Staff, Civil Affairs Division, Western Defense Command and Fourth Army, conceived the method and directed the evacuation. Dillon S. Myer (right), Director of the War Relocation Authority, managed the relocation centers.

Hosokawa quotes Bendetsen as saying in 1968, "Were it not for the pressures, the time, and the circumstances [the evacuation] would not have been done at all."

Only a few remnants of the Tule Lake relocation center remained at the site in 1974. Most buildings had been moved or destroyed. On a horseradish farm a mile from the camp, the house and other buildings used by the Paul E. Christy family since 1947 were constructed from buildings brought from the camp.

On May 25-26, 1974, Japanese-Americans who had been residents at Tule Lake and others revisited the site. This pilgrimage was reported in *Time*, p. 31, and *Newsweek*, p. 28, on June 10, 1974, and in other local and national periodicals.

The Reverend Thomas W. Grubbs of the Sturge Presbyterian Church in San Mateo, Calif., who served as "reconciler" at Tule Lake from 1944 to 1946, has vivid memories of the experience. "I cannot forget," he says, "some of the beautiful people I met in the camp. Tule Lake was a reminder to me that God has far greater plans . . . than we ourselves could ever possibly imagine." (Letter, July 1974).

I-17 attack near Santa Barbara

Walker A. Tomkins, author of *Goleta, The Good Land* (privately printed for the Goleta, Calif., Am-Vets Post No. 55, 1966) approved the paraphrase from his book and provided additional information by letter.

Colonel Bernard E. Hagan (USA Ret.) of Irvine, Calif., the man who was awarded the Purple Heart for the injury he received when deactivating one of the *I-17* shells, says that hundreds of pounds of shell fragments in various sizes were picked up after the attack. One was marked "KOBE" in Japanese, probably indicating where it was made.

Other eye witnesses who provided reminiscences include Mr. and Mrs. W. W. Way of Scappose, Ore., and Emmett M. Roche, Temple City, Calif.

Other sources:

Edmonds, George W. ". . . and the Shells Came." *Noticias*, Bulletin of the Santa Barbara Historical Society, Vol. III, No. 1, Spring 1961, pp. 3-6.

Los Angeles *Times*, Feb. 25, 1942. "Southland Alert for New Sub Raids as Hunt Pushed for Marauding Ship," p. 6; "Here's Damage Caused by Sub's Shelling of Elwood Oil Field," p. B.

Reynolds, Clark G., "Submarine Attacks on the Pacific Coast, 1942." *Pacific Historical Review*, May 1964, pp. 183-193.

Santa Barbara *News-Press*, Feb. 24, 1942; Nov. 8, 1959; Feb. 21, 1965.

Schrader, Del. "The Anxious Days on California Shores Following Pearl Harbor." Los Angeles *Herald-Examiner*, July 14, 1974, p. A-11.

Nobukiyo Nambu was an officer on *I-17* when that submarine attacked *Emidio* in December 1941 and shelled Goleta in February 1942. He commanded *I-401* at the end of the war (see p. 164).

"Battle of Los Angeles"

The controversy over what really happened over Los Angeles on the night of February 24/25, 1942, is still very much alive. Records show that 1,440 rounds of antiaircraft ammunition were shot skyward that night. But at what? A Japanese bomber? No bombs were dropped. A Japanese reconnaissance plane? The *I-17*, which had shelled Goleta the night before, had a GLEN aircraft aboard, but according to Nobukiyo Nambu, First Officer of that submarine, the plane made "no flights on this cruise." (Letter, Sept. 19, 1974.)

Was it an American military plane? "The AAF kept its pursuit planes on the ground, preferring to await indications of the scale and direction of any attack before committing its limited fighter force." (Craven and Cate, p. 283). An American commercial plane? A plane from one of the nearby aircraft plants being tested? If so, where did it come from; where did it go?

Following a radio broadcast from station KGO in San Francisco in 1974, in which a request for information from eye witnesses was made, I received more than two hundred letters and telephone calls. They confirmed the oft-quoted description that "the air over Los Angeles erupted like a volcano" Some observers said they *knew* planes were in the sky that night. The former secretary to a movie star wrote, "Huge spotlights were on one plane and oh—my!—the artillery guns were really shooting." A Community Air Raid Warden of the time says he saw a group of planes, about ten, directly overhead, "forming a perfect V, like a flight of wild geese flying very high."

Some who wrote or called said they *knew* a plane was shot down. Dan Tryon of Redding, California, was a 10-year-old magazine peddler at the time. In an attempt to impress him, Air Corps personnel showed him a newly wrecked plane that had just been trucked into Mines Field. "This is the Jap bomber that was shot down last night," they told him. As he filled his magazine shoulder bag with souvenir parts—including a piece of blood-stained parachute harness—Dan said, "Heck, I know a P-38 when I see one." When he went back the next day, the wrecked plane was completely gone.

Several writers have pointed out that weather balloons were being released regularly in the area. An anti-aircraft searchlight might have caught one of them. One seasoned observer, First Sergeant Everett H. Buckley of the 3rd Coast Artillery (now a resident of Mill Valley, Calif.) was not on duty that night but watched the firing. "I wouldn't swear there wasn't an airplane up there," he says, "but it looked to me like a green outfit firing at its own air bursts and searchlight beam spot."

The greatest verifiable damage done that night was the result of falling shell fragments, traffic accidents in the blackout, and a blow to the prestige of the military defenses against aerial attack. It was a dramatic illustration of the panic which could be expected if any of our cities came under actual enemy attack.

Coastal alert

Extinguishing fires in the wigwam burners in sawmills with water damaged the metal walls and fire-block liners, and restarting a burner required several barrels of crude oil. Ultimately a fog-making apparatus was developed by the West Coast Lumberman's Association, which would damp a burner fire in about two minutes, would not damage walls or liners, and would retain coals for quick re-kindling. (Ellis Lucia in *Head Rig*, Overland West Press, 1965, pp. 212-213.)

"Beach Patrol History," War Diary Office, 13th Naval District, Seattle (unpublished manuscript, n.d.), p. 50.

Interview with Albert Trudell, former Coast Guard radioman, June 1973. ☐

Chapter III: The War in British Columbia

Aikman, Bill and Dave Cossette. "The Attack on Estevan Lighthouse," *Sentinel*, Vol. 10, No. 7, 1974, pp. 11-14. Ottawa: Directorate of Information Services, National Defence Hq.

Gregson, Harry. *A History of Victoria 1842-1970*. The Victoria Observer Publishing Co., Ltd., 1970, pp. 88-92.

Nicholson, George. *Vancouver Island's West Coast 1792-1962*. Morriss Printing Co., 1962, pp. 35, 37-38, 97.

Tucker, Gilbert N. *The Naval Service of Canada: Its Official History*, Ottawa: The King's Printer, 1952. Vol. II, pp. 217-218, 231-232.

Victoria, B. C., *Daily Colonist*: Archie N. Wills column, Aug. 10, 1969; magazine section, May 7, 1967, pp. 3, 15; George Nicholson in Sunday magazine, Sept. 18, 1966, pp. 10-11; June 10, 1970, p. 1.

Wood, Amos. *Beachcoming for Japanese Glass Floats*, 2nd ed. Binfords, 1972.

In regard to the Estevan Point attack, see Morison, IV, pp. 161-162, 169, 183; Hashimoto, p. 270; Ito, p. 226; New York *Times*, June 23, 1942, p. 9, and June 28, 1942, sec. 4, p. 6.

Mr. Hasegawa says that a shipboard rumor persisted after this attack that a sand-filled practice shell had been fired. When it was wanted later, it could not be found. Saburo Hayashi, chief gunner on *I-26*, says that torpedomen and machinists assisted the gunners and that it was possible that the practice shell was fired by mistake. (Letters, 1973-74.)

Personal recollections of the Estevan Point shelling were provided by Edward T. Redford, Victoria; Mrs. Brian Harrison, White Rock, B.C.; Mrs. Clarence C. Evans and Arthur E. Rupert, both of Prosser, Wash.; Mrs. Marjorie H. Renfroe, Seattle; and Otto Freytag, Riviera Beach, Fla.

A translation of entries in the log of *I-8* were provided by Admiral Samejima.

Charles Ells of Port Orford, Ore., wrote in 1974 that he was at the wheel of his commercial fishing boat off Estevan Point on June 20, 1942. "At daybreak I saw a big submarine about three or four miles ahead. I had no radio to report it. The submarine submerged within one minute; then I turned and left the area at top speed. I hailed another fishing boat, the *M. V. Fairfax*, whose skipper broke the seal on his transmitter and called the Coast Guard."

Headlines in the Portland *Oregonian*, June 22, 1942, indicate the relative importance of the Estevan Point attack in a world at war: TOBRUK FALLS; NAZIS GAIN ON SEVASTOPOL AT HIGH COST; SUB SHELLS VANCOUVER ISLAND; OREGON COAST DIMS OUT; JAPS LOSE TRANSPORT BUT ESTABLISH BASE IN ALEUTIANS.

On June 8, 1973—nearly 31 years after the attack— the lighthouse keeper at Estevan Point reported a shell warhead that had been found on the beach, where it had been exposed by the tide twice a day. A crew from a Canadian demolition unit arrived by helicopter on July 3, 1973, examined it, found that it contained picric acid, and detonated it. Fragments are in the possession of the lighthouse keeper and the Maritime Museum in Victoria. (George McBride, Head of Reference Dept., Greater Victoria Public Library). ☐

In addition to his many other occupations at Zeballos (1935-1960) a mining town on the west coast of Vancouver Island. Major George Nicholson, M.C., was a balloon spotter and is a published author on the history of the region.

Sandra Harrison Kruger in 1973. She was a babe in arms at the Estevan Point light station at the time it was shelled by the *I-26*.

CHAPTER IV: PACIFIC NORTHWEST HARBOR DEFENSES

Fourth Air Force Historical Study No. III-2, p. 147.

Hanft (1973), pp. 37-53.

Harper, Mary Howard. "Fort Hayden," in *Jimmie Come Lately*, ed. Jervis Russell. Clallam County Historical Society, 1971, pp. 391-393.

Kirchner, D. P. and E. R. Lewis, "American Harbor Defenses: The Final Era." United States Naval Institute *Proceedings*, Jan. 1968, pp. 95-98.

Lewis, Emanuel Raymond. *Seacoast Fortifications of the United States*. Smithsonian Institution Press, 1970, pp. 79-81, 114-121, 141-142.

McLaughlin, Robert W. "The Harbor Defenses of Puget Sound." Mimeographed, n.d., pp. 6-15.

Page, Robert M. *The Origin of Radar*. Anchor, 1962, pp. 22, 33ff, 127, 133.

Portland *Oregonian*, editorial, June 25, 1942.

Seattle *Sunday Times*, Pictorial feature, Oct. 8, 1972, p. 27.

Thompson, George R., and others. *U.S. Army in World War II—The Technical Services, The Signal Corps: The Test*. Chief of Military History, U.S. Army.

Tillamook *Headlight-Herald*, Apr. 16, 1953. News story on mine explosion on Cape Meares beach.

Zahl, Harold A. *Radar Spelled Backwards*. Vantage, 1971, p. 83.

Individuals who provided information include Neil M. Cochran, Gene Hopkins, Herb Hubbell, Stan Lilian, Homer L. McLaughlin, Vardel Nelson, Daniel Newhouse, Don St. Thomas, Don Spoon, Joe Stanley, C. B. Washburne, Robert H. Watkins; personnel of the U.S. Army Corps of Engineers office at Fort Stevens; former members of the 248th and 249th Coast Artillery.

According to Mrs. Harper and the *Sunday Times* feature, a sign was erected on Cape Flattery after construction for the 16-inch gun emplacement was discontinued in 1943: "In memory of the expenditure of five million dollars at this site." The amount is undoubtedly a gross exaggeration. E. R. Lewis estimates that this installation was less than 10 percent completed and that no more than $200,000 was spent at this site. Complete installations of 16-inch batteries were running about $1.5 million at that time.

Howard P. Sherwood provided the photograph of the mine which exploded on Cape Meares beach, which was sent to Ottawa for identification. A UPI release on Sept. 10, 1974, reported the Japanese mine found off Brookings in 1974.

Amos L. Wood, Seattle author, tells of the discovery of four "migrant mines" along the British Columbia coast in recent years. One was found lodged in driftwood on

The casemate at Fort Hayden, which once held a 16-inch coast artillery gun, as it looked in 1973.

Prince of Wales Island in 1968 and left there. Another, also in 1968, was found on top of a pile of driftwood two miles north of Estevan Point lighthouse. It made a huge hole in the sand when detonated by Canadian Navy men. Two other mines were found in 1972 on the west side of the Queen Charlotte Islands. "The possible dangers associated with migrant mines," Mr. Wood says, "should be publicized whenever possible due to the large number of people who are now beachcombing our Pacific shores." (Letter, Oct. 11, 1974.)

Charles S. Hawkins, Fort Point National Historical Site, Presidio of San Francisco, introduced me to the literature on Coast Artillery weaponry: *Encyclopedia Britannica*, 11th ed. (1910), vol. 19; Wm. H. Tschappat, *Textbook of Ordnance and Gunnery* (Wiley, 1917); Frank T. Hines and F. W. Ward, *The Service of the Coast Artillery* (Goodenough, 1910); *American Coast Artillery Material* (U.S. Army Ordnance Dept., Document No. 2032, 1922); William Crozier, "The Disappearing Gun Carriage," in *Army Ordnance* July/Aug. 1932, vol. XIII, No. 73; Emanuel R. Lewis, "A History of San Francisco Harbor Defense Installations: Forts Baker, Barry, Cronkhite, and

Funston" (Division of Beaches and Parks, State of California, 1965), pp. 146-150.

A letter from the U.S. Army Ordnance Museum, Aberdeen Proving Ground, Maryland, in June 1972, provided detailed information about the two 10-inch guns, model 1900, at Battery Russell.

Interviews with Col. Carl S. Doney (USA Ret.); Bennett Loftsgaard, Sacramento, Calif.; and Col. Vernon D. Greig, Oregon Army National Guard; and letters from Herbert Goldwag, U.S. Army Electronics Command, Fort Monmouth, N. J.; Col. D. M. Copp, U.S. Army Materiel Command, Washington, D. C.; and Robert M. Huston, Marianas Islands, provided additional information.

THE HARBOR ENTRANCE CONTROL POST

Batteries Mishler, Walker, and Lewis, each with two 10-inch disappearing guns, were completed in 1898 as the West Battery at Fort Stevens. After firing, the Mishler guns recoiled into cylindrical pits or "tubs," which differed in shape from the usual concrete DC gun emplacement. When the Mishler guns fired, I have been told, the whole emplacement rocked and nothing was secure. The concussion was so great that at least one man reportedly was killed in the late 1930's. As a consequence, the battery was declared unsafe, and was not manned in World War II. The underground rooms, however, were converted into the Harbor Entrance Control Post (HECP). After the war began, the Mishler guns were hidden by filling the tubs, guns and all, with sand. This act later caused salvage crews to cuss up a storm when the guns had to be dug up before they could be scrapped. Instead of refilling the tubs after the guns were taken out, the salvage crew covered them with planks and dumped sand and soil on top of the planks.

Don Millar and Carl Roth, equipped with flashlights and accompanied by Corps of Engineers men, inspected the dark, wet, moldy underground sections in Sept. 1973. They found no guns, squelching rumors that they had not been removed. ☐

CHAPTER V: UNINVITED VISITOR AT FORT STEVENS

Reminiscenses of participants related in this chapter were acquired mainly in 1972 and 1973 and consist of conversations, taped interviews, and letters from those mentioned in the text. Additional details and background information were supplied by Gerald W. Frank, son of the late Aaron Frank, who provided *Mañana II* for Coast Guard use in the Columbia; and by many others including Paul Aikins, Sid Boise, Bob Brady, Wilbur Cooney, Platt Davis, Carl S. Doney, Richard Ebi, Ken Evans, Ernest Fieguth, John D. Flynn, Paul Garren, Vernon D. Greig, Henry (Leo) Grossman, William F. Hamilton, Les Hall, George (Dave) Hannaford, Zed Harris, Walt Heine, Bill and Harry Hoxie, Robert M. Huston, Art Johansen, Charles McKeen, Bennett Loftsgaard, Lyal Massey, Don Millar, Lynn Neeley, Vardell Nelson, Dan Newhouse, Gil Ogden, Howard V. Parker, Warren Poling, Sam Redkey, Jim Ridders, Lee Rohrbaugh, Cliff Ross, Carl Roth, Laurence Rude, Henry K. Scott, Joe Stanley, Carl Sundbaum, Jack Wood, Bob Yantis—all of Army units; Mrs. Burton De-Graw, Al Phillips, Bill and Cassie Schults, Clifford Hitchman, Mrs. Wayne (Ardith Hitchman) Severson— all civilians at the time of the attack. Also Fred Gold, Ben Norman, Milo A. Jordan, Otto Freytag, Mrs. Albert F. Padgett (writing for her husband), and George W. Cooper —all of the Coast Guard—and Jerry Cassidy and Gordon Sammis.

Rolf Klep, curator of the Columbia River Maritime Museum, and Bruce Berney, Clatsop County Librarian, provided valuable assistance.

In regard to the threat to shoot out the Cape Disappointment light, there appear to be two incidents. Zed Harris is certain of his recollections concerning his orders to a Coast Guardsman to turn off the light or have it shot out. Lt. Tom Barrett, Public Information Officer at 13th Coast Guard District in Seattle wrote: "According to Cape Disappointment Log, at 12:35 a.m., June 22, 1942, the CO of the light station received a call from Base Astoria to extinguish Cape Disappointment and North Head lights and the Columbia River entrance range lights. He complied and these lights were extinguished at 12:46 a.m." Milo A. Jordan, a Commander in the Coast Guard in 1973, was a Coast Guard enlisted man standing watch that night at Cape Disappointment. He wrote that he did not recall such an incident but said, "It was during this same period when the Duty Officer at Fort Canby alerted his search-light groups advising that unidentified objects were offshore. Tensions ran high, and in an effort to be 'first on the line' a sergeant ordered 'Turn it on! Let's go!'—and the light came on. An Army Officer sent an order via field telephone, 'Turn that G _ _ d _ _ _ _ _ light out or I'll shoot it out.'

Details of the power line breakage on the DeLaura Beach Road are contained in "1942 Submarine Attack on Oregon's Fort Stevens Remembered" in *Pacific Powerland,* (Pacific Power and Light Company, Portland, Ore., issue No. 4, 1972).

At the request of Admiral Russell, Admiral Samejima made inquiries in Japan about the attack. Admiral Samejima says that Commander Tagami positioned *I-25* at "13,000 yards range where the water depth was 30-meters —the approaching limit from the viewpoint of escape from attack by [an] enemy vessel . . . There is no track chart of submarine *I-25* showing her firing runs on June 21, 1942, while shelling the fort at the entrance to the Columbia River. Commander Tagami did not know that Battery Russell had 10-inch big guns at mouth of the Columbia River. Commander Tagami, with whom the War History Division had contact, has no personal papers concerned with the mission."

I sent Commander Tagami a photocopy of a 1935 British Chart with Japanese overprinting showing the "alleged course of Japanese submarine to Fort Stevens area in 1942," which was published with Marshall Hanft's article in *Oregon Historical Quarterly*, Dec. 1964 and in reprint in 1973. Tagami immediately replied, declaring it is *"not my chart!"* He said that he was using a "very, very old chart printed in U.S.A." that has not been preserved. In his letter of Feb. 1974, he sketched the river entrance from memory and marked "fortifications" on the *north* side of the Columbia River, and then he drew in the location of a "destroyer and submarine base" at Tongue Point, about 15 miles upriver. In an interview with a newsman in 1950, Tagami had said he was firing in the direction of the submarine base.

Although the Naval Station at Tongue Point was never equipped to service submarines, and over the years only a few submarines ever docked there, its development into a submarine base was contemplated at one time. A 1918 revision of an 1898 navigation chart indicates Tongue Point as a "Proposed Submarine Base." Commander Tagami had some reason to believe that he might be shooting in the direction of a sub base, but could hardly have expected to reach it with his 14-cm deck gun.

In the National Archives, Joan Olson of Grants Pass, Ore., with the help of Fred Crawford, dug out information about the lightship *Relief*, No. 92, which was on the Columbia River light station on the night of June 21/22, 1942. The ship's log indicates that flashes were seen 10 miles south-southeast at 11:45 p.m., but does not identify the source. Ben J. Norman, Seattle, a Coast Guard fireman on the coal-burning *Relief* at the time, was on the bridge when he saw the flashes. "The beacon lights on the lightship were off," he says, "and the ship was blacked out except for our very small anchor light. We were unarmed. If the *Relief* had been attacked, all I could have done was to throw coal at them!"

Commander Tagami did not see the blacked-out lightship, but even if he had seen it, he probably would have ignored it. "Japanese submarines were trained to attack big-sized targets, such as the major battleships or aircraft carriers," says Mr. Hasegawa, commander of the *I-25's* sister ship, the *I-26*. "In many cases torpedoes shot at shallow-bottomed boats were apt to jump out from the surface like, say, a dolphin, and be wasted without any result. Captain Tagami, my classmate, said that he did not see the Columbia River lightship and therefore he has no memory of approaching it."

News of the Fort Stevens attack made the front page of the New York *Times,* June 23, 1942, "Foe's Shells Fall on Oregon Coast," pp. 1, 9. In "Enemy Off Shore Stirs West Coast" (*Times,* June 28, 1942, sec. 4, p. 6) Richard L. Neuberger and Lawrence E. Davis wrote, "It was the first personal taste of war for residents of the Oregon coast, who, contrary to Tokyo's imaginative version of the incident, watched and listened to the 'show' and kept their heads, no matter how much their hearts might have been thumping." ☐

CHAPTER VI: MISSION: RETALIATION

Tolan, John, *The Rising Sun: Decline and Fall of the Japanese Empire 1936-1945*. Random House, 1970, p. 426.

This chapter is based on translations of several of Mr. Fujita's publications and on correspondence with him It was approved by him for publication here on Dec. 12, 1974.

Nobuo Fujita was about 21 years of age when he was conscripted into the Japanese Navy in 1932. He began flight training a year later and eventually rose to rank of Warrant Officer. After the tour of duty on *I-25* described in this chapter, he served as a flight instructor throughout the remaining years of the war.

A comment by Admiral Samejima in a letter in 1972 that "*I-25* escaped by a hair breath from the aircraft attack" on September 9, 1942, is substantiated by letters from crew members Shoji Aizawa, Sadao Iijima, Moriichi Kikuchi, Kou Maki, Togoro Okomoto, and Sensuke Tao.

Maki says that the last man down the hatch caught his clothing in the water-tight hatch cover and it would not lock. With the American bomber already diving on the vessel, great anxiety swept through the submarine as men pulled and tugged and swore at the hatch cover. Finally, with the door released and locked, the submarine dropped to 70 meters as bombs fell from above.

In his diary, Aizawa recorded, "Tremendous explosion at depth about 25 meters; second explosion at 30 meters with very big shock to us caused leaks and some lights went out."

Iijima says that the switchboard room was flooded as sea water poured in through a broken electrical conduit tube. Several of the crewmen mentioned that the only personal injuries sustained were bumped heads and some scrapes, which were attended by the submarine's physician, Dr. Hoshi—who, incidentally, in civilian practice was a gynecologist.

As a further development of the concept expressed by Mr. Fujita that submarines could carry bombers as well as reconnaissance aircraft, the Japanese in 1943 started construction of the largest underwater craft ever built. The *I-400* series (Type STo) submarines were designed to carry three SEIRAN torpedo-bomber seaplanes, expressly for the destruction of the Gatun Locks at the entrance to the Panama Canal. About 16 of the 400-foot-long monsters,

each with a cruising range of 37,500 miles, were planned. Construction started on five of them. Four were launched and three actually completed. The *I-400* was ready by Dec. 30, 1944, the *I-401* on Jan. 8, 1945, but midway in construction *I-402* was converted to a fuel tanker and was not commissioned until July 24, 1945.

Because of the acute fuel shortage in Japan, *I-401* was ordered to Manchuria for oil, but as it left Kure it hit a mine that exploded and had to go back into port for repairs. Its first and only combat mission was to attack U.S. carriers in Ulithi lagoon, but the war ended before the action started.

Lt. Commander Nobukiyo Nambu, who had been First Officer on *I-17* when it attacked S. S. *Emidio* and shelled Goleta, was commander of *I-401* when all three of the giant submarines surrendered late in August 1945. All three were sunk by the U.S. Navy after the war. (Holmes, pp. 472-473; Watts and Gordon, pp. 351-353; letters from N. Nambu, 1974.) ☐

CHAPTER VII: AIR STRIKES ON OREGON

Caiden, Martin. *Forked-Tailed Devil: The P-38*. Ballentine, 1971, p. 128.

Crescent City, Calif., *Del Norte Triplicate,* Sep. 18, 1942.

Everts, A. B. "The First Enemy Bombs," *Timber-Lines* (U.S. Forest Service Region 6 30-Year Club), June 1971.

"History of the Western Defense Command," Vol. I, OCMH File 8.2.2 AA, VI, n.d., pp. 18-23.

Maki (1956), p. 64.

Marshall, Edward. "Service Log," Sep. 12, 1942; and "Report of Bomb Believed to Have Been Dropped from Jap Plane," Sep. 29, 1942. Filed in the Chetco District Office of the Siskiyou National Forest, Brookings, Ore.

Northwest Sea Frontier. "Enemy submarine activity—Report of," letter to Commander in Chief, U.S. Fleet, file A16-3(6) Rs Serial F222095, 12 Sep. 1942.

Portland *Oregon Journal,* "Jap Plane Drops Incendiary Bomb on Oregon Forest," Sep. 15, 1942, p. 1.

Webber, Bert. "The Forest Service and the Japanese Attacks of World War II," *Timber-Lines,* July 1974, pp. 117-122.

Western Defense Command and Fourth Army. G-2 Summary No. 97, entries for 9 Sep. 1942, pp. 1-2.

Those who provided information by letter, telephone, interview, and/or field trips include Edward Marshall, Leslie Colvill, Claude E. Waldrop, John Zlock, Allen Ettinger, Robert H. Ruth, Raymond L. Proctor, Hamilton C. Dowell, C. Otto Lindh, and Jean H. Daugherty.

When I went to Brookings nearly thirty years after the air raid to interview people who remembered the bombing, I heard conflicting recollections. Many of them centered around the type of airplane and where it came from. Even though I could find no one who actually saw the plane, some people insisted it had one engine and two pontoons. Others said it had two engines and one pontoon. Some declared it had two wings; others said it was a monoplane—a big bomber. One man insisted it came from California. A housewife told me she knew all about the airplane, how it was wrecked, and how some men found the wreck and buried half a dozen bodies of the invading force who had been killed in the crash. It turned out that the conflicting reports were the result of a mixed-up time sense. On Jan. 31, 1945, a Navy PBY patrol bomber crashed in the Brookings area, killing all eight aboard. This incident started the rumor, that has now become a firm belief in the minds of some Brookings area residents, that the whole affair was a ploy by the U.S. Navy to shake the United States out of its complacency about the war. (See Bert Webber, "Navy Monument in Wilderness Real Surprise Item," *Oregon Journal,* Jan. 31, 1972, feature sec., p. 1.)

Both Robert Larson, one of the men who saw Fujita's plane on Sep. 9, 1942, and Captain Keith V. Johnson, who helped put out the fires one of Fujita's bombs started, said that they had never before been asked to relate their stories for publication. When I contacted them in 1972 and 1973, Larson was living at Clackamas, Ore.; Johnson was on duty with the U.S. Navy in Hong Kong. I was able to put Captain Johnson in touch with Mr. Fujita, and they met for a visit in Tokyo on Jan. 24, 1974. This unusual meeting was photographed and the Associated Press released a story that was carried in newspapers throughout the United States (e.g., Seattle *Times,* Jan. 25, 1974, p. A2; *Navy Times,* Mar. 6, 1974, p. 26).

In regard to the potential danger of Fujita's incendiaries, the "History of the Western Defense Command," p. 19, says: "Ordinarily the forest fire hazard in the area bombed is greatest during September. However, the area had been drenched by an unseasonable rain the day before the bombing and the amount of moisture in the trees and underbrush undoubtedly retarded the action of the phosphorus pellets in the bomb as well as the spread of the small fire that was started . . . The fact that a strict ban was in force on the broadcast of weather information concerning the Pacific coast at that time may or may not have averted a large fire. Had the bombing taken place a week earlier or a week later it would have occurred when the fire danger was much greater. Had the enemy been able to pick up radio reports of inland weather conditions he might have used that information to his advantage in timing the bombing."

ATTACK ON THE *I-25*

Colonel Jean H. Daugherty (USAF Ret.), Dallas, Texas, insists, "I did not at the time of the attack nor do I now claim that I destroyed or even hit anything." Not until the accounts of survivors of *I-25* were collected for this book did it become known that he not only made contact with an enemy submarine off the Oregon coast but also that he damaged it.

The A-29 he was flying that day belonged to the 390th Bomb Squadron (M), 42nd Bombardment Group (M), stationed at the Army Air Base, McChord Field, Wash. It was one of the modified Lockheed Hudson twin-engined bombers that had been built to British specifications for the RAF but which were assigned to the U.S. Army Air Corps in the early months of the Pacific war.

This is Col. Daugherty's story of his historic flight of 9 Sep. 1942:

"We took off from McChord Field about daybreak on a routine antisubmarine patrol. The co-pilot was 2nd Lt. Otto F. Kuhl, who was fresh out of flying school. We also had a gunner, Sgt. Conrado Garcia, and a radio operator.

"By way of Chehalis, the Columbia River, and Astoria, we followed the usual route out to sea. About 50 miles out, we turned south and flew parallel to the Oregon shore.

Nobuo Fujita and Captain Keith V. Johnson, USN, met face to face for the first time in Tokyo in January 1974. As an 18-year-old Forest Service lookout in 1942, Johnson helped put out fires one of Fujita's bomb caused.

The weather that day was mostly cloud banks at various altitudes plus puffs of low fog with a few bright spots between. It was our practice to fly between 15 and 50 feet above the ocean, angling from one bright spot to the next looking for enemy activity on the surface. If we flew any higher we would have been in or above the overcast with little or no chance to see anything.

"In the southwest portion of the patrol sector, nearing the Oregon-California border, I sighted something dark in the water ahead. It was near the fringe of one of the bright areas and I flew over it on a quartering run. It seemed larger than the pictures of the Japanese submarines we had been briefed on. At first I suspected it was an unreported derelict.

"My course took me into a fog bank, where I started an immediate tight left turn right down at the water level. Still in the fogbank, I headed back toward the object and opened the bomb bay doors. As we leveled out, I moved my thumb to the bomb release switch and peered ahead. While still in the fog, I could dimly see the object in the water slightly to the left and about 300 yards away. Suddenly we broke into the bright morning sunlight.

"I throttled back to reduce speed, lost a little more altitude, and headed straight in toward the long, low object. When I felt I could get the best shots alongside the target or possibly straddle it with bombs, I pressed the release button, dropping two 300-pound general purpose demolition bombs with fuses set for 3 to 5 seconds delayed action.

"With my speed still low, I went into another turn, still in the sunlit area between the puffs of fog, and dropped another bomb. As the turn was completed we saw the object again but it was less clear and much deeper in the water. The dark clouds were closing in.

"On this run I pulled up sharply over the object to allow the gunner, who was in the rear of the airplane, an opportunity to fire. He didn't shoot! I was amazed! There were no barrels in his guns! After the previous mission they had been removed for cleaning and I had not checked before taking off that morning to make sure they had been brought back!

"Still not knowing why the guns had not been fired, I banked around again for another approach, but the

165

target was rapidly closing with fog. We did not see the shape in the water again nor did we see any evidence of damage or oil on the water. We searched the area closely, but found no results of our attack.

"We radioed in to Bomber Command, reporting what had happened and giving the approximate location. We also radioed in for coastal clearance before flying over land, to avoid being mistaken for an approaching enemy plane. We flew back to McChord Field via the Columbia River and landed, having been in the air 4 hours and 30 minutes.

"The 42nd Bomb Group intelligence officer who debriefed us was Lt. Robert Cohen. Everyone in the squadron shared our disappointment. We were fairly sure it was a Japanese submarine but we had no means of positively identifying it and no basis for a claim of having made contact with the enemy." (Letter, J. H. Daugherty, Dec. 1974; Individual Flight Record, Form 5, Capt. J. H. Daugherty, 9 Sep. 1942; U.S. Navy Operations Letter, 9 Sep. 1942, pp. 39-40; Associated Press dispatch, Sep. 25, 1942.)

Other patrol planes along the U.S. and Canadian coasts dropped bombs on what they took to be enemy submarines, but Capt. Daugherty's A-29 attack on the *I-25* appears to be the only instance in which even a near miss or any damage resulted. ☐

Wilbur L. Perez, the sole survivor of the U.S. Army B-17 that crashed on Cape Lookout on August 2, 1943, brought his wife Maude and son Ken back to the site in 1966. Near the monument marking the location, they found fragments of the aircraft. Other remnants are on display in the Pioneer Museum in Tillamook.

CHAPTER VIII: PATROLLING NORTHWEST BEACHES

"Beach Patrol History," compiled by the War Diary Office, 13th Naval District, n.d., a copy of which was made available by Lts. Thomas J. Barrett and Bruce B. Stubbs, Public Information Officers, 13th Coast Guard District, Seattle.

The Coast Guardsman's Manual, 4th edition. U.S. Naval Institute, 1964.

Gibbs, 1962, pp. 41-43.

"History of the U.S. Naval Air Station, Tillamook, Oregon," n.d.; "History of Blimp Squadron Thirty-Three," n.d. U.S. Naval History Division.

Light List, Pacific Coast and Pacific Islands, Vol. III. U.S. Coast Guard, 1972.

McWade, John. "Lone Ranch Borax Mine," *Monthly Bulletin*. Curry County Historical Society, Apr. 1, 1974, pp. 4-5.

NAST, Naval Air Station, Tillamook, Vol. 1, No. 8, Dec. 4, 1943.

Pacific Builder and Engineer, Oct. 1943, pp. 60ff.

Seattle *Post-Intelligencer*, "Russian Freighter is Wrecked by High Seas on North Pacific Shore." Apr. 7, 1943.

Tillamook *Headlight-Herald*, Aug. 19, 1943.

U.S. Coast Pilot 7, Pacific Coast, 8th edition. U.S. Coast and Geodetic Survey, 1959.

Webber, Bert. *What Happened at Bayocean—Is Salishan Next?* Ye Galleon, 1973, pp. 12-13.

Through interviews and correspondence, useful information for this chapter was provided by the following: Headquarters, U.S. Coast Guard, Washington, D.C.; Col. E. J. Parke, Washington State Patrol, Olympia; Walter F. Krath; Carl McCormick, Sr.; Dean C. Allard, Head, Operational Archives of the Naval History Division, Washington, D. C.; Glenn Barkhurst, Jr.; Capt. Keith V. Johnson, USN, Hong Kong; Carol B. McGuire; Mrs. Paul W. Arbeiter; George W. Cooper; E. C. Waldrop; Victor M. Califf; Laurence Rude; Charles R. Dederick; E. C. Fontaine, U.S. Forest Service, Portland, Ore.; Edward H. Marshall; Leslie L. Colvill; and Wilbur L. Perez.

The inlet patrol stations established by the Coast Guard were at these river mouths and estuaries: In Washington at Neah Bay, Quillayute River, Grays Harbor, Willapa Bay, and Columbia River; in Oregon at Nehalem Bay, Tillamook Bay, Netarts Bay, Sand Lake, Nestucca River, Salmon River, Siletz Bay, Depoe Bay, Yaquina River, Siuslaw River, Umpqua River, Coos Bay, Coquille River, and Port Orford.

For the line dropped by Coast Guardsmen to the stranded crew of the *Lamut*, Gibbs (1962, p. 42) says that boot laces were used. The "Beach Patrol History" says the line was made of gauze bandages, presumably from first aid packets. The latter method seems more plausible, because all of the laces from the rescue party's boots would not reach the required distance. The gauze bandages, however, would provide dozens of yards of light line. ☐

CHAPTER IX: THE RIVER OF DEATH

Statements by the following Forest Service personnel were provided by the office of the Fremont National Forest, Lakeview, Ore.: Richard R. Barnhouse, Bly, Ore., May 5, 1945; Fairbeorn H. Armstrong, Bly, Ore., May 6, 1945; L. K. Mays, Lakeview, Ore., May 7, 1945; and Merle S. Lowden, Lakeview, Ore., May 7 and 8, 1945. Herbert L. Hadley was interviewed at Bly on April 27, 1971. Responding to an inquiry in July 1974, Mr. Armstrong wrote from Poulsbo, Wash.: "I took no photos, saved no souvenirs. It was a very serious, very trying, rather gruesome affair—traumatic. We went up to render first aid but when that was not possible we did what we could to cover the bodies—locate parts, etc., until the [others] arrived."

The report submitted to Army Intelligence by Navy Lt. H. P. Scott, bomb disposal officer, was provided by Naval Ordnance Station, Indian Head, Md.

Copies of the "Coroner's Examination" reports by James A. Ousley, May 9, 1945, were obtained from the files of Lake County, Ore.

Larry Winters of Port Angeles, Wash., provided a copy of his unpublished manuscript, "Death via Paper Bag," a copy of his sister Elsye's last letter dated at Bly, Oregon, May 4, 1945, and other information.

Additional details and background information were provided by Dr. Mark W. Lee, President of Simpson College, San Francisco; Mrs. Glen E. Mitchell (Archie's mother), Ellensburg, Wash.; Mrs. Archie (Thelma Winters) Helgesen, Port Angeles, Wash.; Mrs. Archie (Betty Patzke) Mitchell, Vietnam and San Diego; Mrs. Elmer ("Dottie" Patzke) McGinnis, Klamath Falls, Ore.; Mr. and Mrs. Ed Patzke, Bly, Ore.; Mrs. Floyd Pollock and her daughter Irene Pollock Ragsdale, Eagle Point, Ore.; Jess Faha, Lakeview, Ore.; Les Shaw, Editor of Lakeview *Examiner*, Lakeview, Ore.

Typical of news releases was one appearing in the New York *Times*, June 1, 1942, with pictures of Rev. and Mrs. Mitchell and a statement that "The tragedy . . . was kept a strict military secret until today [May 31, 1945]."

"An Act for the Relief of Frank J. Patzke and Others" is included in the Congressional *Statutes at Large*, Vol. 63 (1949). □

This scorched dime, found by Herb Hadley in the rubble of the Bly bomb explosion, gives mute evidence of the intensity of the blast.

CHAPTER X: THE UNGUIDED MISSILES

JAPANESE SOURCES

Adachi, S. and K. Tanaka. "An Explanation of the Balloon Bomb," *Bungei Shunju* (Special Edition) Vol. 28, No. 5, Mar. 11, 1950, pp. 42-51. This was first major scientific article on the subject published in Japan. In 1974, Mr. Tanaka still considered it "correct except for number of balloons launched and [the number that] reached [North America]."

"FUGO Was Planned 13 Years Before Lauching: Japan Attack on Mainland of United States," *Chunichi*, Jan. 16, 1946. This was first popular magazine article about the subject published in Japan.

Kusaba, Sueki. "All About Balloon Bomb; Its Principles and Power," *Maru*, Jan. 11, 1961, pp. 72-76.

Kusaba, Sueki and Kiyoshi Tanaka. "Amendment of Mr. Teiji Takada's article on "Balloon Bomb' in *Shizen*, Vol. 6, Nos. 1-3, Jan.-Mar. 1951." (Unpublished manuscript; copy provided by Mr. Tanaka.)

Nozaki. "Laughable Balloon Bomb—Material is Paper and Paste!" *Chunichi*, Apr. 28, 1946.

Takada, Teiji. "Balloon Bomb," *Shizen*, Vol. 6, Nos. 1, 2, and 3, Jan., Feb., and Mar., 1951, pp. 24-33, 44-54, 70-79. Three major articles by a former Army Technical-Major, who worked on the project during the war. Translated by Ken Suda, Central Meteorological Observatory, Apr. 1953.

U.S. AND CANADIAN MILITARY SOURCES

Army/Air Force. *Japanese Explosive Ordnance: Army and Navy Ammunition.* Dept. of the Army TM 9-1985-5; Dept. of the Air Force TO 39B-1A-12, 1953.

Army Service Forces. "Japanese Free Balloons," Headquarters, Fourth Service Command, Atlanta, Ga., 10 Jul. 1945.

Canadian National Defense, Department of. File No. HQ. 1475-2-c (D-Hist) Historical Section, Army Headquarters, Ottawa, Canada.

Fourth Air Force. "Japanese Balloons," Historical Study No. III-2, n.d., Ch. X, pp. 501-516.

Three of the victims of the Bly bomb explosion are buried in the Linkville Cemetery, Klamath Falls, Oregon.

Naval Research Laboratory. "Japanese Balloons," TAIC Special Report No. 1, Technical Air Intelligence Center, Naval Air Station, Anacostia, D. C., 9 Jan. 1945. This NRL report and subsequent analyses are consolidated in "Japanese Balloons and Attached Devices," TAIC Report No. 41, May 1945 (OPNAV-16-V-T241); includes tabulation of data from reporting forms from 11 Nov. 1944 to June 1945.

War Department. "General Report Number One on Free Balloons and Related Incidents," General Staff-Military Intelligence Division G-2, 29 Jan. 1945. Also supplemental reports Nos. 2 through 8, Feb./Sep. 1945.

War Department. "Report to V. Bush on the Japanese Balloon Problem by an OSRD Special Committee," June 1945. Discusses costs of defense against balloons by antiaircraft weapons in shore installations and on ships.

War Department Bureau of Public Relations—Press Branch. "A Report on Japanese Free Balloons," a joint Army-Navy release for broadcast after 8:00 p.m. EST, 8 Feb. 1946.

Western Defense Command. "G-2 Periodic Report No. 188," 4 Aug. 1945.

Western Defense Command. "History of Japanese Free Balloons," Ch. 5 History of the Western Defense Command, Vol. I (OCMH File No. 8.2.2AA, VI), n.d.

Western Defense Command. "A Study of Japanese Free Balloons," Intelligence Study No. 1, Assistant Chief of Staff G-2, Presidio of San Francisco, Calif., 10 Feb. 1945. Also No. 2, c. Aug. 1945.

Western Sea Frontier/Western Defense Command. "Plan Covering Defense Against Japanese Free Balloons" (short title "BD-1"), 15 Aug. 1945. Annexes outline plans to provide defense against biological warfare; for "Firefly Project," defense against forest and grass fires; for ground, naval, and air defense; and for bomb disposal operations.

OTHER SOURCES

Clark, Neil M. "Paper Detective," Saturday Evening Post, Feb. 27, 1954, p. 27.

Conley, Cornelius W. "The Great Japanese Balloon Offensive," Air University Review, Feb./Mar., 1968, pp. 68-83.

Hayashi, Saburo and Alvin D. Cox. Kogun: The Japanese Army in the Pacific War. U.S. Marine Corps Association, Quantico, Va., 1959, pp. 118-119, 208. First published as Ta'heiyo Senso Rikusen Gaishi (in Japanese), by Iwanami Shoten Publishers, Tokyo, 1951.

Mikesh, Robert C. Japan's World War II Balloon Bomb Attacks on North America. Smithsonian Annals of Flight No. 9, Smithsonian Institution Press, 1973.

Rahm, Neal M. "The Fire Fly Project," Fire Control Notes, U.S. Forest Service, July 1946, pp. 4-7.

Stathos, Joanne. "The Japanese Balloon Invasion of the United States During World War II." Unpublished manuscript, University of Nebraska at Omaha, 1969.

Spilhaus, Athelstan F., C. S. Schneider, and C. B. Moore. "Controlled-Altitude Free Balloons," Journal of Meteorology, Vol. 5, No. 4, Aug. 1948, pp. 130-137.

Wilbur, W. H. (Brig. Gen. USA Ret.). "Those Japanese Balloons," Reader's Digest, Aug. 1950, pp. 23-26.

The Japanese code name for the balloon project was FUGO. Teiji Takada explains that the name was derived from *fusen, fu* meaning "wind" and *sen* meaning "ship." "*Go* is a general word," he says, "to which a variety of meanings might be assigned. *Go* could be a pen name, a number, or for the case in point, a weapon. Thus FUGO means, "windship-weapon.'" (Takada, p. 24.)

The FUGO project, from beginning to end—research, development, launchings, and landings—was shrouded in secrecy during the war on both sides of the Pacific. That is one reason documentation is relatively scarce. Another is that most Japanese records were destroyed purposely or accidentally. At the time of surrender, it was the policy to incinerate the files of the Imperial Headquarters and of the general staffs of the Army and Navy (Bergamini, p. xxxiii).

The leaders of the two FUGO development teams, Kusaba for the Army and Tanaka for the Navy, both stressed the fact that they worked in secrecy and that few records survived. According to Tanaka, the Navy development team wore civilian clothes and worked in a secluded laboratory. A fire, probably caused by one of the B-29 raids, destroyed the records kept in the central office. A duplicate set of some of the records, however, especially the Navy flight records, had been provided to the Navy Meteorological Department and escaped destruction.

It was not until five years after the war that those who had worked on FUGO thought the time was ripe to describe the project for the Japanese people. In March 1950, Adachi and Tanaka published the article cited above "for the benefit of science." Mr. Tanaka told me, "We had been quiet long enough and felt it was time to tell the story, because people were laughing about the project. In reality, the Naval balloon project was a long, difficult, serious study."

A basic source by an American on the Japanese Army's type A balloon and the secrecy surrounding its development is the material collected by Cornelius W. Conley between 1961 and 1965, especially his correspondence and interview with General Kusaba. Conley started his investigation when he was a noncommissioned officer in the U.S. Air Force stationed in the Philippines. While studying for a degree in history at the University of the Philippines, he undertook the balloon offensive as a class project but found it too large to complete in one term so extended the study over a period of years.

When Sergeant Conley first wrote to General Kusaba, he received encouragement and offers of assistance. In April 1963 he interviewed Kusaba in Yokohama within two weeks of the General's death on May 3, 1963. Conley made inquiries at the Veterans Administration in Tokyo but that office could find no one other than Kusaba who had first-hand knowledge of the paper-balloon project. Because he was able to question Kusaba before the General's death, Conley recorded information that does not appear to be available elsewhere.

In his letters and interview General Kusaba explained why few records of the type A balloon were preserved. It was in a 1961 letter that he wrote, "It is with great regret that I have to tell you that there are no records or documents, for at the end of the war they were *entirely destroyed by us*" (italics mine). The Japanese public was not informed that the project was going on—except for exaggerated propaganda claims. Photographers were ordinarily excluded from testing and launching areas; however, a motion picture was filmed for a record of a launching, but it was destroyed by fire in Tokyo before it was developed. At the end of the war many private and official records were destroyed to prevent them from falling into the hands of the army of occupation. The launching sites were abandoned until discovered by the U.S. Army First Cavalry on maneuvers in April 1947.

General Kusaba did, by chance, keep a set of photographs of the launching of an extra large (15-meter) paper balloon. He loaned these photos to Mr. Takada in 1950 for use in the *Shizen* articles, then turned them over to Conley in 1961 for whatever use Conley might make of them. These pictures are published here on pages 100-101 for the first time in an English-language publication.

Neal Conley, who now lives in Pittsburgh, has served as a valued consultant and provided for this book a complete set of the materials he collected—photographs, documents, notes, and correspondence—and copies of two unpublished manuscripts. His manuscript "The Great Japanese Bomb Balloon Offensive" was cleared for release by the Dictorate for Security Review, Department of Defense, on Aug. 12, 1965, and copies were filed in the Smithsonian Institution and in the Department of Defense. His other manuscript, "Summary of Positive Balloon Incidents," introduced the numbering system used in this book and in at least one other publication for identifying the balloons which reached North America. Some of his findings, but not the incident list, appeared in the *Air University Review* article cited above.

I have been fortunate in being able to meet Kiyoshi Tanaka and to spend parts of two days with him in San Francisco. He has enthusiastically delved into records, into his own memory, and into the memories of his wartime colleagues to bring to light new information about the Navy side of the FUGO project. The following notes are based largely on material which he has provided or called to my attention.

TEST LAUNCHING OF RUBBER BALLOONS

When asked in Jan. 1975 to describe the balloon testing that he took part in Kiyoshi Tanaka consulted Mr. Kazuo Nishida in Kobe, Mr. S. Adachi, and Mr. Hirota (formerly Captain Nakamura, whom Tanaka had not seen since 1944), and then provided the following summary of their testing program:

"After the decision by Prime Minister Tojo and Admiral Shimada that the Army (A-type) and Navy (B-type) research be consolidated under Army supervision in July 1944, several of us undertook a special study.

"Tsingtao and Ooita experiments (flights 7-19) convinced us that we must use pressurized balloons. Whether or not they would be successful depended on the amount of superheating and supercooling of the hydrogen gas, in other words, on the inner pressure of the balloon.

"At the beginning, we estimated temperature rise of gas was 50° C. But measurement showed temperature below 30° C and inner pressure around 45 mmHg when a balloon was charged with hydrogen so as to give free lift of 10 kg.

Cornelius W. Conley interviewed former Major General Sueki Kusaba in Tokyo in April 1963 to obtain information about the FUGO project.

The author with Kiyoshi Tanaka in San Francisco in October 1974.

Captain Kazuo Nishida, launching officer (second from right), observes flight of a test balloon in 1943 at Ichinomiya test site. On his right is Mr. (later Captain) Hiroharu Orii, who like the others were civilian workers in the Noborito Laboratory.

Parts recovered from type-B rubber balloons in the United States and Canada: ballast gear (left); altitude switch and radiosonde from the San Pedro balloon (above); and gas relief valves from the San Pedro balloon (below left) and from the Queen Charlotte Island balloon (below right).

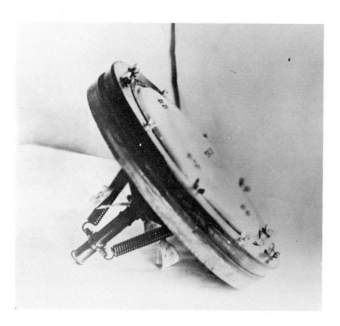

"We recognized the distinguished research of the Army in radio sonde and gas relief valves. We decided to install an Army sonde as the main radio sonde instead of our Navy sonde and to produce a gas relief valve for easy launching and for burst prevention. The use of the Navy sonde was limited to measuring inner pressure.

"Between August 17 and November 5, 1944, fifteen type-B rubberized-silk 9-meter balloons were launched. These were flown in three phases, all from the Ichinomiya test site in Chiba Prefecture on the east coast of Honshu.

Phase I	Aug. 17-Aug. 31	Flights 20-25
Phase II	Sep. 29-Oct. 9	Flights 26-29
Phase III	Oct. 29-Nov. 5	Flights 30-34

"After the six test balloons in Phase I were launched, with radio sonde transmissions varying from 2 to 22 hours after launching, we believed that half of the balloons had

burst, because of an inner pressure rise when too much ballast was released.

"Theoretically, the strength of the envelope was computed to withstand 110 mmHg, but in pressure tests the strength did not exceed 90 mmHg. Mr. Sekine of the Fujikura Rubber Company investigated and found the defect to be in the rubber cement used on the seams. The balloons were physically coming apart at the seams between the panels because of the increase in pressure.

"Also, the pressure test showed 40 mmHg. I asked that the launching test be discontinued. The remaining balloon envelopes were sent back to the manufacturer for refabrication.

"The balloon envelopes for Phase II experiments not only had recemented seams but, beginning with flight 26 on September 29, they also had gas relief values, which were made from Mr. Sekine's special design and had been set at 45 mmHg. In Phase II, four balloons were sent aloft. The most notable, flight 26, returned radio sonde signals for 87 hours—a record.

"In Phase III, five balloons were launched by Army personnel under Navy supervision. For flight 32, we installed a gas relief valve and a modified meteorological radio sonde for measuring altitude, temperature, and pressure differences, plus a special Navy sonde built by Mr. Adachi of the Navy Meteorological Department. This one was for measuring altitude and pressure differences and was capable of sending a maximum of 24 different signals.

"With the two transmitters and full ballast equipment, flight 32 was launched at 2:51 p.m. on November 2, 1944. Signals were received for only 5 hours, after which time there was only silence." (Letter Jan. 7, 1975.)

Thirty years later, in Dec. 1974, it was established for the first time that flight 32 was the balloon that had been salvaged from the ocean west of San Pedro, Calif., on Nov. 4, 1944 (Incident No. 1). The positive identification was made by Messrs. Tanaka, Adachi, Koma, and Sekine after I supplied photographs of some of the recovered apparatus and a copy of the Naval Research Laboratory analysis of the San Pedro balloon (TAIC #1). They identified in the photographs the radiosonde as one built by Mr. Adachi, the gas relief valve as one designed by Mr. Sekine, and an aneroid altitude switch as one designed by Mr. Koma.

With the help of Mr. Adachi, Mr. Tanaka rechecked "the unfinished flying records, flying curves, and meteorological considerations" that had escaped destruction after the war because a copy had been filed in the Navy Meteorological Department. They came to the conclusion that flight 32 could have been gone from Japan "two days and twenty hours in November by the time recovered at sea."

The flying records also show that only two of the 15 balloons launched in the Ichinomiya tests, numbers 23 and 32, had the special Adachi radiosondes.

Flight 23 did not have a gas relief value, but number 32 did. The NRL report notes that the valve on the San Pedro balloon had the number "6" or "9" painted on one side and penciled on the other. Mr. Tanaka says, "On the valves used in the Ichinomiya tests, there were pairs of 'mating' numbers used as guides in final assembly. The pair on flight 32 could have been either 6 or 9. There were only nine of these valves made."

The NRL observed that the ratchet switch which controlled ballast dropping was in position number 6, which indicated to Mr. Tanaka that "the balloon consumed all the ballast it carried (10.5 kg) and fell down and drifted for about one day." NRL salinity tests of the wooden platform carried by the balloon indicated that it had been in the water about one day.

It seems reasonably certain, therefore, that the rubber balloon launched from Ichinomiya on Nov. 2, Tokyo time, was the same one recovered off San Pedro on Nov. 4, Pacific time.

According to U.S. records, only three of the rubber balloons reached—or nearly reached—North America: San Pedro (No. 1), Yerington (No. 1a), and QCI (No. 232). In October 1974, when I showed Mr. Tanaka a photograph of the Yerington balloon (page 102), he exclaimed, "That's my balloon!" He did not know until that moment that any of the balloons he launched in the Ichinomiya tests had reached the American continent.

After checking records in Japan, Mr. Tanaka concluded, "This balloon is either flight No. 20 or No. 22 launched at

Ichinomiya in Phase I. The others in this series we suppose to be burst. The ballast was six 3-kg bags of sand. I imagine it took about six days in summer to cross the ocean and reach Nevada."

Charles Ragsdale says the balloon landed on his ranch sometime in August but that military authorities paid no attention to it until many months later.

Early in 1945, according to Mr. Tanaka and Kazuo Nishida, Capt. Nishida launched three more of the 9-meter rubber balloons. These had gas relief valves which had been developed by Capt. Nakamura and radio transmitters but no bombs. The rubber balloon recovered west of the Queen Charlotte Islands on Apr. 23, 1945 (No. 232), had a gas relief valve numbered 15. Mr. Hirota (ex-Nakamura) told Mr. Tanaka that the number was not a serial number, but designation for type or size—Nakamura's modified Army valve (50 mmHg) for B-type balloon (45 mmHg). They came to the conclusion that the Queen Charlotte rubber balloon was one of those launched by Capt. Nishida in February 1945.

Ballast gear on the B-type balloon

The system for releasing ballast as developed by the Navy research team was somewhat different from the Army system described in the text. For the B-type balloon the system consisted of three components: a low-temperature storage battery, an aneroid altitude switch, and sandbags. When the balloon dropped to a certain altitude, a 12-volt, 40-amp-hour Japanese naval aircraft battery weighing 25.3 kg supplied power to the aneroid altitude switch, which ignited a small black-powder charge, which released one of the sandbags. There usually were 8 sandbags, each weighing about 3 kilograms.

The storage battery was encased in a water jacket to utilize the latent heat of water at freezing point as protection for the battery. The battery also supplied power to the radiosonde. The radiosonde altitude switch was wired so that the transmitter would change broadcast frequencies at each altitude and inner pressure change. The battery was housed within a large celluloid box suspended between the sandbags and below the platform.

On the wooden platform where the radiosonde, the altitude switch, an extra safety switch, an electrical terminal block, and a spring-loaded 8-day clock. If there was to be a payload drop, the clock would make the drop independent of the other systems. The clock was also used for intermittent broadcast of the radiosonde.

"When Army sonde was installed," says Mr. Tanaka, "the low temperature dry cell was used. They were wrapped with black paper and encased in celluloid sheet casing.

"No bombs were carried—or could be carried—by the Navy meteorological observation balloons, because weight of the rubberized silk and the battery was too heavy to carry any bombs. The B-type balloons did not carry any self-destruct explosives."

Biological warfare

From the time that the balloons from Japan first began drifting into the United States, government officials seriously considered them as potential carriers of biological warfare agents. The staff study by the Western Sea Frontier/Western Defense Command cited above (Annex F, p. 1) warned that "While no evidence has been discovered . . . that the Japanese have employed [balloons] as a means of bacteriological warfare . . . the fact remains that such action is a possibility." Balloons, the study pointed out, theoretically could be used to transport bacteria and allied agents to contaminate water supplies and in various ways spread disease among human, animals, and plants.

Sergeant Conley queried General Kusaba on this point, and the General told him that there had been no intention to use the balloons for carrying biological warfare agents. I asked Mr. Tanaka. He reinforced Kusaba's statement and added that no techniques had been developed for carrying such payloads on balloons.

ENDING THE OFFENSIVE

The FUGO project was originally planned as a year-round offensive. The balloon was intended as a subversive weapon to cause great forest fires then self-destruct at high altitudes, never having been seen from the earth (Takada, pp. 24-25). The 10-meter paper balloons would be used for the season of most favorable winds, the five-month period from November through March. The 15-meter paper balloon, which required calm weather for launching, and the 9-meter type B rubber balloon, which theoretically had greater endurance, would be used in the spring and summer. Then in the winter of 1945-46 the offensive would switch back to the 10-meter type A balloons.

Various opinions have been expressed as to why FUGO was terminated in March or April 1945, before the 15,000 projected launchings had been completed. Conley (1965, p. 76) says it was "because a wall of silence was formed by the American people." Wilbur (p. 26) says, "Toward the end of April, General Kusaba was told to cease all operations. The dictum of the [General] Staff was, 'Your balloons are not reaching America. If they were, reports would be in the newspapers. Americans could not keep their mouths closed this long.'"

Mikesh (p. 38) says, "The Japanese had one thousand more balloons in readiness, but further launches were suspended in the early part of April 1945, primarily because the Showa Denko Company and other hydrogen sources were being disrupted by B-29 raids."

Takada (p. 73) says that even though a trainload of hydrogen cylinders might be ready to move, air raids on the railroads forced trains to "suspend departures frequently and unexpectedly for a long time."

Kusaba ("Amendment," p. 17)says, "To my great regret, the progress of the war was faster than we imagined. Soon after the campaign began the air raids against our mainland were intensified. Many factories which manufactured various parts were destroyed. Moreover, we were not informed about the effect of FUGO throughout the war-time. Due to the combination of hardships we were compelled to cease operations."

Tanaka (letter, Nov. 10, 1974) gives these reasons for the termination of FUGO:

"1. A-Type balloon cannot reach United States in spring and summer.

"2. B-Type balloon might be able to reach and cause forest fire in spring and summer. However, most of them were destroyed by B-29 bombardment."

A SCIENTIFIC ADVENTURE

"In military history," Teiji Takada wrote in his 1951 series in Shizen, "there has been no comparable operation to FUGO. It was a scientific adventure—a conquest of low temperature, low pressure, and distance." (p. 24)

As with many adventures, this one was dangerous. One of the greatest hazards during launching was the danger of fire and explosion. The hydrogen-filled cylinders and bombs were stacked near each launch pad. During the mass releases in February and March 1945, there were as many as "two or three hydrogen fires a day." (p. 74) On one occasion, Capt. Hiroharu Orii, a supervising scientist, was "seriously wounded when shot by a blow-plug." (p. 50-51)

Near the end of the war, the Army Minister presented a Letter of Commendation to General Kusaba, Majors Otsuki and Takeda, and Captains Orii and Nakamura for their outstanding work on the transoceanic balloon. Takada (p. 79) summarizes the long-range effects of FUGO in these words:

"The balloon bomb made by us can never be said powerful as an offensive weapon. The devotion to the project of those who were concerned to the project might perhaps have not been rewarded. But, I believe that the study in technical divisions required to complete this FUGO have achieved a rapid progress. Its results are enough to be utilized also in the peace time and their further development can be expected. Those who engaged in the study of the balloon bomb, which was a product of the extraordinary condition of war, seem to be displaying their ability in their respective fields, with their experiences acquired in the war. Only when these experiences, which could be called precious experiences, whatever they might be, are utilized for the future development of our country and for the benefit of the mankind, then we could say that the way we passed was 'not useless.'

"Every time when I see an advertisement balloon floating in the sky, I remember our FUGO with a smile." □

CHAPTER XI: SILENCE—THE BEST DEFENSE

"Air Victory over Japan," Flying, Feb. 1946, p. 72. Discovery of jet stream.

Beals, Ray. "Record of Events, 1945," U.S. Forest Service, Trinity National Forest, Hayfork, Calif.

Buck, Robert N. Weather Flying. Macmillan, 1970, pp. 98-102. Description of jet stream.

Groueff, Stephane. Manhattan Project: The Untold Story of the Making of the Atomic Bomb. Little-Brown, 1967, pp. 309-310. Hanford balloon.

Naval Research Laboratory. "Balloon, Japanese, Rubber, from San Pedro, Calif.," TAIC Report #1, Technical Air Intelligence Center, Naval Air Station, Anacostia, D. C., 9 Jan. 1945, pp. 1-7.

Naval Research Laboratory. TAIC Report #41: "Kalispell Paper Balloon," 8 Jan. 1945, pp. 25-33; "Estacada Paper Balloon," 15 Jan. 1945, pp. 34-36; "Balloon . . . from Kailua, Hawaii," 15 Jan. 45, pp. 37-47; "Balloon . . . from Sevastapool," 18 Jan. 1945, pp. 48-51; "Balloon . . . from Alturas, Calif.," 2 Mar. 1945, pp. 60-61; "Balloon . . . from Hayfork, Calif.," 10 Mar. 1945, pp. 62-63; "Balloon . . . from Tremonton, Utah," 29 Mar. 1945, pp. 75-76; "Radar Test of Inflated Balloon," 7 Mar. 1945, p. 102.

Owsley, Cliff. "A Great and Necessary Undertaking," Southern Lumberman, Aug. 15, 1971. H. H. Arnold as an aerial fire patrolman in 1921.

Reynolds, Clark G. "Attack of the Paper Balloons," Airpower, Apr. 1965, pp. 51-55. Use of 81-mm mortar shells as balloon payload; President Truman's decision to use the atomic bomb.

Ross, Irwin. "Sheriff Hyde and the Balloon of Death," The Elks Magazine, May 1968, pp. 36, 37, 45. Tremonton balloon.

"Target Tokyo," *Brief*, Publication of AAF, Pacific Ocean Areas, Dec. 12, 1944, pp. 3-11. Discovery of the jet stream.

NEWSMAGAZINES

Newsweek, "Balloon Mystery," Jan. 1, 1945, p. 36; "Trial Balloons?" Jan. 15, 1945, p. 40; "Mustn't Touch!" June 4, 1945, p. 34; "The Balloon That Killed," June 11, 1945, p. 35.
Time, "What Next, Please?" Jan. 1, 1945, p. 14; "Picknickers, Beware," June 4, 1945, p. 22; "Balloon Bombs," June 11, 1945, p. 56.

NEWSPAPERS (in chronological order)

Yerington, Nev., *Mason Valley News*, Nov. 17, 1944, p. 1.
Worland, Wyo., *Northern Wyoming Daily News*, Dec. 8, 1944, p. 1.
Thermopolis, Wyo., *Independent Record*, Dec. 14, 1944, p. 1.
Libby, Mont., *Western News*, "Jap Balloon Found in Timber," Dec. 15, 1944, p. 1; "Gives More Detail About Jap Balloon," Dec. 21, 1944, p. 1.
New York *News*, "Jap Balloon Found in Montana Forest," Dec. 18, 1944; "F.B.I., Army, Study 3rd Mystery Balloon," Jan. 1, 1945; Jack Doherty, "Japan Balloons Carry Bombs to West U.S." and "Jap Balloons Bearing Bombs Blown to U.S.," May 23, 1945, pp. 1, 2; "Blast of Jap Balloon Fatal. . . ." June 1, 1945, p. 1.
Portland *Oregonian*, "F. R. Knows Only Little About Balloons," Jan. 3, 1945, p. 3; Don Woodman, "Late By-Line," Aug. 25, 1972, p. 15.
Vancouver, B. C., *Province*, "Jap Balloons Reach Canada; Do No Damage," May 22, 1945, p. 1.
Spokane, Wash., *Chronicle*, "Japanese Balloon Fell in Michigan, the Army Reports," June 6, 1945, p. 1.
Marysville, Kan., *Marshall County News*, "Story of Jap Balloon Which Fell Near Bigelow Can Now Be Told"; "Army Takes Farmer's Fine Stack Covers," Aug. 23, 1945, p. 1.
London *Illustrated News*, "Japanese Bombing Balloon Sites," May 24, 1947, p. 541; "Balloons Designed to Bomb America Costly . . . Failure," June 7, 1947.
Victoria, B. C., *Daily Colonist*, George Nicholson, "Not Always What They Seem," Apr. 25, 1954; Douglas Leechman, "Beatles and Beetles; Science Takes a Hand," Apr. 5, 1964, pp. 12-13.
Missoula, Mont., *Missoulian*, Al Dorr, "Forester Helped Turn Trick: Why Jap Balloon Gamble Lost," Aug. 1, 1965, p. 12A.
Tillamook, Ore., *Headlight-Herald*, "Army Takes Bomb," Jan. 16, 1966, p. 1.
Medford, Ore., *Mail Tribune*, "Medford Man Recalls Finding Japanese Bomb in Lake County," Sept. 17, 1967, p. A. 7.
Torrejon Air Base, Madrid, Spain, *Alert Strip*, Sgt. Cornelius W. Conley, "Japanese Bomb U.S. and Canada," Mar. 22, 1968, pp. 1, 8.
Portland *Oregon Journal*, Bert Webber, "' Day of Infamy' May 5, 1945—Day Japanese Dropped Balloon Bomb," May 5, 1971, p. 1 feature section.
Vancouver, B.C., *Sunday Sun*, Charles Aitkens, "The Secret Weapon That Was To Set Canada Ablaze; The Great Japanese Fire Balloon Plot," May 22, 1971, Weekend Magazine, pp. 4-5.
Klamath Falls, Ore., *Herald and News*, Jerry Mattoon, "More Japanese Balloon Bombs Still Around, Says Writer," Apr. 9, 1972, p. 37.
Hayfork, Calif., *Hayfork News*, "World War II Bomb Blast Site," May 31, 1972, pp. 1-3.
Goldendale, Wash., *Sentinel*, Jerrine May, "Sentinel Sal," June 15, 1972, p. 2; also June 26, 1972, p. 4.
Hamburg, W. Germany, *Bild*, "Historiker: Japan schickte Bomben mit Ballonen uber den Pazifik," June 22, 1974.

Many people have assisted in providing information for this chapter by letter, interview, and telephone.

Librarians, archivists, and museum curators have been especially helpful. Staff members of the state libraries of Oregon, Washington, Idaho, and Montana have graciously replied to requests. I especially appreciate the help of Ronnie Lee Budge, Jackson County Library, Medford, Ore.; Phillip D. Lagerquist, Truman Library, Independence, Mo.; Larry Marcott, Hot Springs County Library, Thermopolis, Wyo.; George McBride, Greater Victoria Public Library, Victoria, B.C.; William Burke, former curator, Klamath County Museum, Klamath Falls, Ore.; James N. Eastman, Jr., Simpson Historical Research Center, USAF, Maxwell AFB, Ala.; Dean C. Allard, U.S. Navy Historical Division; Capt. Roger Pineau, Curator, Washington (D.C.) Navy Yard Museum; Leona Hanson, Yerington, Nev.; Kaye M. Sheltren, Bridgeport, Calif.

Former FBI agents who provided information include Leigh B. Hanes, Jr., James H. Morrow, Orville R. Wilson, Paul W. Haviland, and Archie J. Richardson.

Insight into the discovery of the jet stream was provided by Brig. Gen. R. D. Steakley (USAF Ret.), Annapolis, Md., and T. R. Gillenwaters, president of the Oceanic Research Institute, Newport Beach, Calif. Col. Edward C. Conley (USAF) gave advice and assistance.

Individuals with personal knowledge of balloon/bomb incidents who added pertinent detail include:
(Alaskan incidents) George H. Corey, Pendleton, Ore.
(Incident No. 1a) Charles F. Ragsdale, Los Angeles, Calif.
(Incident No. 8) David Horner and Larry Miettunen, Estacada, Ore.; Don Woodman, Portland.
(No. 10) Evelyn Cyr and J. A. Dollarhide, Medford, Ore.
(No. 15) Mel Barron, Ashland, Ore.; Roland Sherman, Alturas, Calif.; J. F. Green, Palos Verdes, Pen., Calif.
(No. 68) Sheriff Warren W. Hyde, Brigham City, Utah.
(No. 70) Editor Byron E. Guise, Marshall County *News*, Marysville, Kans.; Edwin R. North, Cedaredge, Colo.; Mrs. P. L. (Linda North) Smith, Spokane, Wash.; and Lena K. Potter, Vermillion, Kans.
(No. 77) Jerrine Brooks May, Goldendale, Wash.; and Eldon J. Parke, Olympia, Wash.
(No. 94) Milton R. Cydell, Lincoln City, Ore.; Frank W. Fosnot, Sunnyside, Wash.; Helen K. Gleason, AEC, Richland, Wash.; S. A. McNeight, E. I. du Pont de Nemours and Co., Wilmington, Del.; John R. Ulrich, Bonneville Power Adm., Portland, Ore.
(No. 274) A. C. O'Toole and B. Hillyer, Medford, Ore.
(Post-war incidents) W. F. Hamilton, Klamath Falls, Ore.

Not all locations mentioned in the text and incident lists can be found on current maps. Bigelow, in south central Marshall County, Kansas, for example, no longer exists. It was abandoned to make way for a post-war reclamation project. □

Illustration Credits

3 John F. Green collection

4 Kou Maki

5 J. Larry Kemp collection

6 Oregon State University Library (top); Portland *Oregonian* (center) and USAF

8 USCG photo by Lt. Millard Chappell

9 USN (left) and North American Aviation Co.

10 Grahame F. Shrader collection (top); Nobuo Fujita (center); and Kou Maki

13 Minoru Hasegawa collection (top); Kemp collection (center) and by Saburo Hayashi *NPP*

14 War History Institute of the Japanese Maritime Self-Defense Force

16 Kemp collection

17 General Petroleum Corp. (top) and Del Norte County Historical Society

18 by author

19 Kemp collection

20 The Public Archives of Canada

21 Arnold Lyczewski collection (left) and Kemp collection

22 Kemp collection

23 Military Personnel Records Center, St. Louis, Mo. (probably *NPP*) and USN (bottom)

24 Shrader collection

26 NA

27 by Jay D. Dare

28-29 NA

31 Bernard Hagen collection (left) and Los Angeles *Herald-Express*

32 USASC (top), and Arthur J. Dellinger collection

34 Amos L. Wood collection

35 F. D. H. Nelson collection

36 Edward T. Redford collection

37 Shrader collection (top), and by Saburo Hayashi *NPP*

38 Redford collection (left and center) and Brian Harrison collection

39 Canadian Department of National Defense

40 Marilyn Holsinger and Harley Jessup

42 Bert Kellogg collection (top and bottom), W. C. Dahl, Jr., collection (center)

43 James Ridders collection (top and center) and Shrader collection

44 by Dan Newhouse (top) and USASC

45 by Howard Sherwood (top) and USCG photo by PA3 Vern Brisley

---

46 George D. Hannaford collection (top and center), Ridders collection (bottom left), and 249th Coast Artillery Organization

47 Holsinger/Jessup

48 author collection (top), Newhouse collection (center), and Carl Roth collection

49 Oregon National Guard (top) and Roth collection

50 249th CAO (top), Warren Poling collection (bottom left), Vernon Greig collection (bottom center), and Hannaford collection

51 Otto Freytag collection

52 Ridders collection

54 Alice Wood collection (top left), author collection (top right), Ridders collection (lower left), and Gerald Frank collection (right)

55 by Milo A. Jordan (top), Newhouse collection (lower left), and Laurence Rude collection (lower right)

57 by author

58 249th CAO (top), by author (center), and *Oregonian*

59 by author

60 USCG

62 by author

64 Fujita collection (top left), Tatsuo Tsukudo collection (top right), Meiji Tagami collection (lower left), and Fujita collection

66 Nichimo Mini-Craft Models, Inc.

67 by author (left) and Kou Maki

70 by author

71 Holsinger/Jessup (left) and by author

72 Holsinger/Jessup

73 by E. C. Waldrop (top) and by Frank Sterrett, the *Oregonian*

74 by Sterrett (top) and Waldrop collection

75 Keith V. Johnson collection

77 Lockheed-California Co. (left) and Jean H. Daugherty collection

78 by author

80 by author

81 USCG (top), Poling collection (center), and Glenn Barkhurst, Jr., collection

82 Cathrine Davis Young from USCG map in "Beach Patrol History"

84, 88 USCG

89 USN

90 USN (left), and Wilbur L. Perez collection

91 USCG

92 400th AAF Base Unit, Fourth Air Force, San Francisco

94 Elmer McGinnis collection (top) and Mrs. G. E. Mitchell collection

95 Gifford from family collection, Shoemaker from family collection, others from McGinnis collection

98 Weyerhaeuser Co.

100-101 Cornelius W. Conley collection

102 A. B. Evarts collection

103 U.S. Forest Service (left) and by Kiyoshi Tanaka (right)

104 by Leigh B. Hanes, Jr. (top) and USASC

105 USASC (left) and by author (right)

106 USAAF, Topeka, Kans. (top) and NA (center and bottom)

107 Green collection

111 Wide World Photo

112 *Oregonian*

114 author collection

116 Green collection (left) and USN

117 NA (left) and Green collection

118 author collection (left) and Warren W. Hyde collection

119 Wide World Photo (top) and by Edwin North

120 Linda Kay North Smith collection (upper left), by author (upper right), by Jerrine Brooks May (lower right)

121 USASC (top) and by author

123 Wide World Photo

124 USAF courtesy of the Boeing Company

125 Christian & Missionary Alliance Church

126 by author (top and center) and Weyerhaeuser Co.

129 H. R. Farr collection (top) and by Jerry Baron, Coos Bay *World*

130 Brookings-Harbor Jaycees (top) and by Jerry Baron

131 Brookings-Harbor Jaycees

132 by Fritz Strauss, author collection (top) and by author

134 Holsinger/Jessup

148 by author

149 by author (top left), Evarts collection (top right), by Burford Wilkerson (lower left), and Conley collection (lower right)

150 all from personal collections of individuals pictured

152 Melva Loggins collection

153 Holsinger/Jessup

154 by author (top), and Fujita collection

155 by Hayashi *NPP*

157 Minoru Hasegawa (left) and Kou Maki

158 Hasegawa collection

159 Library of Congress (upper left), Dillon S. Myer collection (upper right)

160 N. Nambu collection

161 George Nicholson collection (left), Brian Harrison collection (right)

162 by author

165 USN photo by M/Sgt John T. Frye, USMC

166 Perez collection

167 by author

169 Conley collection (top), by Yoshito Tsunoda (center), and K. Nishida collection

170 Conley collection

Wrapper design by Marilyn Holsinger

Wrapper photo by Dale Webber

Index

Page numbers in italics refer to illustrations